# COMPETING FOR PROSPERITY

## PROSPERITY

Business strategies & industrial policies
in modern France

# TELESIS

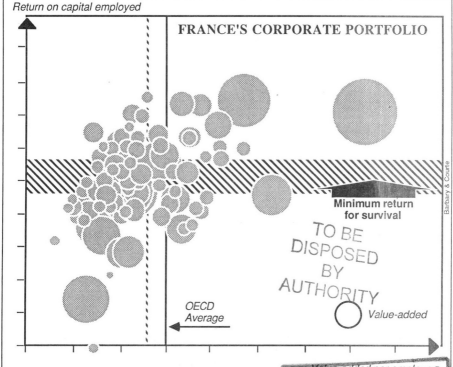

FRANCE'S CORPORATE PORTFOLIO

Return on capital employed

Minimum return
for survival

TO BE
DISPOSED
BY
AUTHORITY

OECD
Average

Value-added

Barbary & Courte

Value-added per employee

Policy Studies Institute

ISBN: 0-85374-273-1

Published by Policy Studies Institute
100 Park Village East, London NW1 3SR
Printed by Bourne Offset Ltd.

# COMPETING FOR PROSPERITY

An evaluation of corporate strategies and government policies in postwar France ; an assessment of French competitive position based on company analysis and case studies ; a prescription of the broad changes necessary throughout French society to keep the country in the leading pack of advanced industrial nations in the decades to come.

TELESIS

# THE AUTHORS

This book has been written by Bertrand DECHERY and a team of consultants from TELESIS. It is largely based on the experience accumulated by the firm over the last six years in advising the top management of some of the largest French corporations as well as various departments of the French government.

TELESIS is an international consulting firm created in 1979, which specializes in business strategy and industrial policy. The firm has offices in Paris, Munich, Providence (USA) and affiliates in Sydney and Melbourne, with a total of more than sixty consultants. TELESIS advises some of the most prominent corporations in Europe, the USA and Australia, helping top management to develop and implement strategies which improve their competitive position, growth and profitability. The firm also advises national and regional governments around the world as well as international organizations such as the EEC, on sectoral strategies and development policies.

Bertrand DECHERY is a founding partner of TELESIS. He worked during four years for French industry, and three years for the Boston Consulting Group in Boston and Paris. During his consulting career, he has managed business strategy assignments in a variety of industries, including automotive, consumer electronics, electrical engineering, offshore, aeronautics and chemicals, for European and American companies. He has also advised governments and public agencies in Sweden, Ireland, Belgium and France as well as the EEC in several economic sectors and development policies. He was a member of the Commission de l'Industrie during the preparation of the IXth Plan in France. Bertrand DECHERY is a graduate of Sciences Po and the Faculté de Droit of Paris, and holds an MBA from Harvard Business School. He is the author of 'Les Mécanismes Fondamentaux de la Compétitivité', Editions Hommes et Techniques, Paris 1980.

# ACKNOWLEDGEMENTS

The author gratefully acknowledges the invaluable research and analysis conducted by Caroline Arrighi de Casanova as well as her creative contributions to the ideas developed in this book. She has been assisted by several TELESIS consultants, in particular Thierry Coulange and Philippe le Hodey. The author also acknowledges a large debt to his partners at TELESIS for their guidance, contribution and encouragement over many years.

Precious editorial assistance has been provided by Janet McDonald and Laurie Oldfield and the best secretarial support has been given by Barbara Gaymay, Geneviève Fremon and Nadine Grandjean. The graphics have been designed by Jean-Christophe Courte.

TELESIS is most grateful to the Gatsby Foundation for its generous support, without which this work would not have been carried to fruition.

# Contents

# LIST OF FIGURES

# INTRODUCTION

Forty years after the postwar reconstruction, 'modernization' is again the motto of French government and business leaders. Has France's industrial policy come full circle and missed its target ?

The usual indicators of growth, employment and trade balance at the macro-level, as well as the trends in profits, investments and market shares at the corporate level, give a gloomy picture of France compared with the resurrection of the US economy, the unabated emergence of Japan, and the steady solidity of West Germany, not to speak of rather prosperous smaller economies such as Switzerland, Sweden or Austria. Even Italy, once a subject of disdain for many Frenchmen, seems more dynamic, and Great Britain is more and more often cited in favourable terms. What has happened to the 'French economic miracle' ?

Almost everybody in France has forgotten the predictions made by Herman Kahn and his team from the Hudson Institute[1]. The American futurologist expressed the opinion that France's mix of northern and southern European cultures was ideal for continued high growth in the competitive environment which would prevail in the 1970s and 1980s. He stated that a proper understanding of the forces in French society raised not so much the question 'Why is France overtaking Germany today ?' as 'Why has France ever been behind Germany ?' The authors of the study predicted that France would be the most powerful European economy in terms of total production by the mid 1980s and that the French people would enjoy the highest standard of living in Europe by 1990.

It was a time of high confidence and high expectations following 'thirty glorious years' of continuous rapid economic growth, indeed the second best performance in the industrialized world after Japan. It seemed that the country's productive forces had responded to the leitmotifs of successive governments : 'productivity' was the key word of the reconstruction phase, then 'exports' became the objective

------------

[1] L'envol de la France dans les années 80, Hachette, Paris, 1973.

1

of a protectionist nation entering the Common Market. 'Industrial imperative' was President Pompidou's favourite concept, and 'competitiveness' that of President Giscard d'Estaing.

French governments have always used these themes to mobilize the nation's resources in their continuous effort to 'catch up' with the leading industrialized countries. 'Modernization', the Socialists' theme for the 1980s, is rather pessimistic, for it conveys the idea of an obsolete industrial base which requires another period of 'reconstruction'. This in turn implies that earlier achievements may have to be questioned, which would be an even more painful exercise for the nation.

What has then happened to France ? Were the thirty glorious years a true miracle which could end as unexpectedly as it occurred, or have most observers and policy makers been deluded by the exceptional circumstances which France enjoyed in the 1945-75 period ?

This book examines the reasons for the postwar economic 'miracle' in France and why there has been a marked change in direction in the last decade. We present the arguments for reversing this decline and the chances for France to regain a strong competitive position in the international economy. We have not limited the study to industrial policy in the strict sense of the goals set by government for industrial development or the actions taken by public agencies. We discuss the history and future of French industry through a diagnosis of the multiple factors which determine its strengths and weaknesses : French corporate strategies and management practices, French society and traditions, world economic competition and global interdependence and, of course, official industrial policy.

This book has three parts. Part I examines France's global comparative economic performance as an international competitor from 1945 to date. It looks into the paradox of the relative industrial stagnation today in comparison with the first 30 years of growth after the war. Part II presents a framework for reviewing the comparative performances of France's corporations and the value of their contribution to France's standard of living. It reviews the role of business leadership in establishing a competitive industry which could serve as the foundation for a sustainable growth in living standards. Part III examines the role and effectiveness of government actions in the development of industry. It evaluates not only "industrial policy", but also all major policies which directly or indirectly affect the competitive position and the allocation of resources among corporations. The postcript finally indicates the recent fundamental changes which are taking place in French society beneath the surface of politics and ideology, and suggests further changes which are necessary if France is to stay in the league of the most advanced industrial nations. This book wants to demonstrate that prosperity - the goal of any country at peace - is never secure. Prosperity is the result of an ever-renewed process of successful competition.

Paris, February 1986

Figure 1

# FRANCE'S RELATIVE PERFORMANCE IN STANDARD OF LIVING

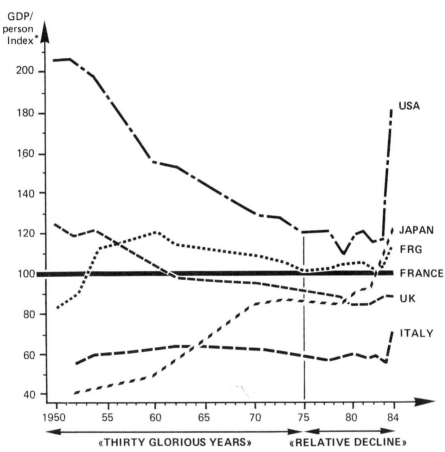

GDP/
person
Index*

- 200
- 180 — USA
- 160
- 140
- 120 — JAPAN
- FRG
- 100 — FRANCE
- UK
- 80
- ITALY
- 60
- 40

1950  55  60  65  70  75  80  84

←————— «THIRTY GLORIOUS YEARS» —————→ ←— «RELATIVE DECLINE» —→

\* In constant 1983 US $
Sources : OECD, IMF

4

# PART I RISE AND DECLINE OF FRANCE'S COMPETITIVE POWER

## 1. CATCHING UP ?

Postwar industrial development in France has resembled a three-act play : first, a period of 30 years of continuous and rapid growth - the result of the Marshall Plan, the internationally acclaimed pl nning system, the post-colonial search for new markets in Europe and elsewhere, the renewed monetary confidence and stability of the de Gaulle years and the accelerated industrialization of the Pompidou era ; second, a decade of relative decline triggered by successive oil price rises but really caused by weakening industrial competitiveness in relation to the US and Japan ; and finally a third act now underway which will take France beyond this decade. The aim is the modernization of whole sectors and regions and success or failure will depend more on managers, creators and workers than on voters.

Successful competition at all levels -individuals, companies and countries - is at the root of economic progress. France realized the benefits of international competition when it overtook Britain and when it edged close to West Germany. Perhaps the most gratifying achievement was the narrowing of the gap between France's living standard and that of the world's wealthiest country : GDP per person was one-third that of the United States in the early postwar years, while by 1974 it had risen to 80 per cent of the US level (Figure 1).

The growth period is important for an understanding of present attitudes. The French economist and social observer Jean Fourastié has called the period France's 'thirty glorious years'. France had moved quickly from its prewar status of an agricultural economy with a protected and uncompetitive industrial sector to a modern industrial economy led by

5

Figure 2

## FRANCE'S RELATIVE PERFORMANCE IN ECONOMIC GROWTH

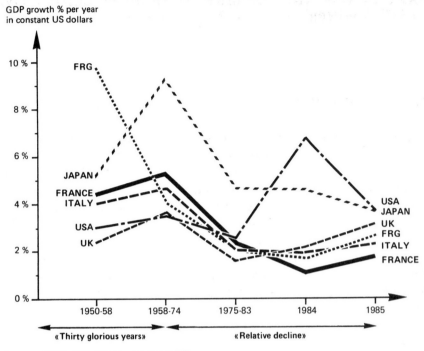

Sources : OECD, IMF, EEC forecast (for 1985)

Figure 3

## EVOLUTION OF FRANCE'S FOREIGN TRADE BALANCE
### EXPORTS / IMPORTS (%)

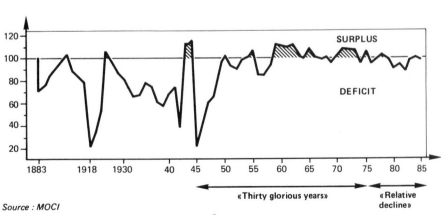

Source : MOCI

6

companies of international size and performance in many businesses such as automobiles, aircraft, power generation equipment, railway equipment, tyres, oil, glass or consumer appliances. The growth rate of total wealth was consistently higher than those of the three industrial leaders, the US, the UK and West Germany, during the period 1958-74 (Figure 2). France managed this in an increasingly open international environment and showed a positive balance of trade through most of the period, in a century of massive deficits (Figure 3).

Unfortunately, since 1974, France has been losing ground compared with its main competitors. The gap in the standard of living between France and West Germany has widened again by a margin of 15 per cent in West Germany's favour. The same is true for Scandinavian economies and Switzerland. The favorable gap which had opened with Britain has begun to narrow since 1983. It is obvious that the US economy is again dominant, and Japan is now at a level just above the French standard of living. Furthermore, France's GDP per person has been sustained at artificially high levels by a dramatic increase in foreign debt, which rose from nothing to 6 per cent of GDP in 1981 and to 12 per cent in 1985 : the annual payments on total foreign debt now amount to close to 2 per cent of GDP per person in France, and will increase automatically for several years unless the dollar continues to fall well below its early 1986 level, which is beyond the control of the French government. This sudden surge in foreign debt - caused by the ill-conceived expansionary policies of 1981 and 1982 - still puts France at a lower debt ratio per capita than Germany, Japan or the US. France however is far from having the same current account surplus as the first two countries or the same financial and currency supremacy as the third one.

The relative economic stagnation of France may be clearly observed in the performance of many of its major companies. The vast majority of the largest industrial concerns are showing low levels of profitability and five out of the top ten have been losing money over the last three years. Peugeot and Michelin, formerly top-performing management models of the private sector, have both been

Figure 4

# WHAT HAPPENED TO THE PROFITABLE COMPANIES OF 1973 ?
## FRENCH COMPANIES LISTED IN THE 1973 TOP 100 PROFITS WHICH BECAME LOSS MAKERS IN 1981

| COMPANIES | SECTOR | 1973 Profits Bill. F. (1983 FF) | % Return on equity | 1981 Losses Bill. F. (1983 FF) | % Loss on equity | 1984 Profits (or Loss) Bill. F. |
|---|---|---|---|---|---|---|
| RHONE-POULENC | Chemicals | 1,67 | 8 | - 0,41 | 5 | 1,80 |
| PEUGEOT-CITROEN | Automobiles | 1,49 | 9 | - 2,45 | 16 | - 1,00** |
| P.U.K. | Non ferrous metals & chemicals | 1,03 | 6 | - 3,10 | 31 | 0,55 |
| USINOR | Steel | 1,23 | 7 | - 5,17 | 48 | - 3,10 |
| THOMSON | Electronics | 0,83 | 16 | - 0,19 | 2 | 0 |
| CDF* | Coal | 0,35 | 8 | - 0,33 | 8 | - 0,60 |
| CII-HB | Computers | 0,33 | 11 | - 0,55 | 34 | - 0,50 |
| LE NICKEL | Non ferrous metals | 0,19 | 4 | - 0,35 | 65 | 0 |
| RENAULT | Automobiles | 0,16 | 2 | - 0,75 | 5 | - 11,50 |
| FERODO VALEO | Vehicle components | 0,15 | 11 | - 0,17 | 10 | - 0,10 |
| SACILOR | Steel | 0,13 | 2 | - 3,53 | 28 | - 8,14 |
| SCOA | Trading | 0,12 | 8 | - 0,14 | 17 | 0,02 |
| SCHNEIDER | Electronics, engineering | 0,09 | 8 | - 0,42 | 23 | 0 |
| HACHETTE | Publishing | 0,09 | 7 | - 0,02 | 16 | 0,19 |
| SHELL Française | Oil | 0,06 | 1 | - 0,20 | 3 | - 1,07 |
| DMC | Textiles | 0,06 | 7 | - 0,09 | 16 | 0,06 |
| SNECMA | Aircraft engines | 0,06 | 4 | - 0,16 | 8 | 0,05 |
| AIR FRANCE | Airlines | 0,04 | 1 | - 0,46 | 12 | 0,90 |
| KLEBER COLOMBES | Tyres | 0,02 | — | - 0,52 | 54 | N.A. |
| TOTAL | | 8,30 | | - 19,10 | | - 22,37 |

* After government subsidies
** Net income before tax carry-back
Source : Telesis analysis from annual reports

8

heavily in the red and burdened with debt with hopes to return to moderate profits only by 1986. State-owned Renault has lost a record breaking 12 billion francs in 1984 when its main international rivals in the US, Japan, Germany and Sweden were making record profits. Large groups like Pechiney and Thomson, which were thought to be wealthy and strong and which had been on the Left's nationalization list since 1972, proved to be much weaker than the Left anticipated when it came to power in 1981. Pechiney has returned to the black in 1984, but Thomson is just breaking even despite drastic measures. In fact, nineteen of the companies which were among the top 100 companies in size of profits in 1973 were losing money by 1981. Their combined profits of 8 billion francs turned into total losses of 19 billion francs in 1981 (Figure 4). The financial results announced by some of these large corporations since 1983 or 1984 show definite improvement, but none of them has reached its 1973 level of profitability, and many are still losing large sums in sectors as diverse as cars, electronics, steel and chemicals, where their leading foreign competitors are announcing historical records of profitability.

French productive sectors can no longer absorb all people of employable age. In the 1960s, the economy was able to accommodate the significant rise in numbers of people seeking work, which resulted from the postwar baby boom, the growing proportion of women working, immigration and repatriation of French citizens from Algeria. Today, however, unemployment has risen to more than 9 per cent from 2 per cent in 1973 and could be well above 10 per cent by 1986 when the breathing air caused by extraordinary social measures like training schemes or 'TUC' fades away. This rate is significantly higher than that of Japan, Germany or even the US and is close to the level of the oldest industrial nations, UK and Belgium. Even more worrying than the overall figures is the structure of France's unemployment, which illustrates built-in obsolescence. The average length of unemployment was 13.4 months in France, 11.2 months in the UK, 8.2 months in Germany and only 3.6 months in the US. Only Belgium surpassed France with 17.3 months. In addition, 43 per cent of registered unemployed people in France have

Figure 5

## CHANGES IN LABOUR FORCE AND JOB CREATION

| COUNTRIES | 1958 – 1973 | | 1973 – 1983 | |
|---|---|---|---|---|
| | CHANGE IN LABOUR FORCE (Millions) | NEW JOBS CREATED (Millions) | CHANGE IN LABOUR FORCE (Millions) | NEW JOBS CREATED (Millions) |
| USA | 22,1 | 22,0 | 22,0 | 15,9 |
| JAPAN | 9,4 | 9,7 | 5,6 | 4,3 |
| FRANCE | 2,4 | 2,0 | 1,1 | 0 |
| UK | 1,1 | 1,0 | 1,1 | - 1,2 |
| GERMANY | 0,3 | 0,8 | 1,0 | - 1,5 |
| ITALY | - 1,0 | - 0,9 | 2,8 | 1,8 |

*Sources : OECD Labour statistics*

Figure 6

## RELATIVE TRENDS IN LEVELS OF INVESTMENT

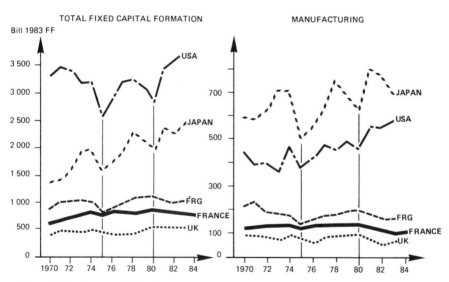

*Sources : National accounts OECD, IMF.*

been out of work for more than one year, compared with 36 per cent in the UK, 28 per cent in Germany, and 13 per cent in the US. Many of France's competitors, notably the US, have been more successful in replacing lost jobs with new ones, albeit mostly in relatively unskilled services which usually provide low wage employment. France's unemployment rate has more than quadrupled in the last decade, despite a much slower increase in the labour force. This has resulted in a net job creation flow close to zero (Figure 5). The traditional creations of service sector jobs can no longer compensate for an increasing shrinkage of industrial employment.

In the last decade, the absolute number of jobs available in the industrial sector in France declined by 870,000 and this trend seems to be long lasting. It is estimated that industry shed some 200,000 jobs in 1984 and almost the same in 1985. In other words, jobs lost through productivity improvements and closure of businesses were not replaced by jobs in new or growing sectors of industry. For example, new jobs created in automobiles, electronics and services in the North and in Lorraine nowhere near matched the losses in steel, coal and textiles. The decline in the total number of jobs represents 20 per cent of positions available in the industrial workforce today and this dramatic shrinkage has been on a par with that in the UK.

A third sign of France's relative economic stagnation is its recent low levels of investment in industry, in comparison with its competitors particularly Japan and the USA. France did not keep up with its level of investment of the early 1970s whilst others were raising theirs (Figure 6). The recent signs of recovery in 1985 are far from restoring plant and equipment investments levels to where they stood in the early 1970s.

These indicators of economic malaise are further emphasized by France's declining position as a major exporter. France has steadily lost its share of OECD trade (Figure 7). The continuing devaluation of the French franc since 1975, which has accelerated since 1981, is the most

Figure 7

## COMPARATIVE EXPORT SHARES IN MANUFACTURING

| Countries | WORLD TRADE (%) | | | |
|---|---|---|---|---|
| | 1958 | 1975 | 1980 | 1983 |
| GERMANY | 26,7 | 18,6 | 18,2 | 18,5 |
| USA | NA | 9,4 | 10,0 | 9,9 |
| UK | 25,8 | 8,5 | 8,4 | 7,7 |
| FRANCE | 12,4 | 9,4 | 9,1 | 8,5 |
| JAPAN | 8,5 | 12,4 | 13,5 | 17,7 |
| ITALY | 5,9 | 6,8 | 7,2 | 7,8 |

*Sources : UNO, OECD*

Figure 8

## NET TRADE BALANCE IN MANUFACTURED GOODS*

% OF MANUFACTURING OUTPUT

| | 1958 | 1975 | 1980 | 1982 | 1983 |
|---|---|---|---|---|---|
| UK | 25,7 | 14,2 | 0 | 0,3 | 5,9 |
| GERMANY | 23,1 | 26,7 | 22,6 | 32,2 | NA |
| FRANCE | 11,5 | 10,2 | 4,3 | 2,6 | 1,0 |
| ITALY | 10,3 | 23,1 | 15,7 | 25,7 | NA |

*\* Definition : Manufactured exports minus manufactured imports as a percentage of manufacturing output.*
*Source : OECD*

12

obvious acknowledgement of France's predicament as a relatively weak competitor in the international industrial economy.

At the same time, French businesses have lost their share of their domestic market. Foreign automobiles have now grown to a steady third of the French market, from less than a fifth a decade ago, despite strict limits on Japanese imports. French consumers are showing increasing preference for imported goods at the same time as foreign consumers are finding French goods less attractive. Figure 8 shows the change in the percentage of manufactured imports in comparison with exports over the past 25 years. The trade deficit was reduced in 1984, dropping to around 25 billion francs, half the figure of 1983 and a quarter of the 1982 total, but trade will still not be balanced in 1985 with about the same deficit as in 1984, to the disappointment of the government who had set the balancing of trade as one its main objectives. The position vis-à-vis competitors can be judged by the fact that the West German trade surplus soared to around 170 billion francs in 1984 and 220 billion francs in 1985. Fortunately the trade deficit is about compensated by 'invisible' exports in 1984 and 1985, namely engineering contracts and tourism. In summary France was able to sustain its standard of living, only thanks to the record revenues of tourism, agricultural commodities, and defence equipment. But these sources of revenues cannot be considered as the most stable and predictable. At the same time the manufactured trade surplus has fallen from 110 billion francs in 1984 to 90 billion francs in 1985 despite growing demand abroad and a stagnant market at home. In the last decade, France trade balance has been positive only once, in 1978.

France's loss of competitiveness has also swollen its external debt. The country had to pay 66 billion francs in 1984 on its total borrowings and 72 billion in 1985. Exports would have to rise by 10 per cent above what they are today to cover this debt servicing. The improvement in the trade balance in 1984 and 1985 will have to be accelerated for a good five years before the cumulative deficits can be absorbed. The recent months do not give much hope in this respect, with the exception of the decrease in oil prices and the dollar.

France, it seems, has been experiencing the 'British syndrome' of relative decline in standard of living. Not surprisingly, the Left accuses the Right of having left behind a mess in the Spring of 1981 and argues with some justification that the financial position of the companies it nationalized came as an unwelcome surprise. It had told the heads of nationalized companies to balance their books by the end of 1985, but it has had to make obvious exceptions - the steel companies, Renault and of course the coal mines.

In turn, the Right blames the Left and the unions for having disrupted the entire production system with nationalizations, higher wages and social benefits and challenges to the authority of the management of large corporations. Some right-wing critics believe that the decline is irreversible and that the French can come to expect a lower living standard than their neighbours. As it is, the various forecasts for growth in 1986 range from one to two per cent which will place France behind most of its competitors.

What are the reasons for the decline of France's relative position as an industrial nation ? Can answers be extracted from the maze of conjecture and blame which cover the economic facts ? More importantly, can a way be found to reverse the trend and avoid a return to the defeatism of the inter-war years ? A more in-depth analysis based on good understanding of the competitive process between nations is necessary.

Competitive activity between companies within the same country has been relatively well understood since the industrial revolution. As companies compete to deliver the same products and services more productively, i.e. at a lower cost per unit, their activity has two effects : prices fall, and the surplus human resources can produce new goods and services, or enjoy more leisure time. The resulting wealth for the society is measured in terms of increased standard of living, as the same goods are available for less work hours, and/or society's resources achieve greater output from the

14

same inputs. If a country is to increase its standard of living steadily, its economic activity must consist of continuous movement both toward improving the productivity of existing businesses and shifting human and financial resources to new, more productive uses.

Until the last 20 years, most competitive activity took place within the boundaries of each particular country or group of similar countries (like the EEC). The world trade that existed before this time simply represented a complementary exchange of goods. For example, France and the UK traded with their colonies, exchanging manufactured goods for minerals, grains, wool and cheap labour. Even developed countries had a similar pattern; the US primarily exported to Europe products such as aircraft, computers, pharmaceuticals and defence electronics, which could not be produced locally.

Trading between nations for the same goods, or head-on competition between companies from different countries, is a recent phenomenon. It gives a new layer of complexity to the achievement of a higher standard of living by any nation. Wherever the products of companies of one country are traded openly in competition with the products of companies in other countries, the story is different. Companies in any society can only create wealth for their society if they can achieve higher productivity which gives them a stronger competitive position relative to rival companies in other countries. The fundamental mechanism for wealth creation through trade is better called competitive advantage than comparative advantage in the same business.

As world trade increasingly represents head-on competition between countries, industrialised countries, particularly those which rely heavily on sales of manufactured products and related services for GNP growth, face increasing challenges in seeking to increase their standard of living. The challenge must be taken up by companies and by governments. First, companies within industrial nations must find goods and services which are competitive in world markets. Second, the governments of industrialised nations must orient their policies in ways which best assist the movement of human and financial resources, through the medium of the nation's companies, towards increasingly productive uses.

## 2. 1945 - 1975 'THIRTY GLORIOUS YEARS' OF GROWING PROSPERITY

Within this context, France's rapid growth in standard of living between 1945 and 1974, relative to its OECD partner competitors, may be seen to have resulted from a network of particular circumstances within its competitive spheres. These circumstances allowed it to make gains of a size which seem "miraculous" when compared with achievements of competitor nations over the same period and when compared with France's more recent achievements in improving its standard of living. The circumstances, broadly speaking, were that :
- France's overall productivity was very low in relative terms in 1945,
- France had resources for rapid improvements in productivity after 1945,
- the organization and strategies of enterprises and governments made a more efficient and effective use of resources than had been experienced before the war,
- international competition was not of a kind to impede France's growth potential or its progressive opening to world markets.

### Overall prewar productivity relatively low
At the end of World War II, France could, in a sense, go in no direction but a positive one in terms of its productivity. Postwar annual productivity gains per year were 5 per cent to 6 per cent in agriculture (the highest after Germany), between 3 per cent and 5.7 per cent in industry (the highest after Japan) and between 1 per cent and 3 per cent in services, which have brought France up to a very good position among OECD countries (Figure 9).

First, in 1945, France was still primarily an agricultural economy. Its agricultural resources have always been a source of wealth, of course. In the late eighteenth

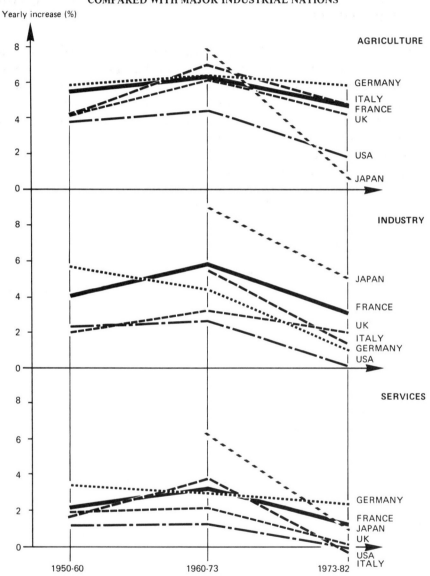

Figure 9

FRANCE'S RELATIVE GAINS IN PRODUCTIVITY
COMPARED WITH MAJOR INDUSTRIAL NATIONS

Yearly increase (%)

AGRICULTURE

GERMANY
ITALY
FRANCE
UK

USA

JAPAN

INDUSTRY

JAPAN

FRANCE

UK
ITALY
GERMANY
USA

SERVICES

GERMANY

FRANCE
JAPAN
UK

USA
ITALY

1950-60          1960-73          1973-82

*Sources : Angus Maddison - Economic growth in the West, OECD, Historical Statistics*

18

Figure 10

## CHANGES IN FRANCE'S ACTIVE POPULATION IN PRODUCTIVE ACTIVITIES

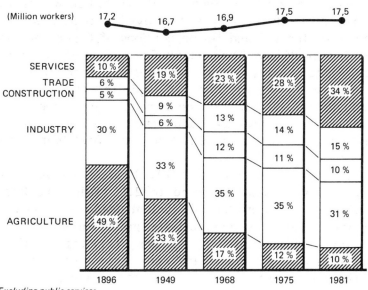

Excluding public services
Source : INSEE

Figure 11

## AGRICULTURAL WORK FORCE IN ADVANCED INDUSTRIAL NATIONS

DECREASE IN % OF TOTAL CIVILIAN EMPLOYMENT

|  | 1950 — 1982 |
|---|---|
| JAPAN | − 32,3 |
| ITALY | − 27,6 |
| FRANCE | − 19,7 |
| GERMANY | − 19,5 |
| USA | − 9,4 |
| UK | − 3,3 |

Source : Labour Force Statistics  OECD

19

century, France's agriculture made it the wealthiest country in the world with the ability to feed the largest population of Europe. Today, France is still self-sufficient in most commodities grown in the northern hemisphere, and the world's third largest exporter of agricultural products. Nevertheless, in the late 1940s, France's agricultural industry was relatively unproductive. France had 5.6 million workers in agriculture, or a third of the employed population. This compared with the UK and US proportions of 6 per cent and 13 per cent respectively. These countries had made a major structural shift away from agriculture and towards manufacturing much earlier; they had exploited the technical breakthroughs of the late 19th century in organic chemicals, electricity, engines, telephones, radio, etc., and had gained a large presence in world markets during the first half of the twentieth century.

In the 30 years up to 1974, France reduced its population employed in agriculture to 2.1 million workers, representing 12 per cent of the civilian employed population in 1974 (Figure 10). The productivity gains were achieved through the application of modern farming methods (agricultural machinery, fertilizers and agro-chemicals) and through the concentration of land into larger units, as other advanced countries had done earlier.

It is a credit to the different political regimes and to French society that such a large productivity gain was achieved in such a short period without major disruptions and without dislocation of the social fabric. Today, France is an industrial economy with the benefit of the long stability (and sometimes the resilience) of its agricultural traditions. Only Japan and Italy, which were both more recent industrial economies, had higher reductions in their agricultural work force (Figure 11).

Second, France's industrial production in 1945 was virtually at rock bottom, both in comparison with its former output and with its competitor countries at the end of World War II. France was the only large industrial economy whose output had diminished between the two wars. In 1938, French output was 20 per cent lower than in 1929, while Germany's and the UK's were 50 per cent and 27 per cent higher, respectively. French industry continued to decline during World War II while other European countries (including some neutral ones such as Sweden) were operating at full speed for the war effort. The decline in France's industrial output between the wars was largely a result of sluggish demand, protectionist attitudes, and low investment rates in all sectors of the economy including of course military equipment and transport infrastructure. Again in this period, other industrial countries were gearing up for the war and developing their economies aggressively.

The end of World War II created conditions which strongly stimulated growth in French industrial production. Industrial plant and equipment were in great need of replacement, since the industrial capacity which was not destroyed was not renewed at all during the war years. More importantly, France's infrastructure of roads, railways, bridges and ports suffered a severe degree of destruction. The country's widespread need for physical reconstruction provided an unprecedented demand for production of goods and services throughout the 1950s and 1960s. Productivity gains in industry were rapid, peaking in the 1960s and early 1970s; only Japan made greater gains in the period.

France was able to meet the demand over the next 30 years for three major reasons. The first was that it had ready access to the resources it required for the task. The second was the dynamic response to the challenge of industrial reconstruction by corporations and the government; management used strategy and organization efficiently and effectively, with a strong sense of national responsibility. The third reason was that France did not face intense competition from other countries.

## Resources available for productivity growth

France enjoyed access to the resources it needed for the reconstruction of its infrastructure and for industrial growth.

First, France had access, although at high cost, to domestic raw materials such as coal and iron ore, necessary for the production of basic manufactured commodities, such as steel for construction, and for the manufacture of ships, aircraft, and consumer goods such as automobiles. It also had

Figure 12

# RELATIVE TRENDS IN LABOUR COSTS

ESTIMATED HOURLY COMPENSATION FOR PRODUCTION
WORKERS IN MANUFACTURING 1960 - 1984

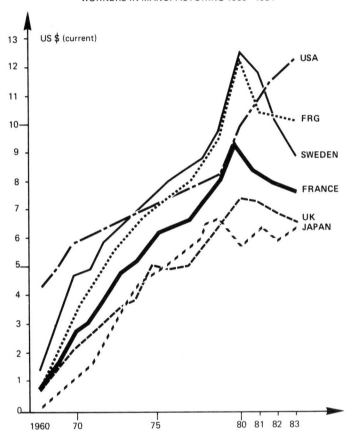

*Source : US Department of Labour*

22

access to lower-cost raw materials from its colonies and protectorates, such as iron ore from Mauritania, phosphate from Morocco and oil and gas from the Sahara for industrial production.

Second, France had access to plentiful sources of relatively low-cost labour (Figure 12). Labour for industrial activity came from the movement of 5.4 million people from agriculture in the 30-year period, from immigrants in particular of former French colonies and southern Europe, from the postwar "baby boom" growth in population, and from the massive resettlement of 1.1 million Algerian French after 1962.

Third, France had access to very low-cost capital for basic investment, from the Marshall Plan. It received 21 per cent of the US $ 12.8 billion given to Europe by the US, or the equivalent of one and a half years of industrial investment made in France in the late 1940s. This low interest money gave France the ability to invest heavily in plant and equipment in capital intensive industries such as railways, cement, steel, electricity generation and petrochemicals. With this investment, France was able to gain advantage over the UK for example, which retained older, less efficient industrial stock after the war. In addition to low-cost foreign capital, France had access to low-cost capital from the banking system. Throughout the period, France had one of the highest savings ratios of western countries, with depositors earning very low (or even negative) real interest rates on savings accounts and bank term deposits. In fact, combined with high inflation, this has caused a continuous transfer of resources from the French public and its savers to its enterprises.

The fortunate combination of resources spurred the development of some remarkable champions of industrial enterprise. At the same time, successive governments pursued policies which assisted many new and growing companies to make the most productive use of their resources for the benefit of France.

## Champions of enterprise

The French car industry was already developed before World War II ; brilliant engineers and daring entrepreneurs like André Citroën and Louis Renault had pioneered many new technologies and successfully launched new products. After the war, three companies, Renault, Peugeot and Citroën, grew rapidly. They supplied the new mass market at home and began in the late 1950s to export to other European countries. These companies had the finance and expertise to put together technical resources (engineers and technicians), invest in new facilities and set up distribution systems. They symbolized the new wave of postwar French industrial leaders.

Similar leaders emerged in the aircraft companies of Dassault, Breguet, Sud-Aviation, Nord-Aviation, Turbomeca, Snecma, etc. from a long and fertile history of technical inventions and commercial successes. In power generation and distribution equipment, France benefited from the rise of many companies such as Alsthom, Jeumont, Merlin-Gérin, Télémécanique, Legrand, etc. Michelin, Kléber-Colombes and Hutchinson supplied tyres to the growing automobile industry. CFP and SNPA supplied petroleum and oil products for automobiles and all manufacturing industry. BSN and St Gobain supplied glass to the booming construction and automobile industries. Brandt, Moulinex, SEB and Thomson responded to the growing demand for domestic appliances and household goods. Companies like Progil, Kuhlmann, Pechiney and Rodiaceta invested in petrochemicals, fibres, and other organic chemicals, to fill traditional gaps in French industry, frequently using foreign technologies and product licences.

## Government policies

The successive French governments of the 30 year period 1945-1975 assisted the process of shifting France's resources to new, more productive uses, in several ways. First, the government provided businesses with a domestic market through public investment in infrastructure (roads, bridges, housing) and purchases of equipment by government controlled utilities (electricity, railway, telephone). Second, it provided cheap capital, either directly in the form of soft loans and investment grants to particular regions or State owned companies, or indirectly through the interest rate structure controlled by the Treasury and the largely State controlled and State regulated banking system. Third, it encouraged exports, through the tax system (France invented the value added tax in 1954 which indirectly favours export sales) and through low cost credit provided by private and State owned banks (BFCE was created in 1945) following government directives.

A fourth measure was funding a major part of French research and development through public programmes in defence and aeronautics, and later in nuclear energy and digital telecommunications. In this area, the government also promoted knowledge and innovation in technology and product development by concentrating resources in targeted areas of France, with a mix of research centres, universities and high-technology companies in the same field of industry. Before the war, Paris was almost the only French centre of scientific knowledge; subsequently, Grenoble was developed around electrical engineering and electronics, Toulouse around aerospace industries, and Rennes to a lesser extent around telecommunications.

Finally, in recognition of the need for skilled labour, the government raised the general level of education by extending the compulsory age for education to 14 years and then in 1959 to 16 years, and by increasing university enrolment. As a result, while the population between 15 and 20 years of age rose by 46 per cent between 1950 and 1982, the number of young French students completing high school rose by 530 per cent.

By the end of the 30 'glorious' years, France's position as a world industrial power seemed assured. The standard of living was one of the highest in the world and progressing more rapidly than in the older industrialized countries. Furthermore, all the trends indicated that France was not resting on the laurels of these years, but building to reinforce its position : total investment ratios remained higher than those of all competitors except J pan, shares of

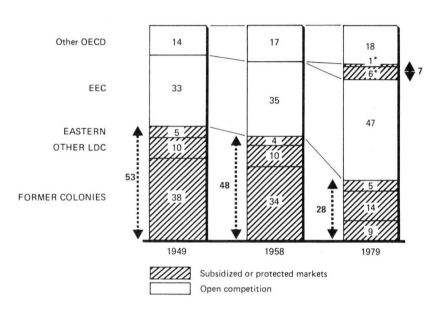

Figure 13

# FROM A SHELTERED TO A TRADED ECONOMY
## RELATIVE IMPORTANCE OF PROTECTED MARKETS
### IN FRANCE EXPORTS
(%)

*Note : Subsidized markets include agricultural commodities exports
supported by the Common Agricultural Policy of the EEC*

*Source : Telesis analysis from OECD trade statistics*

26

export markets were up, R&D expenditure ratios were reasonably high although decreasing, and most large corporations looked profitable and strong.

With hindsight however, it can be seen that the speed and height of France's rise in standard of living were made possible by the particularly favourable competitive environment.

## International competition relatively unthreatening

France's position in the European and the international economies gave it a unique opportunity to realise its growth potential after 1945.

As has been said earlier, France's strength as an industrial producer at the end of World War II was relatively poor. It was mainly an exporter of agricultural commodities to industrial nations, but its manufactured goods found their main markets in French colonies and other protected markets (Figure 13). The United States, UK and Germany had a greater overall capability to compete with French companies on any open market, and smaller countries like Sweden, Switzerland or the Netherlands also had stronger companies in their key industries. France therefore faced the task of opening its economy to world trade without being swallowed up by stronger players.

Despite this relatively disadvantaged position, French corporations were able to supply France's domestic demand for goods and to export an increasing volume of manufactured goods without encountering fierce competition. The reasons for this relative lack of competition may be found through examination of the competitive environments of the stronger countries during the period.

First, the United States' own domestic demand was large enough to absorb virtually all its growth. In addition, while it was the most innovative and efficient producer of many manufactured goods and the only producer in many new businesses, it did not flood European markets with exports, but rather established local production subsidiaries in Europe in cars, chemicals, pharmaceuticals, etc. US companies assisted France and other European countries to develop competitive industrial strength : by 1950, the US had established more than 200 subsidiary companies in Europe, with one-quarter located in France. These companies brought new technology and new production management processes, and generated employment in France.

Second, the UK continued to trade principally with its traditional imperial markets in Africa, South-East Asia, India, Australia, New Zealand and Canada after World War II. As the countries of the former British Empire gained independence, the UK lost ground in the markets of the former colonies, which were anyway growing slower than the European markets. Fortunately for France, the UK was slow in coming to terms with the economic consequences of the political changes of the 1950s and failed to join the EEC on its formation in 1958. For the remainder of the period in question, the UK posed little threat to France, being excluded from the EEC and unable to restore its previous competitive position in world markets on its own. When the UK finally joined in 1974, France had surpassed it.

Third, German competition was accommodated within the protective mechanisms of the EEC which prevailed during the period under review. The mechanisms for resource allocation among the member nations were based on mutual recognition by the two major powers, France and Germany, of their respective needs. After the EEC was formed, Germany accepted the Common Agricultural Policy, despite the fact that it had the effect of German consumers subsidising French commodity exports. De Gaulle recognised that the EEC could give France a fighting chance to renew its industrial strength, since it would have, in particular, Germany as a powerful economic partner, as well as a competitor.

Fourth, the EEC agreements protected France, together with all member countries, from competition from nations with the potential to penetrate markets for industrial products inside the EEC. The protection of the common external tariff against countries like Denmark, Sweden, Switzerland or indeed the US, constrained imports in steel, paper, chemicals and other goods, allowing France to produce manufactured goods which would otherwise not have been competitive.

Finally, during this period France did not feel the effects of the manufactured exports which would later come from Japan and from the assortment of international manufacturers producing goods in South-East Asian and Latin American countries. In the early 1970s, Japanese producers had just begun to affect western markets, in businesses such as steel, shipbuilding, automobiles, motor cycles and cameras. Again, in 1970, imports from the newly industrialising countries represented only 4 per cent of OECD manufactured imports, which was only 1 per cent more than in 1963.

How, then, can France's position be summarised at the end of the 30 'glorious years' ?

First, France had, without doubt, achieved a momentous rise in its standard of living, both through radically improving the productivity of its agricultural base and through shifting human and financial resources to new more productive uses across a wide spectrum of industrial sectors. By 1974, those sectors comprised a fully developed national network of businesses in manufactured goods and supporting services. France had thus achieved a definitive transition from an agricultural to an industrial base for its economy. It could expect its future GNP growth to come largely from growth in employment and productivity in the industrial sector and growth in goods and services in the sub-supplier sector.

Second, within the protected environment of the EEC, France had made successful steps in international competition in the industrial sector. For example, French companies started to establish distribution networks, brand image and after-sales service in other EEC markets. In 1974, Renault had become the leader in European market share for cars, and Michelin for tyres with the invention of radial technology. Other French companies made acquisitions in other countries to achieve improved economies of scale in production and greater control of distribution and pricing. St Gobain, for example, became number two in the European glass industry behind Pilkington. Finally, companies engaged in high technologies acquired knowledge from their competitors through licensing agreements and joint ventures in businesses such as pharmaceuticals, specially chemicals, aircraft, computers, etc. Some like Aerospatiale (helicopters and missiles) and Dassault (light jet fighters and business jets) had even gained worldwide positions in their segments.

France's success within the relatively sheltered environment of the 30 glorious years may have lulled corporations and the government into a false sense of security about the long-term sustainability of France's postwar position. France had established an industrial base in a harbour protected, as it were, from the storms at sea by the reef of the EEC. As international competition intensified later in the 1970s, it became clear that France did not have Germany's strength to weather the incoming waves. In 1974, no-one realised that France was not ready for the aggressive head-on competition which now constitutes international trade.

# 3. 1975 - 1985 A DECADE OF RELATIVE DECLINE

No industrialised country has escaped the effects of the sobering economic forces of the last decade. In an environment of open international competition, free flows of capital and accelerating productivity improvements from technological development, companies in developed countries have experienced severe pressures on their efforts to sustain competitiveness, while European governments have found it increasingly difficult to achieve growth or even stability in standards of living.

First, companies which have supplied manufactured goods requiring relatively unskilled labour, such as segments of clothing and shoes, ships or electronic assembles, have been seriously affected by the establishment of large-scale manufacturing operations in developing countries. These countries have had a cost advantage in mass production, in relatively low-cost labour, as well as in up-to-date production technology and appropriate production volumes.

Second, in higher skilled labour businesses such as automobiles, steel or machinery, competition on a world scale has intensified at the same time as increasingly rapid technological development has accelerated productivity improvements in many of these industrial sectors. Many companies with long-established profitability in their businesses have found their market shares eroded by competitors in their own traditional areas of competition and, more particularly, from competitors who have emerged on the open market of world trade, particularly Japan.

At a company level in all developed countries, there have been and continue to be winners and losers in all industrial sectors. At a national level, some developed countries have found their growth and employment more seriously affected by these forces. While countries struggle to restructure their manufacturing industries, young people find that the jobs they might have expected to have a decade ago no longer exist, either because businesses no longer exist or particular jobs no longer exist. At the same time, many companies and governments are finding that they are prevented from building new high-skill businesses by the lack of a broad spectrum of essential technical, marketing and management experience.

In this period of dramatic "shakeout" on the world scene, we can see that France has lost more ground than its main competitors, except the UK, as illustrated by the decline of market shares and corporate returns, increasing foreign debt and stagnating standard of living.

Industrial growth in France in the postwar era took place principally in two of the three broad arenas for competition in industrial activity. The three arenas are : (1) raw materials businesses, which involve fundamentally the exploitation of natural resources; (2) low wage-rate businesses, which involve fundamentally the exploitation of cheap unskilled labour; and (3) complex-factor businesses, which involve fundamentally the optimization of all elements of the production system, including purchasing, manufacturing, marketing and distribution, applications engineering, and research and development. France's industrial development took place initially in what were then low wage-rate businesses and gradually moved to complex-factor businesses.

In broad terms, France's relative decline in the last ten years has resulted from four major factors :

- France had less raw materials for production of energy or basic industrial commodities than its competitors, at a time when their prices had soared ;
- France became exposed to new competition in low wage-rate businesses ;
- France was more vulnerable to open competition in complex-factor businesses ;
- France had less strategic restructuring of industry at the national level.

## Not enough natural resources

The basis for determination of a country's wealth has
historically been its natural endowment. When food was the
major item of consumption, France was one of the wealthiest
countries in the world because of its agriculture. With coal
and iron ore serving as the base materials for the first
industrial revolution, the UK, Germany, Belgium and Sweden
developed rapidly. In times of chronic energy shortages, oil
and gas rich countries like the US, Australia, Norway, Holland
or the UK have an economic advantage.

Natural resources increase national wealth in three
ways. First, and quite obviously, endowments of raw materials
reduce a country's imports and generate exports. They allow
the country to live off its natural heritage and exchange
products of its soil, its seas or its mines for other goods and
services. Natural resources were the basis of the Ricardo
theory of comparative advantage, with the famous example
of Portugal trading wine in exchange for British textiles.
While France has its natural resource of agriculture, or its
"green oil", its net trade balance of agricultural commodities
is somewhat erratic and quite insufficient to cover the
continuous increases in the cost of materials such as energy,
ores, tropical commodities or timber. Figure 14 shows the
growing deficit of France's total commodities trade balance
over the decade. Not even Japan had to finance a larger
negative commodity trade balance in proportion to its GDP.
The US, German and British economies had resort to more or
lower cost natural endowments to weather the increase in
commodity prices (Figure 15).

France's 'green oil' exports also face a new competitive
challenge. The Common Agricultural Policy of the EEC keeps
European prices at artificially high levels (Figure 16) in order
to sustain production and employment in agriculture. This is a
particularly important protection for the least efficient EEC
producers, including French small dairy farms and low
quality vineyards. The "price umbrella" maintained by CAP
has in turn attracted efficient producers in Germany, the UK
and Ireland, which have resulted in overproduction. The
financial crisis resulting from chronic EEC surpluses in
products such as butter and wine will undoubtedly result in

Figure 14

### FRANCE'S TRADE BALANCE IN RAW MATERIALS AND ENERGY

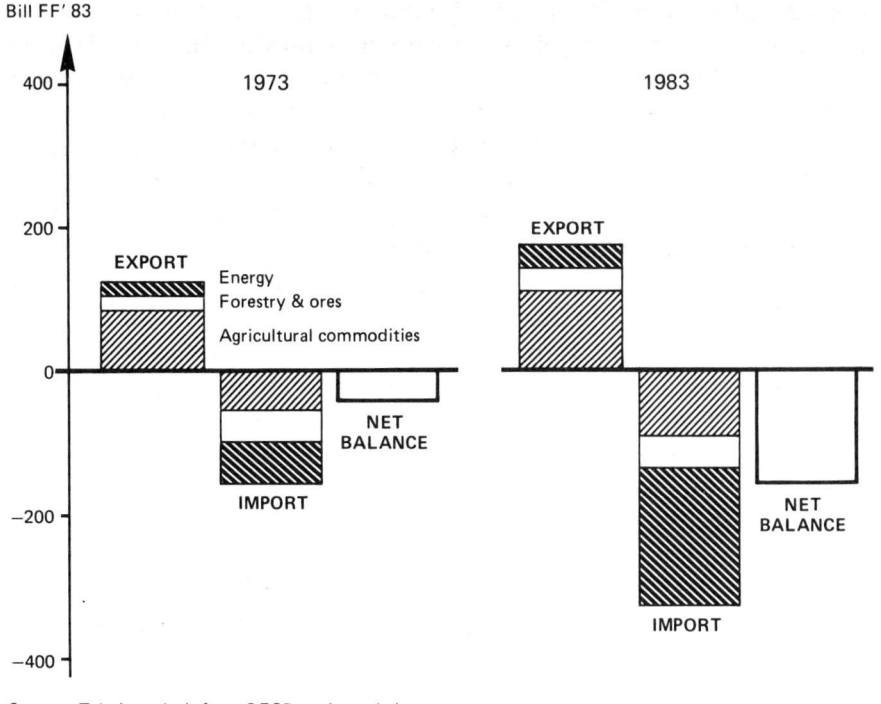

Source : Telesis analysis from OECD trade statistics

Figure 15

### NET TRADE BALANCE IN RAW MATERIALS AND ENERGY

|  | Change 1973 - 1983 as a % of GDP |
|---|---|
| UK | 7,46 |
| USA | - 1,02 |
| JAPAN | - 1,59 |
| FRG | - 2,02 |
| ITALY | - 2,64 |
| FRANCE | - 2,73 |

Source : Telesis analysis from OECD statistics

## EEC PRICES COMPARED WITH WORLD PRICES
## FOR MAJOR FOOD PRODUCTS

Figure 16

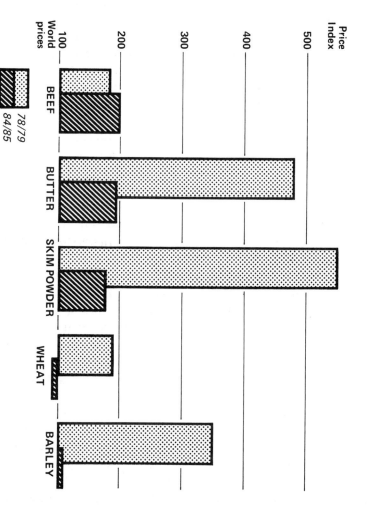

Price
Index

Sources : EUROSTAT, EEC

renewed pressure for reduced European production, at the expense of the least efficient producers. In these circumstances, French agriculture and processing agro-industries will only maintain (or increase) their share of exports if they can achieve productivity and quality improvements which make them competitive with II producers. France is thus living with a 'green petrol' crisis in the wake of the oil crisis. It will have to cut down on overall production and exports to salvage the common agricultural policy.

Second, natural resources can provide low cost inputs for domestic production and make domestic industry more competitive on world open markets. For example, Dutch and Norwegian fertilizer producers have a cost advantage over France in ammonia derived from locally sourced natural gas. This new competition has displaced jobs and wealth from France to Holland and Norway. A second example is the recent Gulf based ethylene and polyethylene production, which outperforms, on the basis of locally sourced raw materials, France's optimum scale cracking-unit built in Dunkirk just before the oil crisis. France is now disadvantaged in all industrial commodities where the main source of competitive advantage is the proximity of a local raw material or energy source. For example :

- Fossil fuels and naphtha determine the cost of most refined oil products, petrochemicals and thermoplastics. The dramatic increase in oil prices has given an extra cost advantage to traditional low-cost producers (Gulf) and encouraged new higher cost producers (North Sea), making French as well as main-land Europe refinery and petrochemicals capacity redundant very soon after a period of massive investments on French territory in Dunkirk, Le Havre, Etang de Berre and Lyon. All oil companies refining in France are now losing money, and capacity will have to be reduced further.

- Natural gas exploited in Holland, Ireland and Norway has stimulated competitive production of ammonia-based fertilizers. All but one French fertilizer company are losing money, and must continue to reduce workforce and capacity. France's only source of natur[al] gas is at Lacq in the South-West. The Lacq field has enabled SNPA (now Elf-Aquitaine) to generate significant spin-off businesses (in sulphur-based chemicals and fertilizers) and has helped the company fund a large part of its investment programme. Lacq will, however, be depleted within the next decade.

- Cheap electricity for electrolytic processes is a major source of competitive advantage in the production of aluminium, chlorine and derived products. Pechiney recently invested in modernizing its aluminium plants on the condition that it would have guaranteed electricity at a significant discount, and took a share in a new nuclear plant built for EDF as part of the agreement. Elf-Aquitaine is asking for the same treatment in chlorine production. Thanks to its nuclear power plants which now produce 50 per cent of its electricity, France has the lowest cost power inside the EEC. While this appears to be a rational method for maintaining domestic production and employment, it is not clear that France can compete with non-EEC countries like Norway with its cheap electricity from hydro sources, even at discounted domestic rates.

- Quickly grown and efficiently exploited forests, such as those developed in North-West America and Brazil, are the critical source of low-cost production in pulp and certain grades of paper like kraft paper where the input of mechanical pulp is very high. Without these local inputs, all French producers of mechanical pulp and derived grades of paper are losing money, except when the dollar exchange rate reaches exceptionally high levels. They are unable to overcome this fundamental cost disadvantage.

The above list is not exhaustive but gives a clear indication of the cost handicaps which French commodity industries suffer, in terms of world competitiveness, as a result of France's relative lack of natural resources.

Third, the exploitation of natural resources can spawn a network of complex-factor businesses in sub-supply and support services. Historically, for example, Swedish participation and skills in many mechanical engineering businesses go back to the challenges of exploiting deep iron ore mines and forests in rocky terrain. Atlas Copco developed drilling equipment, Sandvik developed high speed steels and cemented carbide, and others developed continuous pulp digesters and pulp dryers to solve new technical problems; this was the practical basis for world leadership in very specialized and profitable machinery businesses. In this respect, France's engineering companies have not had the benefits of domestic exploitation of mines and oil fields. The successes to date of French off-shore engineering and service industries are therefore remarkable. It is significant that they are now feeling the negative effects of the activities of Norwegian and British companies which are taking advantage of their booming (and often protected) local markets.

In summary, France's relative lack of natural resources has been a major contributor to its negative trade balance in commodities, its declining competitiveness in raw-material based businesses, and its relative lack and even absence of growth in many complex-factor businesses. When the relative size of France's economy is taken into consideration, it can be said that France has paid the highest toll of developed countries over the last decade, on this account.

## New competition in low wage-rate businesses

All industrializing countries develop new businesses, increase market shares and generate cash flows for investment on the basis of their relatively low wage-rates, which gives them a cost advantage over more advanced countries. This strategy is the first major step in the ever renewed process of industrial evolution : successful 'newly industrialized' countries achieve a higher standard of living, with higher wages, and are inevitably attacked by newly competing countries making the first step to industrialization. Korean companies are now seriously attacked by Malaysian or Indonesian competitors in relatively unskilled businesses such as radio assembly or clothing. Virtually all businesses in all European countries paid low wages compared to US businesses after the war, and France used this advantage very successfully for 30 years. Over the last decade, however, three sources of new competition have arisen to take low-wage based production away from France.

First, 'newly industrializing' countries have emerged in Europe itself and have systematically and aggressively used their relatively low-cost labour to attract US and Japanese off-shore investments. Ireland and the UK (particularly Wales and Scotland) have been the most successful in securing these investments and creating a large number of low-skill jobs in, for example, electronic assembly (including semiconductor packaging and testing and computer assembly) and pharmaceutical compounding and packaging. This activity has had an opportunity cost for France in terms of jobs not created. In addition, it has created a new source of potential low-cost competition for all manufacturing inside the EEC. Undoubtedly, as low-wage countries such as Spain, Greece or Portugal enter the EEC, France's competitive advantage in its relatively low wage rates is being further eroded.

Second, new competitors outside Europe have combined lower labour costs and longer working hours with increasing levels of skill and effective organization. New low-cost producers of this kind from Korea and Taiwan have made large inroads into businesses like consumer electronics, construction engineering, textiles and plastic manufactured goods, and are now heavily investing in semiconductors, industrial electronics and automobiles. Korean companies are certainly the most dangerous competitors today. Korean labour costs are still one fifth of French levels for production workers as well as for engineers; in businesses like TV colour tubes this can give a total factory cost advantage of 30 per cent (Figure 17). In addition to this advantage, Korean consumer electronics companies such as Daewo, Samsung and Gold Star have built modern world-scale facilities, while their engineers obtain almost the same yields as producers in developed countries, and their product design is rapidly improving. Even with transport costs and duties

Figure 17

## COMPETITION FROM NEWLY INDUSTRIALIZED COUNTRIES

COLOUR TV TUBES (Small size)

|  | Cost per tube (FF. 1984) | |
|---|---|---|
|  | European plant | Korean plant |
| MATERIALS AND ENERGY | 205 | 205 |
| LABOUR COSTS : Direct labour on purchased parts | 76 | 14 |
| Direct labour of tube factory | 32 | 6 |
| Overhead | 40 | 8 |
| TOTAL LABOUR COSTS | 148 | 28 |
| DEPRECIATION | 33 | 33 |
| TOTAL FACTORY COST | 386 | 266 |

Note : The two plants have similar size, production processes and yields
Source : Telesis client study

Figure 18

## NEW COMPETITION IN COLOUR TV

|  | JAPANESE COMPETITION % of market | | KOREA & TAIWAN % of market | |
|---|---|---|---|---|
| MARKET | 1980 | 1984 | 1980 | 1984 |
| USA* | 33 | 36 | 3 | 18 |
| UK* | 25 | 28 | 2 | 12 |
| FRG | 5 | 6 | 0 | 5 |
| FRANCE | 5 | 3 | 0 | 0 |

* Includes local assembly
Source : Telesis client study

40

(approximately 20 per cent in this case) taken from the factory cost advantage, the Koreans still have an overall cost advantage.

France has responded to this pressure with quotas and 'voluntary' restraint agreements, and to date the share of imports in the French domestic market taken by these competitors is, as a result, much smaller than in the US, UK and Germany (Figure 18 illustrates the TV example). Nevertheless, the imports have forced many French producers to lower their prices, with an adverse effect on profits. However, France cannot hope to artificially contain this tide for ever, particularly as it increases in volume with further developing countries like Malaysia and Thailand entering the world competitive scene with manufactured goods. Even the world leaders in Japan are likely to suffer, while higher-cost producers like Philips or Thomson, who employ several thousand people in France in consumer electronics, face potentially drastic consequences.

The third source of new competition for low-wage based businesses in France has been the relocation of production by French companies to still lower-cost sources of labour. For example, in the last ten years, several French apparel and fashion designers like Gaston Jaunet or Bidermann invested or set up joint ventures in manufacturing in North Africa and Mauritius. As another example, Thomson began TV and radio assembly in Singapore in 1975 and is now moving to Malaysia. However, French off-shore investments have generally been less significant than similar US, German or British investments and in many cases have failed to give French companies a sustainable cost advantage. The reason is that French companies relied for too long on domestic unskilled labour (immigrants in particular), instead of automating the production and when they have moved off-shore, they have done it haphazardly without reorganizing the whole production process. The German clothing industry, for example, started in the late 1960s to differentiate between long production runs which could be either automated or sent abroad to inexperienced subsuppliers, and shorter runs, more dependent on fashion, which had to be kept at home. This planning allowed the German textile industry to

Figure 19

# RELATIVE STRENGTHS AND WEAKNESSES
## OF FRANCE AND GERMANY'S FOREIGN TRADE

CUMULATIVE NET BALANCE IN MANUFACTURING
1974 – 1983

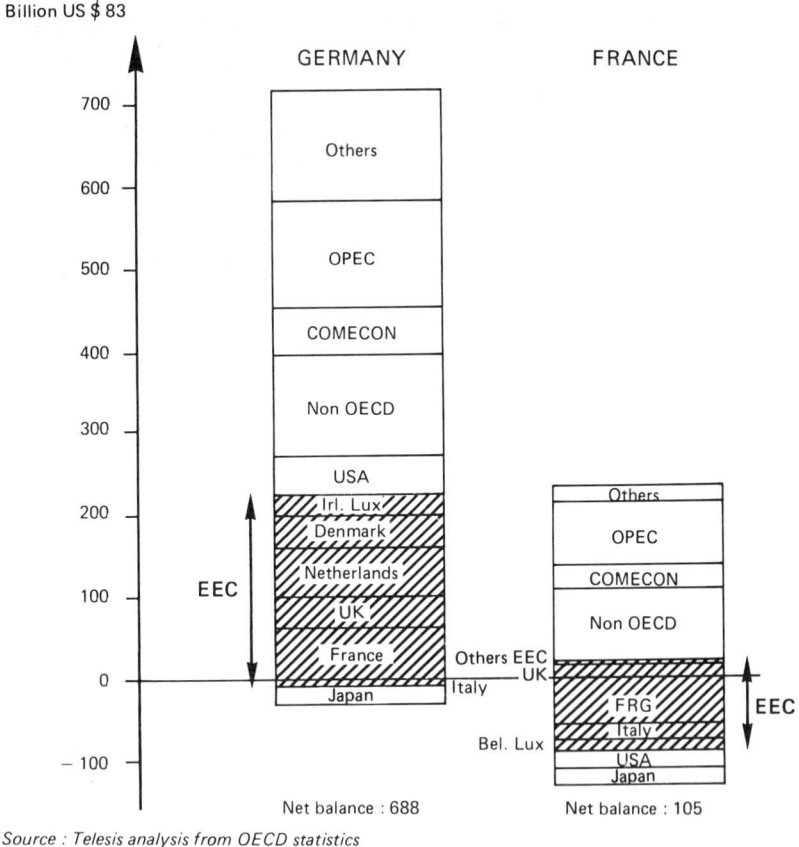

Source : Telesis analysis from OECD statistics

42

keep its natural market for upstream materials in fibres, spinning and weaving. The French clothing companies, in contrast, did little to reduce labour costs until they were in crisis and thereby jeopardized the domestic market for upstream businesses.

## Structural weaknesses to open competition in complex-factor businesses

Complex-factor businesses are the predominant basis for the standard of living of developed economies with insufficient natural endowments, that is all OECD countries except Norway and to a lesser extent Australia and Canada. In these businesses, it is the combination of intelligent strategies, efficient organizations and investments which bring a higher productivity than for competitors, and therefore create wealth.

France, more than most other developed countries, had to rely on a strong base of complex-factor businesses which would generate foreign income, skilled employment and profits for the investors. Because it had less natural resources than the UK, Holland or even Germany and a higher proportion of low wage-rate businesses vulnerable to new competitors, France like Japan had to force the pace of resource shift into higher skilled, technology based businesses. The country, however, has been squeezed severely in its complex-factor businesses by a lower growth rate in world markets, and increased competition at a time when its companies were not yet ready for full battle. Its overall market shares have slightly declined (as illustrated in Figure 7) and French industrial trade surplus (which is one of the measures of the contribution of complex-factor businesses to the country's economic health) has not grown enough to pay for unavoidable and growing deficits of raw materials, energy and cheap goods. This has been mainly true after the second oil shock.

The composition of France's industrial surplus is even more worrysome as it demonstrates a more fragile competitive situation than other European economies, in three dimensions. First, France registers a surplus only with OPEC, Comecon and developing countries, whereas a more diversified and competitive industry like Germany is able to generate permanent surpluses also with other developed economies (Figure 19). This shows weaker performance of French companies to penetrate foreign markets and defend their domestic positions against competitors with similar resources and skills. OPEC and Third World markets are also subject to wider fluctuations than developed markets. Second, a good part of French industrial exports have been and still are concentrated on sectors of a higher volatility and cyclicality than Germany or Japan i.e. aerospace, defence and large engineering contracts. Since 1978, each of these items has fluctuated by a ratio of 1 to 3. The brutal fall of construction and engineering contracts (including off-shore) which brought a bonanza to many large French firms has been somewhat compensated by an increase in aerospace (Airbus and Ariane) but mainly by a few very large military orders from Saudi Arabia, Greece, India, Egypt. This concentration on a few politically sensitive export businesses makes France's foreign income more dependent on its foreign policy, oil prices and wars, than on the performance of its companies. Third, the more steady sources of exports in complex-factor businesses like automobiles, chemicals or steel have suffered from the weakening competitive positions of French companies. The automobile sector in particular, which has always been the single largest exporter, has lost share abroad and domestically.

If French industry is not able overall to earn a trade surplus with other developed economies, it is due to structural deficiencies in many areas of business strategy, investments and organization which we will review in part II. Four areas of weaknesses have an impact nationwide and across most sectors of industry, and should be stressed in this section.

a) Insufficient attention to production management

France has not developed the skills in production management which are essential for head-on competition with world leaders in complex-factor business particularly Japanese. French engineers have been traditionally educated to pursue conceptual excellence and brilliant invention, as embodied in the Concorde. Engineering schools in France, possibly with the exception of Arts et Métiers and Centrale, do not teach production management. Nor have French companies traditionally provided enough training in production management or offered high rewards for excellence in this area. Meanwhile, businesses and engineering and management schools in competitor countries like Germany, US, Sweden and Japan have focussed attention on critical although often mundane aspects of production like yield, maintenance costs, inventory control, quality control and material flows. The lack of production management skills brings in its wake a corresponding relative lack of skill development in the entire labour force. This is a major reason for the decline of many traditionally respected French complex-factor businesses, such as cars, trucks or machine tools which have faced in recent years the unhappy choice of losing market share or lowering prices for lack of quality.

France in the last decade has found itself to be the victim of over-reliance on its postwar sources of unskilled labour. French labour costs were significantly lower than those of the US, Germany, Sweden or Benelux until the mid-1970s, because of an historical lag in the comparative standard of living of the French people, particularly of blue collar workers, uneducated women and immigrants. This relative gap gave an initial boost to labour intensive production such as car assembly, after the war. Unfortunately, it also gave French car manufacturers the illusion that this labour would last for ever and be a continuing source of advantage. They made less of an effort to improve productivity or working conditions. In 1980, the average wage-rate of the French car industry was, in US $, 10/hour in comparison with $ 13 in Sweden, $ 15 in Germany and $ 16 in the US. Competitors like Volvo, Mercedes or BMW, in higher labour cost countries, had much stronger incentive to modernize facilities, automate production, optimize scale, develop quality control skills, and improve working conditions, all with the aim of achieving higher levels of productivity and quality. Today, French car manufacturers face the daunting task of achieving relatively quickly the

Figure 20

# ESTIMATED NUMBER OF RESEARCHERS IN SELECTED INDUSTRIES

1979

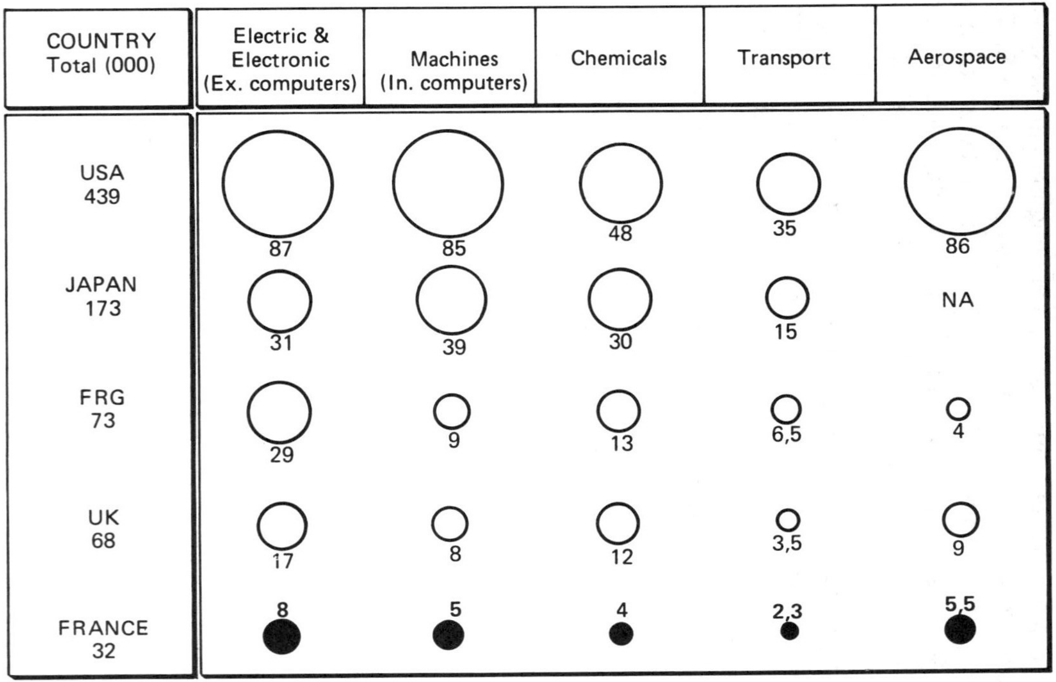

| COUNTRY Total (000) | Electric & Electronic (Ex. computers) | Machines (In. computers) | Chemicals | Transport | Aerospace |
|---|---|---|---|---|---|
| USA 439 | 87 | 85 | 48 | 35 | 86 |
| JAPAN 173 | 31 | 39 | 30 | 15 | NA |
| FRG 73 | 29 | 9 | 13 | 6,5 | 4 |
| UK 68 | 17 | 8 | 12 | 3,5 | 9 |
| FRANCE 32 | 8 | 5 | 4 | 2,3 | 5,5 |

R. & D. scientists & engineers (in 000)
Source : NSF, MITI, BDI, MRI, Business-Monitor, Telesis analysis

46

production management and technical skills and organization that other manufacturers have been steadily working at for the past decade.

b) Diversion of research and development resources from market applications

In the areas of development, France has absorbed its best scientists and technicians into the large publicly sponsored technological ventures of the Fifth Republic : the H Bomb and the Force de Frappe, the nuclear plants, aerospace projects (Mirages, Concorde, missiles, helicopters, Ariane), digitalization of the telecommunications network and the modernization of the railways. These ventures have produced some world technological leaderships, for example in fast breeder-reactors, high-speed trains or missiles, and have contributed to the building of a modern infrastructure and independent defence capability. However, as they were developed for non-economic objectives with less cost constraint, they have not generated enough products and services suitable for competition in open world markets. It remains to be seen if the French nuclear engineering capacity can be exported to many countries and if the most recent aerospace ventures now conducted on a European level can be eventually profitable (Airbus or Arianespace). Meanwhile, other countries like Japan and Germany, which were banned from many defence industries, have used a significant proportion of their most talented scientists, engineers and other skilled technicians in the development of competitive products for world markets. France now lacks crucially needed engineers and scientists in fields like microelectronics, computers, process control, production automation and new materials (see Figure 20). Government support in R&D in these applications has been later and much less important than in countries like the US, Japan and Germany.

The other reason for the often disappointing business spinoffs of brilliant engineers is that French technical culture has paid little respect traditionally to "applications engineering", which can be an important source of competitive advantage in complex businesses. There is a tendency to "reinvent the wheel" and surpass the development of other countries, often for its own sake rather than for gaining any commercial advantage. More pragmatic engineering cultures like Japan, Germany and Sweden have focused their efforts on the commercial application of breakthroughs of foreign origin (generally the US) to achieve business success. The Japanese did not invent either the transistor or the cathode ray tube ; however, they were working at the business domination of radio and TV while French engineers were reinventing colour TV in the Secam system. While Secam produced a better quality image than the NTSC standard used in the US and Japan, it had the immense disadvantage of putting non-Secam export markets, all in developed countries, at higher cost.

c) Nationally-focused management

French culture and traditions have also caused top management of companies to be disadvantaged in a world competitive arena. French managers do not know international markets outside Europe as well as their German, Swedish, Dutch or Swiss colleagues and it is still not uncommon to meet top managers who do not speak English, while very few have lived outside France. French head hunters still use foreign multinationals based in France as their best source of recruits. French true multinational companies like Air Liquide or l'Oréal, which have also become "management schools", are still exceptions, and they are medium-sized companies, by world standards.

France's relative lack of internationally focussed top management meant that its corporations did not have the organizational structures to meet the head-on competition of the last decade. In particular, they had not established competitive knowledge of international markets or international distribution networks, and were disadvantaged in exploiting new opportunities for export and in redesigning product lines in time to match competition on domestic markets. In addition, very few French companies have established international alliances to gain access to new products or processes in exchange for markets. Where partnerships have been formed, France has in general not had an equal position and could not exploit them to gain market share outside France. In computers, for example, CII-HB has

48

not been able to exploit its relationship with Honeywell to its advantage. Companies like Siemens, ICL, Olivetti and Philips formed relationships with US or Japanese partners on a more advantageous basis.

d) Insufficient profitability and financial reserves
    Finally, French corporations have found themselves not profitable enough and with too little financial reserves to weather downturns and still invest in R & D, new plants and equipment at a time of increased pressure for technological innovation and automation. The growth period has been financed with an unreasonable use of debt, not through internally generated cash flows or well-remunerated equity. After years of insufficient levels of profitability and when real interest rates soared, too many French companies found themselves with negative leverage, earning less than their cost of capital. They had no other options than cutting investments and "strategic expenses" (like R & D or advertising) or being bailed out by the State or by stronger (sometimes foreign) companies.

**Less strategic restructuring of industry at the national level**
French leadership of government, business and labour together, did not become conscious of the structural decline of the country's competitive power until very recently. Former Prime Minister Raymond Barre, for example, was among the very few political leaders to base his programme on the renovation of industry. It is a healthy paradox for French society to see the Left in power implementing similar (or sometimes more stringent) policies and encountering little opposition to the necessity of a more competitive traded sector. But France has wasted precious years for several reasons.
    First, its general economic policy has been systematically counter-cyclical with its major trading partners, therefore creating trade deficits at times of demand stimulation (1975-76 and 1981-82) and slowing down growth at times of world market upswings (1976-78 and 1983-85). Monetary and budgetary policies have also been too lax and too centred on the domestic market to be used as

49

incentives for industrial restructuring. The continuous devaluation of the French Franc against stronger currencies (D Mark, US dollar and yen) has led to a vicious circle of fundamental lack of competitive position compensated by temporary cost advantages.

Second, government policies and the general attitude of the labour movement have not helped prepare the social transitions away from uncompetitive businesses, as in countries like Germany, Japan or Sweden. The structural and unavoidable decline of resource-based or low wage-rate businesses surpassed by new competitors has not been clearly understood or well accepted by public opinion. The State has rapidly expanded its financial bail-out schemes to respond to the increasing number of corporate failures, regional dislocations and unemployed people. France is now trapped in a self-defeating process of rigid employment pattern, heavy taxes and public deficit which do not encourage the evolution of enterprises towards more competitive or higher value added positions. Entire sectors of industry such as steel and shipbuilding or even automobiles and telecommunications now face massive overstaffing, growing corporate losses and decline in market share.

Third, the development of strong and sustainable positions in complex-factor businesses in world markets has not always been supported as efficiently as in other countries. Export financial assistance has been too concentrated on large 'political' contracts such as aircraft, defence hardware or infrastructure for LDCs and Arab countries, and not enough on encouraging a stable flow of manufactured goods to more solvent developed countries. Furthermore, international alliances have sometimes been impeded or slowed down by nationalistic attitudes, as in the case of Thomson-JVC in video cassette recorders, Pechiney-Occidental Petroleum in chemicals or Thomson-Technicare in medical equipment.

Finally, resource allocation within the country has favoured the public sector and sheltered businesses, at the expense of the private traded sector. The capital markets have been mostly used by the dramatic increase in government and quasi-government bond issues to finance public deficits and investments ; real interest rates have soared partly as a consequence, putting already highly geared enterprises in a financial squeeze. Also, the rates of return have remained consistently higher in the sheltered sector (insurance and banking, distribution, food and local and professional services) than in the traded sector, despite lower levels of risk. This is due in many areas to the lack of domestic competition, price regulation or price fixing and also the tax system. In turn, this lower rate of return in the traded sector has discouraged the flow of capital and skilled people.

## 4. THE APPROACH USED IN THIS BOOK

Chapters 1 to 3 have traced France's economic development and relative competitive position as a developed country since World War II. We have shown that in today's environment of open world competition in traded goods, France is experiencing difficulty in maintaining a rate of increase in its standard of living similar to those achieved by other developed nations. This is particularly true since 1980, and will further deteriorate for the next three to five years, owing to the debt burden which the country has accumulated.

As we stated at the beginning of chapter 1, the standard of living of citizens of any country can rise as a result of improvements in the productivity of existing economic activity and/or by the shifting of human and financial resources to new, more productive uses. In this context, we explained in broad terms in chapters 2 and 3, why France's rate of growth was more rapid for 30 years after World War II but slower over the last decade.

In this chapter, we shall outline in greater detail our conceptual approach to understanding why a country's standard of living is growing, stagnant or declining, both in relation to its past performance and in relation to the performance of other economies. This outline will lead us into a detailed examination, in part II, of where France's major corporations stand in the framework, and what this means as a whole for the future rate of growth in France's standard of living. Following this examination, we shall, in part III, examine how government policies have contributed to the situation.

The approach states that a nation's relative growth in standard of living depends on the efficient combination of corporate strategies and national policies :
- Increase in national wealth depends on increased productivity of employed resources :
    . the wealth of a nation is the total value created by all people in employment ;

52

- a nation continually increases its wealth if people of employable age can eng ge in incre: singly productive activity.
- Corporate competition and national policies are required to increase national wealth :
  - the natural process of corporate competition guarantees increased wealth for the nation only from sheltered activities, which are those not subject to open international competition; the only national policy required for these activities is to maintain fair rules of the game and efficient competition ;
  - in traded activities, corporate competition from abroad can have special characteristics which may render national policies, either direct or indirect, necessary at certain times, in particular to help the resource allocation process and the competitive positions of the country's enterprises.

## Wealth increase dependent on relative productivity growth

The wealth of a nation is the total value created by all people in productive employment. Within each enterprise, the total value, or value added, of each corporation represents the difference between output (total sales revenues) and inputs (cost of raw materials, energy, and purch sed parts and services such as accounting and data processing). People's standard of living will increase if these corporations can extract a higher value for the work performed by their employees.

Value added is embodied in the goods and services produced by a country's employees across the full spectrum of activities, from small farms and businesses to the largest corporations. If the value added per work-hour is to increase for a nation, its people must work increasingly productively. In practice, this means that the productivity of existing economic activity must improve, that resources must be moved to new, more productive uses, and that an economy must develop enough enterprises to employ people displaced by the achievement of increased productivity.

## Corporate competition and national policies needed to increase wealth

Productivity gains within any sector of business occur as a result of normal competition between corporations. However, these productivity gains do not necessarily lead to a rise in the overall standard of living for a particular country; the dividing factor is the nature of the competitive arena.

The first arena contains business sectors where a country's competing corporations are sheltered for any reason from open competition with corporations in other countries. Here, productivity gains resulting from normal competition lead to an increase in the overall standard of living, as the surplus resources are put to some other productive use and losses of value added by one company are replaced by gains made by its more efficient competitors in the same country. These businesses may be called the non-traded or sheltered businesses of an economy. Typical sheltered businesses are services such as goods distribution, house construction, or highly perishable foods. Foreign competition in these goods remains unattractive as long as productivity improvements from increased production scale are outweighed by the costs of distributing the goods to the country in question. For example, the cost of transporting heavy commodity goods like custom-bent steel reinforcing bars is an economic barrier to outside trade. In goods distribution, the cost of penetrating local systems constitutes the economic barrier to outside entry, and in any case is a local employment activity.

The second arena contains business sectors where a country's competing corporations are engaged as well in open competition with corporations of other economies. Here, the country's standard of living will rise only if its corporations can achieve productivity gains which keep their products at a marketable and profitable price in competition with goods from other economies. In our framework, these businesses are called traded businesses. For corporations involved in traded businesses, the critical measure of productivity is that of all competitors in all countries. For example, steel producers in two countries with similar real wage rates in steel production must achieve similar productivity gains to hold their market share and remain profitable. If one producer is gaining market share on the basis of lower labour costs, while at the same time is making, say, a 2 per cent annual productivity gain, the other producer must make gains higher than 2 per cent to compensate for higher labour costs if it is to hold margins and market share.

Governments may have different roles to play in each arena. Sheltered businesses can take care of themselves perfectly well, and should be left to guide their own economic growth. Companies in sheltered businesses will achieve productivity gains in the process of normal competition, as they manipulate whatever levers they can to gain a sustainable cost advantage over other companies in supplying goods and services. Government involvement should be limited to setting broad rules to limit inflation and promote competition.

Traded businesses present a different picture, and an extremely complex one for developed countries. Today, more and more developing countries are moving into the manufacture of commodities and goods for industrial and domestic use, and trading them on the open world competitive market. Even with the most strenuous efforts to achieve productivity gains, competitors in developed countries may not be able to match the prices of the developing countries which are based on a wide labour cost advantage. In recent years, all developed countries have watched large traditional industries which have constituted major employment bases suffer serious decline in competitiveness, with significant social consequences.

In response, developed countries re seeking to move resources increasingly into complex-factor businesses where companies may establish a source of sustainable competitive advantage on the basis of their management and technical skills. For most countries, including France, these difficult structural adjustments must be achieved in the face of relatively slow national growth and within an interdependent world economy where sharp and sudden changes in supply, demand and technology occur, causing wide 'ripple effects' across economies, industries and businesses. Overall, countries which are involved in traded businesses face three sources of challenge in the management of their national resources to achieve a steady increase in standard of living.

First, countries which have a source of competitive advantage in natural resources or their use must plan for the time when they are exhausted and/or displaced by newly developed lower cost resources in or used by another economy. For example, a major factor in the success of the Japanese steel industry over European steel producers has been its exploitation of low cost coal and iron ore from relatively new Australian mines. The challenge involves the development or application of new technologies to lower the cost of exploitation or processing of domestic resources, as in the case of Swedish deep-mining techniques and Norwegian off-shore oil deep-sea drilling. But in many cases, the country should plan for a smooth social transition away from the uncompetitive resource-based industries, such as French coal mines.

Second, more developed countries face the challenge of the inevitable displacement of their unskilled labour-intensive businesses by competition from less developed countries which use their source of competitive advantge. The challenge, if taken seriously, involves increasing the skills of large numbers of people and investing in businesses where they can be employed. Skills and capital should be used in two ways. They should be incorporated in existing businesses threatened by lower-wage competition, to increase automation, product quality and innovation. This process of segmentation has taken place in consumer electronics (for example radio and black and white TV are totally dominated by Taiwan and Korea while colour TV and VTR are still mostly produced in Japan, US and Europe) and will probably continue. Other industries like cars or semiconductors will follow the same pattern. To stay competitive, corporations have to invest in barriers to entry such as skilled labour, proprietary products and production processes, distribution, brand image or after-sales network, depending on the nature of the business. These barriers are typically more sustainable than plant scale or available technology. When low wage competition cannot be contained by barriers of this kind, the challenge is to plan smooth social transitions and new business development.

Third, developed countries which are increasingly dependent on complex-factor businesses face the challenge of strategic management of their resources, particularly through the employment of skills and experience in all elements of corporate businesses, so as to achieve profitable corporations in increasingly higher value added activities (this is developed in more detail in part II).

The government of a developed country, in carrying out its mandate to increase economic growth, may have one of three broad responses to the issue of its corporations' international competitiveness. A government may leave corporations to find areas of business where they can establish a cost advantage which will sustain their competitiveness on world markets. A second, more politically pragmatic choice is protection for declining businesses in the form of tariffs, quotas and 'voluntary' restraint agreements and in the form of subsidization of their costs. As a third alternative, a government can work with the leaders of corporations, trade unions, financial institutions, universities and research establishments, local authorities, etc. to develop policies and practical methods of shifting human and financial resources into more productive and higher value added businesses, in order to increase the nation's standard of living at an acceptable rate. Japan's formidable position as a competitor in world markets is perhaps the most outstanding example of the latter method of response.

With more than one-half of its businesses involved directly or indirectly (as sub-suppliers) in activities which we classify as traded activity, France's standard of living is highly sensitive to changes in the productivity of competitors in all world economies. With this relatively high degree of exposure, we believe that it is unrealistic to expect France to move its resources significantly to higher value added activity through the effect of an 'invisible hand'. France does not have the massive homogeneous domestic market of the United States to cushion it against the effects of rapidly evolving world competition. Nor does it have, like Norway or

57

Australia, the cushion of vast low-cost natural resources which can be worked to increase the country's standard of living while the country gets some 'breathing space' to move resources to new more productive sectors of manufacturing. The national challenge which indeed is the rationale for an 'industrial policy' is therefore to provide corporations with the resources, incentives and flexibility, so as to maximize their chances of becoming competitive in the priority sectors which will generate wealth for the nation. In this process business leaders have a prime role and responsibility. Government policies can only be effective through their performance.

The structure of this book is derived from our conviction that 'industrial policy' is not only government policy, but the convergence of efforts between business, government and all parts of society to shift resources continuously to more productive uses, i.e. to build more competitive positions in high value added businesses within the traded sector.

Part II addresses this challenge to the role of business. It shows to what extent and why France is still lacking the strategic and managerial expertise to continue to progress towards an efficient, modern and open economy.

Part III looks at the role of government in providing the necessary ingredients for successful competition. It demonstrates how successive French governments have not always exploited well the strong levers they had, and in what respect they have misjudged situations where they had few levers. It concludes by offering a framework for a more effective set of policies.

Finally, the postscript suggests the broad changes necessary throughout French society to bring the country in the leading pack of advanced industrial nations during the coming decades.

# 1. CORPORATE PERFORMANCE AND NATIONAL WEALTH

National wealth is the sum of wealth created by each of the country's enterprises from the smallest to the largest. The combined performances of enterprises are therefore the critical determinant of a nation's well-being; it is as important for business leaders to have a method for understanding the ever-changing patterns of performance of their enterprises as it is for chemists to understand changing molecular structures in their search for more effective products.

In a market economy, corporations generate wealth in three ways :
- by increasing global value added, which will then be distributed in more revenues for employees, shareholders (and the State), and will create work for sub-suppliers ;
- by increasing profitability, which can translate into more return for investors and more investments for future growth (either in the same firm or in other businesses) ;
- by raising the average value added generated by each employee in the firm, to a higher skill content and/or less working time for the same output.

This wealth creation process is inherent in any market economy and began to flourish in European nations five centuries ago. The role of business is to exploit these mechanisms. There is no "invisible hand" however which ensures that business success automatically generates prosperity for the nation. Economists recognized a long time ago, for example, that governments should ensure a fair competitive environment in order to avoid the inefficiencies of monopolies and price fixing practices.

More fundamentally, in an economy open to trade, business sucesses in the sheltered sectors cannot ensure an improvement in a country's competitive strength or even in its standard of living. A growing and profitable fast food chain, for example, can contribute to lower prices for consumers, but has no or little impact on the balance of payments, which is a critical constraint for increasing purchasing power in an open economy without significant natural endowments. This impact even becomes negative when its success is mostly based on imported goods.

The success of business in traded sectors is crucial, and is a priority for national policy in any country which has to import goods and services it cannot produce - raw materials, energy, or proprietary technology. Only a handful of countries with very large natural endowments and/or scarce population can prosper without competitive companies in the traded sectors : Saudi Arabia, the Gulf States, Norway. Even the best endowed countries like the US or Australia need them.

This ambitious role assigned to business is not obvious to everyone. Management is generally exclusively evaluated on its ability to generate attractive returns to shareholders over a long period. This is why the corporate leaderships of IBM, Daimler Benz or Matsushita are so widely praised. Of course nobody is indifferent to the fact that they also pay their employees good salaries, advance their skills, rarely lay off people and generate exports. But this is viewed as a natural consequence of performing companies.

In this review of French economic performance, we will make a distinction of prime importance between business success in traded sectors and in sheltered sectors. This is not to say that entrepreneurs and investors in sheltered companies are bad citizens. The creation and growth of Carrefour (distribution) or Bouygues (construction) are indeed a remarkable demonstration of innovation and management skills, and as such should be highly praised as a demonstration of French postwar renewal. It must be remarked, however, that they generate less exports and lower value added employment than modern foreign corporate successes such as Nixdorf, Novo, or BMW not to speak of US Stars like Digital Equipment or Hewlett-Packard.

A prosperous country in today's open environment will be one in which enough business leaders will have managed their companies to reach a high value added and competitive position in traded sectors. All leaders in society - not only in business but also in governments, unions, universities, etc

-must understand this process in order to provide the nation's companies with the necessary resources and incentives for them to strive in the desired direction.

A framework can be developed which enables us to examine how the country's total resources are employed by companies (Figure 21). It shows how those resources are distributed in terms of value added per person employed and in terms of profitability (measured as cash return on total capital employed), which broadly represents the relative competitive position of an enterprise. Within this framework, companies are classified as in one of four categories of contributors to national wealth. The limits of each category are set by the average value added per person employed for OECD economies, which serves as a benchmark for standard of living, and by a range of cash return on total employed capital of 3 per cent to 8 per cent in real terms, which can be considered to be the minimum rate of return required by a company to maintain its competitive position (depending on market growth). Of course, these four categories are not closed 'boxes' but rather intermediate positions in a continuum. Finally, the framework stresses the importance of maximizing net exports (total exports minus imported materials).

On this graphic display, the process of wealth creation by better competition described in part I is brought down to the corporate level.

- Total wealth generated by a corporation is measured by its value added, (circle size in the charts), i.e. the difference between output (sales) and input (raw materials, energy, and purchased parts and services); of course a company also generates wealth indirectly by providing a market to sub-suppliers or locally produced raw materials, but this degree of complexity has not been incorporated in the charts.
- Increase in standard of living is generated by a higher value added per person (horizontal axis). This illustrates the evolution of any company towards a higher intensity of skilled labour or capital away from unskilled labour. Increase in value added per person can be obtained in several ways : by raising

61

Figure 21

## FRAMEWORK FOR ASSESSING A COUNTRY'S
## CORPORATE PORTFOLIO

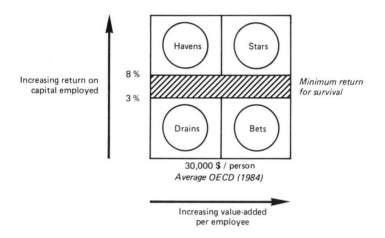

30,000 $ / person
*Average OECD (1984)*

Increasing value-added
per employee

the average skills required, by replacing labour by capit. l and/or by reaching the same output with fewer people.

Competitive position may be measured by the total cash return on capital employed (vertical axis). A corporation which is more productive than its competitors generates a higher profitability, if factor costs (wage levels, interest rates, etc.) are comparable. Cash return on total capital employed is calculated as the ratio of total cash generated (depreciation and operating income before interest and taxes) to total capital (equity, long term debt and interest-bearing permanent short term debt). The capital is estimated at replacement value by adding back five years of depreciation allowances. T king into account market growth rate, capital intensity, real interest rates and tax rates, a company should generate between 3 per cent and 8 per cent "real" annual return on employed capital to maintain its competitive position. This return enables it to sustain corporate growth at a rate at least equal to world market growth, modernize assets as they become obsolete from age or technology, and remunerate shareholders, bankers and other lenders. The range of 3 per cent to 8 per cent is therefore the minimum return required for 'sustainable growth', to use the term pioneered by the Boston Consulting Group.

A country's corporation can fall into one of the four categories displayed on the chart, 'Stars', 'Bets', 'Drains' and 'Havens', which may be described as follows :

'Stars' are profitable businesses with a relatively high value added per person. In high wage economies, Star corporations are typically complex-factor businesses operating in traded sectors like IBM, Mercedes and ICI, or businesses based on competitive natural endowments like Shell or BP. Some very profitable (and very productive) sheltered businesses in low skill labour sectors can be just over the average OECD value added line such as Carrefour in France. This is the case also of high skilled service businesses operating behind language or distribution barriers, like

63

computer custom software, advertising or legal services. From a shareholder's point of view, stars represent the most desirable long-term investment of all businesses. From a nation's point of view, they are the businesses which all developed economies need to increase their standard of living. The nation and private investors therefore share a common interest in direct and indirect investment in Star businesses.

'Bets' are businesses with a relatively high value added per person which are uncompetitive in their markets. They include 'question marks' in high technology traded businesses, such as ICL and CII-HB in computers or British Aerospace and SNIAS in aircr ft, which are up against stronger world competitors and have as yet failed to establish a dependable or leading position. They may also include companies in sheltered and traded capital intensive sectors, such as cement, steel and petrochemicals businesses, which are surviving in low growth markets at marginal profitability.

Farsighted corporations working in the long term interest of their country - particularly in Japan - have decided to invest in new high value added businesses, cut prices and lose money initially in order to gain market share and establish a better position in what they saw as the future base of advanced economies. NEC and Hitachi for example have initially lost on their production of RAM-semiconductors to gain share from established US leaders like Texas Instruments or Motorola.

In general, however, from a shareholder's point of view, the Bets represent a high-risk investment (in the case of newer high technology businesses) or an undesirable investment (in the case of survivors). From the nation's point of view, they might be desirable if they represent a pool of human skills or the replacement of unskilled or unpleasant labour by capital. Shareholders and the nation do not necessarily have a mutual interest in investment in Bets. It may be in the national interest to support start-up and surviving businesses in the face of individual shareholder disinterest. Most developed countries have recognized this, even in the most liberal economies. All governments subsidize advanced research and technologies, and encourage highly skilled businesses, including the US which channels funds mostly through the defence and space programmes. All major

64

European countries have geared their public support programmes to high value added businesses such as aircraft, computers or semiconductors. The MITI in Japan has systematically encouraged the structural evolution of the economy towards 'knowledge intensive' businesses which in start-up phases were not profitable[1].

The evaluation of the competitive opportunities of Bets is of utmost importance for a nation's future wealth : investments in some risky enterprises involved in high technology should be encouraged, but not wasted. In the end, all corporations must become competitive or disappear. For a country, it is important to invest in Bets at the right time, but also to divest from them when they tie up too many resources compared to the likely output. In all cases, they represent one of the most difficult challenges of a nation's industrial strategy.

'Drains' are uncompetitive businesses with a relatively low value added per person. They are typically traded businesses in developed countries which have not been able to make the productivity gains required to retain profitable market share in the face of new competitors. Drains include raw materials businesses which are replaced by the new availability of more economical sources, such as European iron ore mines which are uncompetitive against Australian mines on the basis of ore body; capital intensive businesses such as European steel production which is uncompetitive against Japanese steel on the basis of scale and process technology; and labour and capital businesses such as British and French car manufacturers which are uncompetitive against other Europeans on the basis of lower quality, lower price realization and higher production cost.

From a shareholder's point of view, Drains have no attraction as a form of investment. From the nation's point of view, they tie up resources with the use of subsidies and protection, but cannot sustain high wages. The challenge however is not necessarily to divest from Drains, and invest in Bets, but to invest in Drains so that they become self-sustaining Stars, or at least improve their positions in the

---

1
  See Ira Magaziner (President of Telesis Inc.),
  Japanese Industrial Policy, PSI, 1979.

right direction. When very large companies fall in Drain positions - like the car industry in the UK and France - it may be more important to the country's future to allocate scarce resources to restore their competitive position (as was done for Chrysler in the US), provided that it is done at reasonable cost, rather than to diversify in new (but small) mythical 'high-tech' businesses. Resource allocation decisions should be based on the total value added at stake (macroeconomic analysis), and the chances to become competitive again (strategic analysis), rather than on financial statements or futurology. This also is one of the most difficult challenges for a nation's industrial strategy.

'Havens' are businesses generating a relatively low value-added per person which are operating profitably. In developed countries, Havens are typically partly or totally sheltered businesses; if they were traded, they would be unlikely to sustain their competitive position in the face of competition from newly industrializing countries with a lower standard of living. They include some distribution businesses, some low-skill food businesses, and construction. Some havens can sustain their profitability even in traded businesses, when other barriers exist such as patent protection, brand financial or legal monopolies. From a shareholder's point of view, Havens can be very attractive because they only face competitors operating within the same constraints and the same environment, or no competition at all (patents).

From the national standpoint, despite their success as individual businesses, Havens do not have the same value as Stars, or even as some Bets, because they do not assist a developed nation in its critical task of allocating resources to higher value added businesses in order to sustain an acceptable rate of increase in standard of living. In fact, by attracting shareholders' funds and management talent, both scarce resources in any nation, they may indirectly impede the development of higher value added complex-factor businesses, which need both capital and highly experienced and skilled management to establish strong competitive positions in fast-moving markets. Even from the point of view of employment, Havens make a somewhat ambivalent contribution to the national wealth. The majority of the jobs they create tend to be concentrated in low-skill, low-wage employment.

For example, most of the 15 million jobs created over the last decade in the US have been in service areas such as fast food, cleaning and security. In this respect, the US economy's often praised performance in job creation may not be duplicable in Europe. It is more the result of a large and growing sheltered sector due to the size of the country and its population growth than of the competitive performance of an open economy.

The difference in objective between shareholders and the government is, of course, the result of the difference between individual desire and national responsibility (Figure 22). Desiring the highest possible rate of return for their invested capital, shareholders are concerned mainly that corporations move upwards. They will naturally concentrate their resources on Havens and Stars. The government, however, has responsibility for providing a framework that will facilitate the highest possible increase in the nation's standard of living. Therefore it is concerned that the national resources, embodied in corporations, should move constantly right as well as upwards, since developed nations can only sustain a steady increase in standard of living by moving resources to activities which have increasingly higher value added per person.

With this concern, governments will concentrate the development of policy and the allocation of resources on the nation's traded businesses, or Bets and Drains (Stars being by definition self-sustainable). This is not to say that sheltered businesses are unimportant; growth in absolute value added is an essential ingredient for increased national wealth, and therefore absolute growth in Havens is desirable. Also, more efficient sheltered businesses can help the cost position of traded goods and services for which they supply critical inputs, such as electricity, transport or packaging. Indeed, some Havens are businesses subject to steep productivity gains like modern distribution, and as such increase national wealth. However, a government need not put public effort or money into attracting the movement of resources into Haven businesses because market forces inside the country can take care of it, provided that competition policy is effective enough.

Figure 22

# THE NATIONAL ECONOMIC CHALLENGE

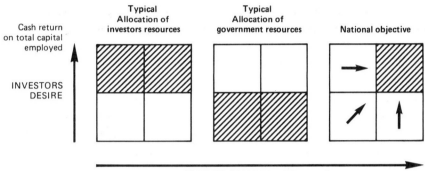

The trade-offs and complementarities between private investors and government constitute the total national economic challenge, to increase the competitiveness of its corporations (as embodied in returns), and to increase the value added per person employed. The nature of the global industrial strategy challenge, and the extent of government's responsibility, will depend on how well the nation's corporations meet these objectives in traded activities, and as a consequence generate profitable exports and sustainable employment. This widely differs among nations.

To illustrate those differences in corporate performance and national strengths, we have positioned on Figures 23 to 27 the largest exporting companies in the advanced industrial economies (annual exports over $ 1 billion in 1984). This display of the largest multinationals already indicates the scope of France's competitive challenge.

- The top exporting companies which France can count on to pay for its imports are mostly below the normal return zone, and more than half are below the OECD value added median (Figure23). France only true "Stars" which generate large exports are in the oil industry. France has also some some good companies, on the border lines with Dassault, Rhône-Poulenc and Pechiney.

- The British portfolio of top exporters (Figure 24) is fairly similar to that of France with an even more contrasted situation between large successfull companies based on natural resources exploitation and fairly low return and/or low value-added manufacturing companies (with the brilliant exception of ICI).

- In the US and Germany, as well as in some smaller European economies (Figures 25 to 27), the Star performers contribute to a larger extent to wealth creation for the whole nation : the same companies which bring good returns for their investors are also in high value added categories and generate large exports. IBM, Dupont de Nemours and General Electric for the USA, Daimler Benz, Hoechst and Bayer for Germany, Nestlé for Switzerland are top performers for their investors as well as for their country.

69

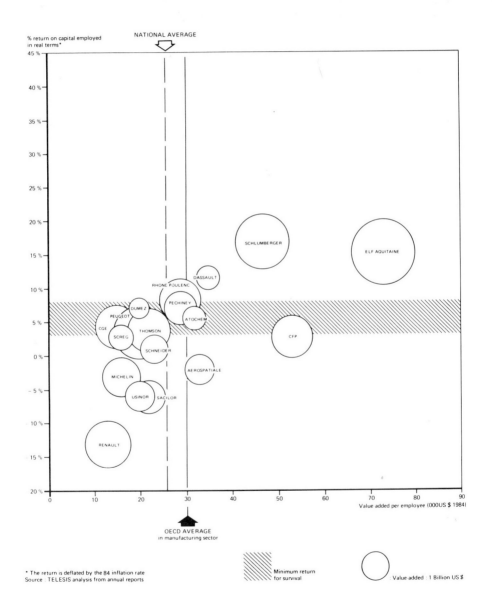

Figure 23

**PROFILE OF THE TRADED SECTOR – 1984**
**Companies exporting more than 1 Billion US $**

**FRANCE**

Figure 24

**PROFILE OF THE TRADED SECTOR -- 1984**
Companies exporting more than 1 Billion US $

UK

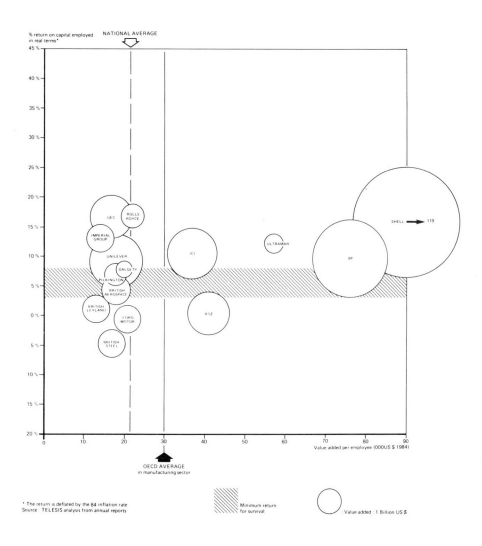

% return on capital employed in real terms*

NATIONAL AVERAGE

OECD AVERAGE
in manufacturing sector

Value added per employee (000US $ 1984)

* The return is deflated by the 84 inflation rate
Source  TELESIS analysis from annual reports

Minimum return for survival

Value added : 1 Billion US $

71

Figure 25

# PROFILE OF THE TRADED SECTOR – 1984
## Companies exporting more than 1 Billion US $

## USA

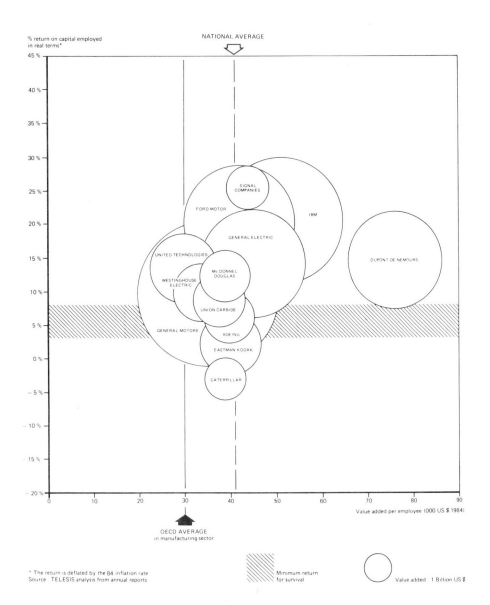

* The return is deflated by the 84 inflation rate
Source   TELESIS analysis from annual reports

Minimum return
for survival

Value added   1 Billion US $

Figure 26

## PROFILE OF THE TRADED SECTOR – 1984
### Companies exporting more than 1 Billion US $

## GERMANY

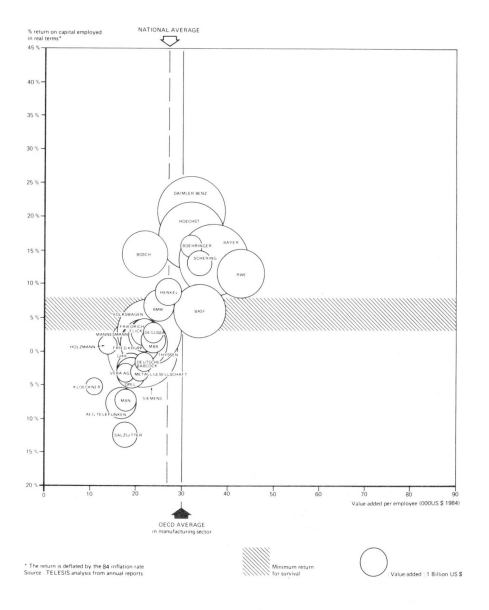

% return on capital employed in real terms*

NATIONAL AVERAGE

Value-added per employee (000US $ 1984)

OECD AVERAGE
in manufacturing sector

* The return is deflated by the 84 inflation rate
Source : TELESIS analysis from annual reports

Minimum return for survival

: Value-added : 1 Billion US $

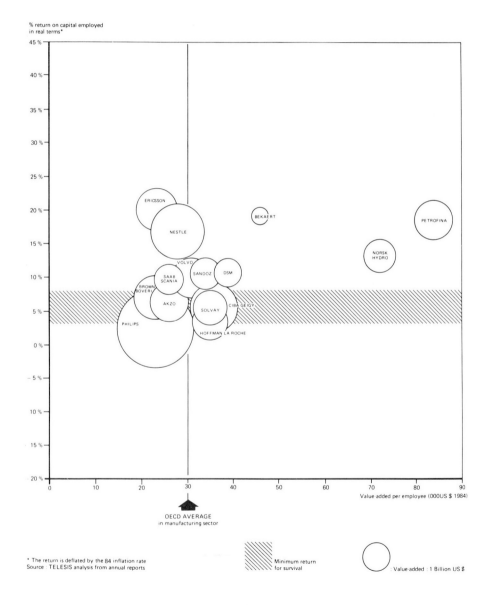

Figure 27

# PROFILE OF THE TRADED SECTOR -- 1984
## Companies exporting more than 1 Billion US $

### SMALL COUNTRIES

% return on capital employed
in real terms*

OECD AVERAGE
in manufacturing sector

Value-added per employee (000US $ 1984)

* The return is deflated by the 84 inflation rate
Source : TELESIS analysis from annual reports

Minimum return
for survival

Value-added : 1 Billion US $

74

The framework allows us to explore France's economy with a focus on the relative value of its corporations. The challenge for France - as for any medium-size high-wage economy open to international competition and with little natural endowment - is to channel resources so as to :

- produce as many Stars as possible without missing growth opportunities, and at the same time, to reinvest available cash in new businesses ;
- improve the competitive positions of Bets, so that they can be financially sustainable Stars, or divest from them when the cash required becomes clearly out of proportion with the value added and net exports which they can generate ;
- turn Drains into more competitive or/and higher value added businesses, or divest when the chances become too marginal ;
- let Havens develop on their own, and encourage them to explore new opportunities in higher value added businesses.

In this permanent structural evolution, the role of business is critical. It is the responsibility of the enterprise to sustain a competitive position in order to maintain its integrity, finance its growth and generate wealth for its employees, its suppliers, its customers and its capital providers. It is a concern of the nation - represented by the government in any democratic society - to ensure that the enterprise does so in the higher value added businesses of the traded sector. The extent and type of government involvement is therefore determined by the successes - or failures - of business on both dimensions. If business 'naturally' evolves in the upper right part of the chart, government need not and should not interfere. This has been the case of successful small countries like Switzerland, for example, and is largely the case also of a larger economy like Germany where the top corporations are in Star positions, and maximize exports. If business follows other directions, there is a case for government responsibility. But in all instances, there is no successful industrial strategy at the national level, without competitive and growing companies.

## 2. PERFORMERS AND LOSERS

The assessment of France's industrial fabric starts with a detailed display of its top 100 corporate portfolio (excluding public services). The performance of the largest corporations is most important to review first, because they 'pull' the rest of the economy, particularly the traded sector, providing more than two-thirds of France's manufactured exports. In this capacity, they sustain jobs in the whole traded sector, and in sub-supplier products and support services, which represent about half of total industrial employment. It is for this reason that large companies are still the locomotives of modern economies, providing the means for shifting resources from declining or uncompetitive activities to higher value added growing and sustainable ones. Net new jobs for an economy are created from the small businesses which develop to supply the changing needs of consumers and the large corporations, but contrary to widespread belief, small businesses generally ride on the back of successful large exporters.

Figures 28 A and 28 B show the relative performance and total value added of the top 100 corporations (some are not represented for lack of data). The year 1981 was chosen as being equally influenced by right and by left governments, and 1984 is the last year for which data were available.

The center of gravity of the portfolio has moved to the upper left quadrant from 1981 to 1984. In 1981 many French companies were below the minimum return required to sustain growth and stay competitive, but most of them were close to the OECD median value added per person. In 1984, a good number have improved in profitability, including large corporations like Peugeot, Rhône-Poulenc, Pechiney or Air France, but the core of French business is now below the OECD average value added line. This is in good part due to the dollar increase, as all figures are displayed in dollars, but it also shows the small real growth of many French companies in the 1980s.

Figure 28 A

# FRANCE TOP 100 CORPORATIONS PORTFOLIO – 1981

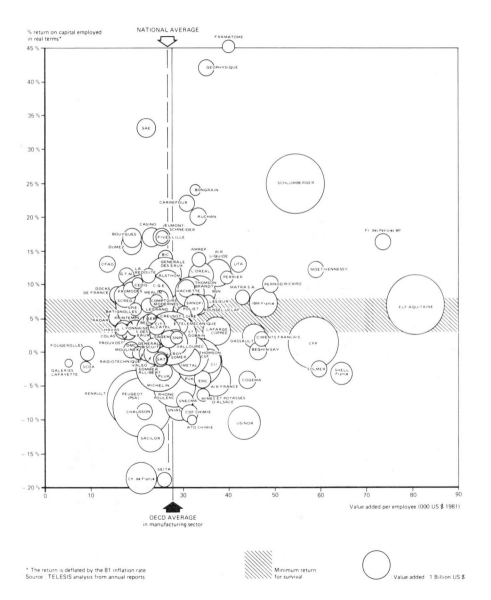

% return on capital employed in real terms*

NATIONAL AVERAGE

Value added per employee (000 US $ 1981)

OECD AVERAGE
in manufacturing sector

* The return is deflated by the 81 inflation rate
Source : TELESIS analysis from annual reports

Minimum return
for survival

Value added   1 Billion US $

Figure 28 B

# FRANCE TOP 100 CORPORATIONS PORTFOLIO — 1984

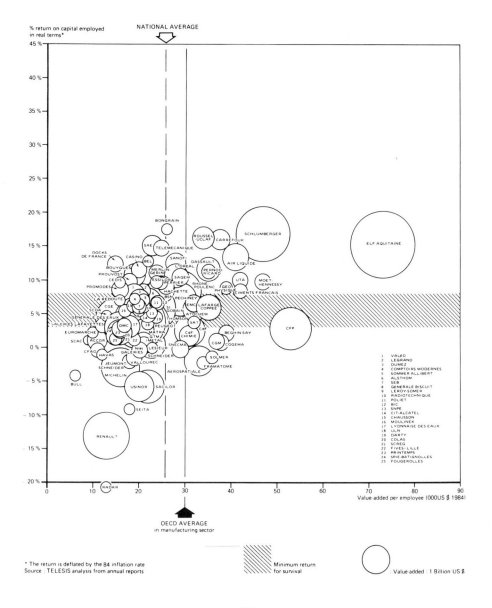

% return on capital employed in real terms*

NATIONAL AVERAGE

OECD AVERAGE
in manufacturing sector

Value-added per employee (000US $ 1984)

1 VALEO
2 LEGRAND
3 DUMEZ
4 COMPTOIRS MODERNES
5 SOMMER ALLIBERT
6 ALSTHOM
7 SEB
8 GENERALE BISCUIT
9 LEROY-SOMER
10 RADIOTECHNIQUE
11 POLIET
12 BIC
13 SNPE
14 CIT-ALCATEL
15 CHAUSSON
16 MOULINEX
17 LYONNAISE DES EAUX
18 DARTY
19 ULN
20 COLAS
21 SCREG
22 FIVES-LILLE
23 PRINTEMPS
24 SPIE-BATIGNOLLES
25 FOUGEROLLES

* The return is deflated by the 84 inflation rate
Source : TELESIS analysis from annual reports

Minimum return
for survival

Value-added : 1 Billion US $

Overall, it can be said that the French portfolio of the top 100 companies has improved over the last three years but remains only average both in terms of return to the investors and contribution to the national wealth. Figures 29 to 31 illustrate the different patterns of the three main competitive areanas :

- traded business in open markets (Figures 29 A and 29 B) have improved in return on capital between 1981 and 1984. The large drains in automobile related business and steel have only marginally improved however, and the exceptional "Star" results of smaller companies like Geophysique, Bongrain, Moëtl-Hennessy or Pernod-Ricard have come closer to the center ;

- sheltered businesses (Figures 30 A and 30 B) have deteriorated in profitability, as a result of a stagnant domestic market and increased competition in industries with overcapacity like retailing or construction. Several companies are now under the minimum return band, while the majority has stayed below the average OECD value added line, as can be expected in markets sheltered from foreign competition. The long established pattern in the French economy of a profitable sheltered sector attracting capital and talents away from a loosing traded sector is changing. Deflationary policies at home contrast with growing export markets (the US in particular) and past returns have attracted too much competition. In distribution and construction, only the best are showing sustained good performances ;

- finally in businesses operating in protected or subsidised markets (Figures 31 A and 31 B), French companies show scattered results, with only Dassault significantly improving its position. The instability of most other companies is due to shrinking or at least cyclical public markets, as the government budget deficit increases and exports do not compensate for volume cost at home.

The nation as a whole should be concerned about such a situation. On the one hand, the best managed companies do not 'automatically' bring in the highest returns for the country in terms of exports and highly skilled personnel when they operate in low value sheltered businesses like distribution or construction. On the other hand, the mainstream of export businesses in an advanced economy (like automotive products, computers, or chemicals) is not competitive and therefore their returns to the country are vulnerable. France's relative decline in the new world arena, described in part I, is largely explained by this structural deficiency. Part II of this book explains why France is not in a situation - like Germany or the US - where market forces alone will naturally improve its economic situation. Rising unemployment, chronic foreign deficits and marginal real growth are not primarily the result of bad economic policy, but of the lack of competitive companies in the high value added quadrants of the traded sectors. In the following sections we examine this situation in more detail and offer some generic explanations of the widening gap between French industry and its strongest competitors. This book does not have the ambition to explain each individual corporate success, but rather to illustrate the strengths and weakenesses of French industry with concrete examples.

## The Stars

The Stars are too few in comparison with other industrial nations, and except for three companies in oil and oil services, they are medium-large rather than very large corporations. Furthermore, their businesses (oil and oil services, traditional French goods, and sheltered activities) produce less spin-off for the nation than Stars of the most advanced industrial nations : Germany, the US or even smaller European countries like Sweden or Switzerland which are shown on the preceding figures.

The Stars of French industry are of four kinds. The first category - oil companies - is the best illustration of a close cooperation and a mutually reinforcing joint venture between business leadership and government policies. Part III gives an account of the government's role. Management responsibility has been decisive in bringing these companies

80

Figure 29 A

# FRANCE'S TOP 100 CORPORATIONS PORTFOLIO – 1981
## Traded businesses in open markets

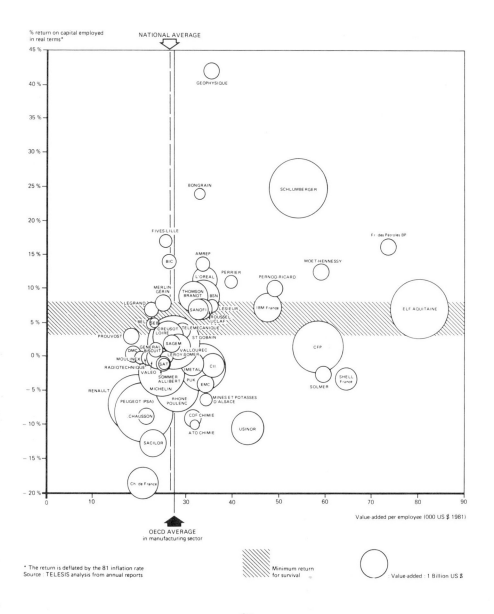

% return on capital employed in real terms*

NATIONAL AVERAGE

OECD AVERAGE
in manufacturing sector

Value-added per employee (000 US $ 1981)

* The return is deflated by the 81 inflation rate
Source : TELESIS analysis from annual reports

Minimum return
for survival

Value-added : 1 Billion US $

81

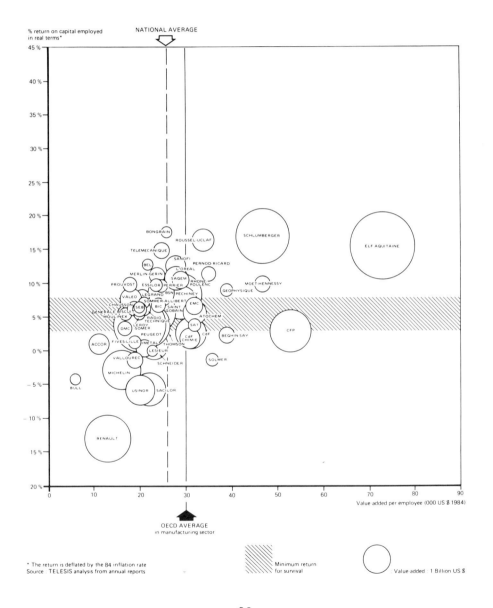

Figure 29 B

## FRANCE'S TOP 100 CORPORATIONS PORTFOLIO – 1984
### Traded businesses in open markets

82

Figure 30 A

# FRANCE'S TOP 100 CORPORATIONS PORTFOLIO – 1981
## Sheltered markets

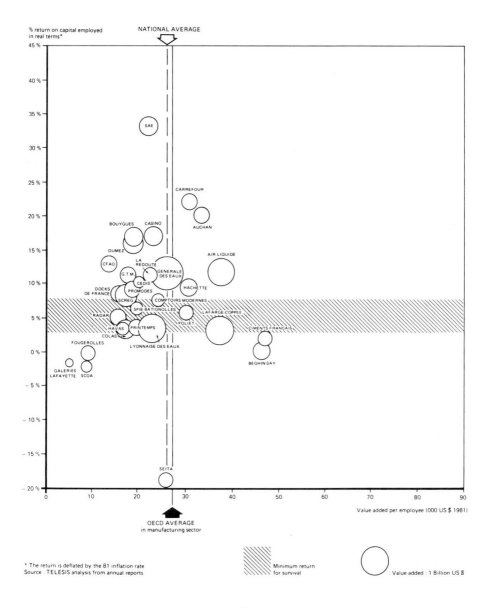

% return on capital employed in real terms*

NATIONAL AVERAGE

OECD AVERAGE
in manufacturing sector

Value added per employee (000 US $ 1981)

* The return is deflated by the 81 inflation rate
Source : TELESIS analysis from annual reports

Minimum return for survival

Value added : 1 Billion US $

Figure 30 B

## FRANCE'S TOP 100 CORPORATIONS PORTFOLIO – 1984
### Sheltered markets

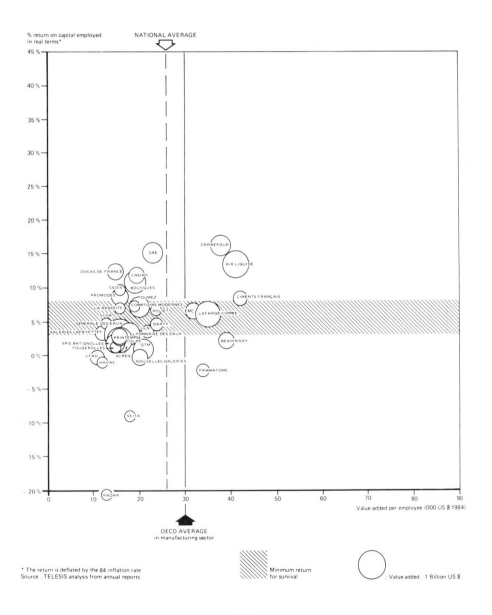

% return on capital employed in real terms*

NATIONAL AVERAGE

Value-added per employee (000 US $ 1984)

OECD AVERAGE
in manufacturing sector

* The return is deflated by the 84 inflation rate
Source : TELESIS analysis from annual reports

Minimum return
for survival

: Value-added : 1 Billion US $

Figure 31 A

# FRANCE'S TOP 100 CORPORATIONS PORTFOLIO – 1981
## Traded businesses in protected or subsidised markets

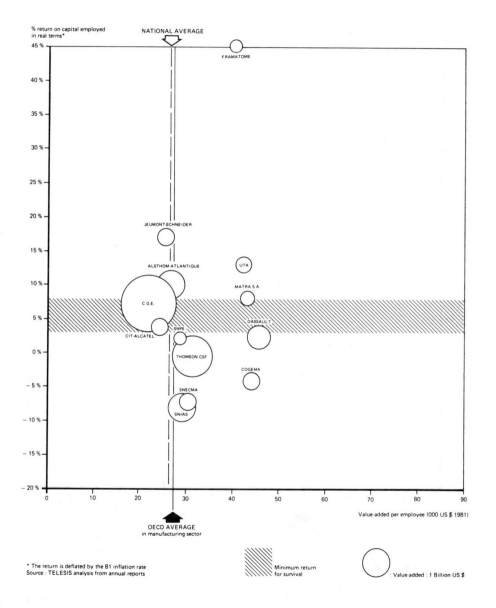

* The return is deflated by the 81 inflation rate
Source : TELESIS analysis from annual reports

Figure 31 B

## FRANCE'S TOP 100 CORPORATIONS PORTFOLIO – 1984
### Traded businesses in protected or subsidised markets

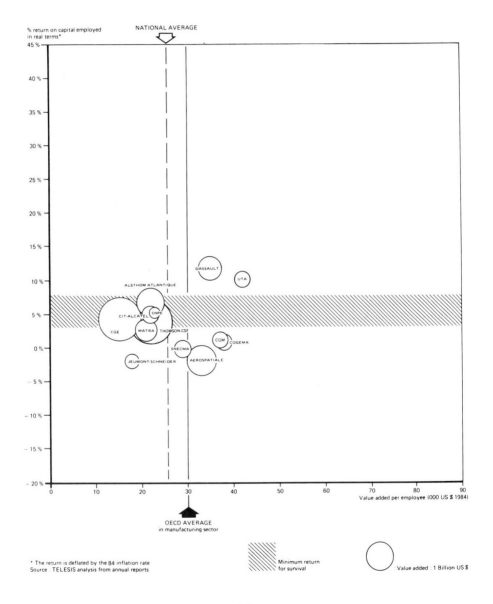

* The return is deflated by the 84 inflation rate
Source : TELESIS analysis from annual reports

into the open international markets, and achieving a financially sustainable growth over the last decades. Government has always played its role of providing the necessary ingredients for successful competition in high value industries : access to technical knowledge, initial risk financing, domestic market regulation, etc. The second category – food and cosmetics – are cases for true capitalism and government-free market economy. The success of those corporations is solely due to their management and employees. The contrast between the two illustrates the versatility which any 'industrial policy' should have in a complex economy like France's. The third category – sheltered businesses – has attracted many entrepreneurs of high calibre in the postwar period, probably in a higher proportion than in Germany, Japan or Sweden. This is reflected also in the relatively small size of the fourth category – high tech – where France lacks the reservoir of successful companies found in other modern economies. The characteristics and relative proportions of these four types of Stars illustrates the renewal of French industry in the postwar period, but also explains its limits.

(a) The oilmen adventure : a case of business-government cooperation

Of the three large oil companies, two are true Stars and one is on the borderline. Schlumberger, the world's leading exploration company and now a diversified oil service and electronic company, is the oldest one and the most brilliant. It was founded by two French brothers before World War I but is now mostly based and staffed by Americans although its chief executive officer has always been French. The two French-owned oil operators, Elf-Aquitaine (SNEA) and Compagnie Française des Pétroles (Total) are more recent. Elf is a postwar creation and a State controlled company, CFP was created in 1926 and had stayed in majority private.

The French success in the oil industry is the result of a combination of daring and talented entrepreneurs, a long established tradition of management and technical invention and commercial creativity, backed by a farsighted and consistent set of government policies (see part III). Its development embodies most factors which typically appear in

87

French corporate successes. Similar or even more important successes in the oil industry of course are found in other countries, but they stem from a long history of investments (UK), newly discovered domestic resources (Norway) or a combination of both (US). No country without a natural endowment, however, has caught up in this industry in the recent period with as great a success as the French industry. In this sector, French corporations surpass their Japanese or German counterparts.

Elf and Total grew as a result of France's long standing objective to compensate as much as possible for its lack of crude oil resources with owner-operation of oilfields. Both companies have benefited from political and national support but have mainly taken up the appropriate challenges of advancing their position at the international level. It is a tribute to their management to have fully exploited public policy and implemented successful competitive strategies.

As early as 1927 the French government regulated the domestic oil industry to allow new French operators to compete with the dominant Anglo-American 'Seven Sisters'. Compagnie Française des Pétroles, which is one-third owned by the State, was then created as the national champion, and today the two French companies control about one-half of the domestic market. However, the two operators could not have grown to their present size without the early focus on international markets. Corporate leadership was not satisfied with the protection they were given at home and took their businesses into the international arena. This was done through consistent investments in new oil fields and a spirit of entrepreneurship in many untapped regions of the world where French industry became    pioneer. While French colonies and protectorates offered accessible sources of exploration before and after World War II, the companies were farsighted enough to prepare for the loss of protected sources by investing in new areas : West Africa, the North Sea, Canada and now China.

After World War II, the government endowed Elf-Aquitaine (SNEA) with a strong source of cash by granting it the exclusive exploitation of very low-cost natural gas at Lacq, which still generates around 1 billion francs net profit per year. The State also assisted SNEA with a strong

Figure 32

# NEW BUSINESS DEVELOPMENT IN THE FRENCH OFF-SHORE INDUSTRY

| COMPANY (by sector) | Sales 1981 (Mill FF) | Origin of the company | World competitive position |
|---|---|---|---|
| **Exploration** | | | |
| Cie Générale de Géophysique | 2.800 | Prewar creation | N. 3 (2 in seismic expl.) |
| **Drilling** | | | |
| Neptune-Forex | 2.000 | Postwar creation | N. 3 |
| Foramer-Forasol | 1.000 | Postwar creation | N. 4 |
| **Construction** | | | |
| AMREP-UIE | 2.900 | Postwar creation | N. 4 in production platforms |
| ETPM | 2.400 | Vallourec subsidiary | N. 4 in hook-up, pipe-lines |
| CFEM | 1.200 | Usinor subsidiary | |
| Bouygues off-shore | 650 | Recent diversification | |
| EMH | 200 | Postwar creation | |
| ACB | 100 | Diversification | |
| CMP | 100 | Diversification | |
| **Engineering** | | | |
| Doris | 700 | Postwar creation | N. 3 (1 in concrete) |
| **Submarine maintenance & repair** | | | |
| Comex | 1.100 | Postwar creation | N. 1 (Innovator) |
| Intersub | 100 | Postwar creation | |
| Anchor system | N.A. | Postwar creation | |
| **Equipment** | | | |
| Coflexip | 1.300 | Postwar creation | N. 1 (Inventor) |

*Source : Telesis client study*

combination of cash and technical knowledge by merging the former BRP (research in petroleum) and SNPA (Lacq operator) in 1966 into the new SNEA. In turn, the management of SNEA used its cash flows to invest in R&D and off-shore technologies and to diversify into speciality chemicals, pharmaceuticals and cosmetics. Those investments, which were sometimes quite risky, proved in most cases sound strategic decisions. New acquisitions of SNEA in France (CECA for instance) or the US (M and T Chemicals) are growing and profitable. Its holding company for diversification, SANOFI, is quoted on the Paris Stock Market and is itself a Star, as shown in Figure 29.

Government policies have encouraged technical innovation in the oil industry through the creation of the Institut Français du Pétrole in 1945 (financed by an excise tax on petroleum) and by various R&D incentives (see part III). In addition, the management and engineers of the two operators (particularly Elf-Aquitaine) pioneered off-shore oil exploration and production in the early 1960s in waters deeper than US competitors could manage at that time. In Gabon and then in the North Sea, where the first platform was French engineered and operated, the corporations gained a technological lead over their competitors, as a result of innovation.

The investments and world expansion of French oil operators have in turn fuelled demand for sub-contractors and small suppliers. The French off-shore equipment and service industry has grown from annual sales of 2 billion francs to 20 billion francs in real terms over the last decade and is now second in the world behind the US. It has become one of the most brilliant high value added and export generating sectors of the economy. Most of these off-shore suppliers have been postwar creations, led by a new wave of entrepreneurs who have managed to seize significant world market share from their much longer-established American competitors (Figure 32).

Compagnie Générale de Géophysique is the oldest as well as the most profitable, and a Star on its own; Comex is the world leader in submarine work, and Doris is one of the largest independent engineering firms specializing in off-shore structures. These companies have generally gained their

90

reputation in world markets, through innovation and quick internationalization. Comex for example has set many world records in deep sea diving and maintenance and has patented many items of equipment. Doris pioneered the first concrete gravity platforms in the North Sea and Coflexip has invented new materials and new production processes to service the needs of oilfields in flexible anti-corrosion pipes. Some of these firms have grown very fast and have sometimes taken too many risks, such as Amrep which filed for bankruptcy in 1983 and is being reorganized and recapitalized by Bouygues. In general, they have developed the new French engineering skills and experience in servicing the large oil operators.

In summary, the oil and oil-related industries are an outstanding illustration of the creation of corporate Stars in France stemming from the combination of technical excellènce, aggressive internationalization, strong corporate leadership, and supportive national government policy. They set a model for what direction and what forms an industrial strategy can take in a country like France.

(b) French social traditions : a case of free capitalism
Among the top 100 corporations are seven Stars which have built businesses from the base of long standing French social traditions. Fine cooking and beauty are an integral part of the French way of life, and French products are desired by people in all countries for their high quality and status. All of them are traded businesses which have developed primarily from strong management, generally individual entrepreneurs rather than large technostructures. Two of them (BSN and mainly Lesieur) have suffered in 1984 from lower growth at home and increased price competition but still remain healthy companies.

The six Star food companies and one in cosmetics have established their source of sustainable competitive advantage through successful marketing and distribution strategies :
- product differentiation : through product innovation (Bongrain's Caprice des Dieux, Danone's creamy yoghurts or l'Oréal shampoo) or unique packaging (Perrier's oval bottle, Lesieur's mini packaging for liquid soap) ;

- brand advertising : Perrier, Lesieur, Danone or Kronenbourg have became generic names for their respective products, in France and in many European markets ;
- dominance in distribution, particularly in modern and fast growth channels, either through longer shelf life (Bongrain, Danone), or with lower cost logistics (Perrier, Pernod-Ricard).

In turn, higher market share has enabled them to lower production costs through investment in large scale facilities and to use the cash generated by this for further investments in new product introduction, and new market penetration.

These Star companies have all been managed with consistency and foresight. Their leaders are strong and charismatic personalities but they have also learned from previous mistakes and have educated their company towards better performance. They have emerged from the vast number of small family owned operations through successful mergers and acquisitions and transition to professional management.

The French corporate Stars in the food industries are of two kinds : companies which have built from a base of natural endowments, and those which have developed primarily from outstanding marketing skills regardless of raw materials. The four Stars of the first kind are Pernod-Ricard, Moët-Hennessy, Perrier and Lesieur. They share the characteristic of not being confronted with direct foreign competition, owing to their unique materials. BSN and Bongrain are the two Stars in food products who have achieved success primarily through marketing strategies without raw materials advantage. Neither however is yet a true multinational trading in full competition on world markets. The following short descriptions illustrate these points.

Pernod-Ricard and Moët-Hennessy have emerged as leaders and the only two truly international companies from the group of internationally known producers of French wines and spirits, including Martell, Courvoisier, Benedictine and Cointreau, and many others which remain relatively small private businesses. These companies have used French grapes or other fruits, the product of the soil and climate, to their advantage and have established competitive positions as world premium producers through constant attention to product quality, distribution costs, advertising and international marketing. The two largest have also made the transition from family run operations to professional organizations after a carefully managed process of mergers and acquisitions.

Pernod-Ricard, still managed by a Ricard heir, is the highly successful result of mergers in 1970 between the two largest anis-based alcohol (pastis) producers, which has become very profitable owing to a dominant position in distribution and brand image. It has since diversified into new beverages and entered new markets and intends to become a large multinational competitor in beverages through acquisitions (in distribution) and new product introduction, particularly in the US.

Moët-Hennessy, now managed by professional managers, is also the brilliant result of a merger in the early 1970s between France's leading Champagne and Cognac producers. It has diversified into other up-market products such as Dior cosmetics and perfumes. It is already a multinational with its competitive position based on brand image and dominant distribution coverage. It has recently embarked in a diversification strategy based on its knowledge of bio-technological processes by acquiring two companies in rose culture in France and in the US.

Perrier, founded and still managed by G. Leven, is likewise able to command a price premium for its bottled water from French springs. It has sustained its position through advertising, dominant distribution and low production cost from a very modern bottling plant on site. Its export successes show remarkable marketing ability, since Perrier has been able to compensate high logistics costs with price premium (and favourable exchange rates). This may not be sustainable in very competitive and distant export markets like the US. Perrier failed in its diversification in the mid 1970s into dairy products (Preval) but has since recovered and has recently acquired another French drink producer (Sellier-Leblanc).

Lesieur, professionally managed, is the result of mergers in the late 1960s between Lesieur and Cotelle and has since then gained the second position in Europe (after Unilever) in cooking oils. It has built on its initial advantage of access to peanuts in the former French colony of Senegal with effective product management, advertising and distribution. It has also diversified into other food and consumer products, based on its distribution presence and marketing skills. It is trying to become the number 1 producer of oil in Spain, Europe's largest market, but also has to face a tough battle with Unilever in margarine.

BSN has emerged as a corporate Star in the late 1960s from a series of acquisitions and mergers which started before World War II when Souchon-Neuvesel, a glass manufacturer, acquired Evian, a source of mineral water. Other acquisitions have included Boussois, another glass producer, Kronenbourg and SEB, the two largest French breweries, Gervais-Danone, the largest French fresh dairy products company, and many other smaller food companies. BSN has been managed for over 20 years by A. Riboud, who has gathered teams in consumer marketing and financial control which can rank among the best in French industry. The company is considered today to be one of the best 'schools' of marketing management in France.

Bongrain shares some similar characteristics. It is the largest French cheese company (outside cooperatives) and a European leader in branded specialties of soft cheese. Although a public company today, Bongrain is still tightly managed by its founder, J.N. Bongrain. After World War II, he developed the concept of nationally branded cheese whereas France only knew generic labels. He built a competitive position based on brand awareness and distribution dominance in new products made for longer shelf life than traditional cheeses. Bongrain has been an innovator (in marketing and production) and is now a cost leader in all elements of the business. The company exports a third of its production, mostly in European markets, and has also invested in foreign production.

Many of these successful food companies were created - or have adopted their present configuration - after the war and even after the Common Market. They have grown mostly within their domestic market and by exporting to nearby European markets. It is still a challenge for most of these French Stars to establish themselves as successful multinationals in more distant export markets like the US or Japan. The most international, Moët-Hennessy, has invested in the US in locally grown sparkling wine, in addition to its exports, but is far from the largest multi-nationals like Seagrams or Cadbury-Schweppes. BSN has acquired control of Dannon (US) and signed a joint venture with Ajinomoto in Japan in fresh dairy products but has never followed the international success of Heineken or Tuborg in beer. Bongrain has recently acquired a loc l cheese producer in the US after several investments in production and distribution in Europe. It rem. ins to be seen whether any of these Stars in the French economy can achieve the size and results of the largest food and beverage multinationals like Nestlé, General Foods or some of the best British food companies.

L'Oréal, now partly owned by Nestlé and who has been managed for almost thirty years but F. Dalle is the largest Star representing the French tradition of beauty products. It is a fully traded business with a presence in all major markets, including the US and Japan. L'Oréal is a world leader in hair products and holds the second largest world market share in cosmetics, after Revlon. It has recently diversified into pharmaceuticals through the acquisition of Synthelabo, the number 4 French company in its field. Of all companies exploiting French traditions, L'Oréal is certainly the only true multinational, competing directly with world class leaders such as Revlon, Avon or Shiseido and generating substantial exports for the country.

In conclusion, the food and cosmetic industries are among the few sectors of the economy which still generate competitive companies with relatively high value added characteristics. This is due in general to the skills, and experience in product development and consumer marketing, which in turn have allowed efficient production methods.

These companies have long been family-owned and founder-managed. The older ones - L'Oréal, BSN, Lesieur - have turned to professional managers to solve internal crises, or to embark on new growth paths, and have become among the best training grounds for French management. Others are still managed by their founder (Bongrain) or by the second generation of owners (Pernod-Ricard), but have integrated a new class of professional managers.

For all of them, effective strategies have been implemented with no support from the State. They represent one of the few sectors in France where modern capitalism has performed effectively in a free market context. As we will see below, this also holds true for smaller companies in the same industries. Indeed, this has been perceived by foreign investors who have in recent years made many acquisitions in those fields.

### (c) Corporate successes in sheltered businesses

The third category of Stars are corporations which operate in sheltered or protected market arenas. Some have become multinationals, not by exporting but by investing in the same businesses in foreign sheltered markets.

These eight Stars are all excellent representatives of fairly well-managed corporations in sheltered or protected businesses. They are protected from international import competition because of logistic cost barriers (cement, industrial gas), language barriers (books and magazines), public purchasing (nuclear engineering), government regulation (airline) or the very nature of the trade (distribution chains). They face exclusively domestic competition in France, which still represents the major portion of their revenues and net income (except for Air Liquide). Abroad, these companies have met new competitors, but with little repercussion on their domestic operations.

Air Liquide is a world leader in industrial gases. It has 70 per cent of the French market and strong positions in many foreign markets, including the US and Japan where it started operations before World War I. Its success is based on original patented processes, and a consistent policy of reinvestment in local capacity distribution (pipeline networks and R&D). It competes in many foreign markets with world leaders such as British Oxygen, AGA, Linde and several US companies.

Carrefour pioneered 'hypermarkets' in 1962, which are stores of very large surface (up to 20,000 m$^2$) in suburban areas, selling food, textiles and other consumer goods, often at discount prices. It remains the most profitable distribution chain in France and has invested in many foreign countries, including the US. Recently Auchan (created by the textile Mulliez family) has followed Carrefour in the same business, with a similar success, while others have been less successfull.

Lafarge-Coppée is the world's third largest cement producer, behind Holderbank and Blue Circle. It has been among the pioneers in dry process technology and has consistently invested in capacity and plant automation. It is the number 2 producer in North America following large investments in Canada and the acquisition of Lone Star in the US. It has diversified with the acquisition of the Coppée Group, a Belgian family-owned holding company for various businesses in biotechnology and engineering. Ciments Français is the number 2 company in France in the same industry, and is following the same geographical diversification in the US. Those two companies may compete in some markets with the two world leaders Holderbank (Switzerland) and Blue Circle (UK), which are more profitable companies.

Hachette is the second largest publishing house in Europe. Starting from a very strong position in book and magazine distribution in France, where it had virtually exclusive wholesale trade through its NMPP subsidiary, it has diversified by acquiring publishers, magazines and distribution chains in many European countries, but is way behind the resources of foreign rivals such as Bertelsman in Germany.

Framatome is the sole French general contractor and engineer for nuclear power plants. It is owned by the CEA (the State owned atomic agency) and Creusot-Loire (the now bankrupt subsidiary of Empain-Schneider). Its renowned technical leadership has developed from the strong investment programme of EDF in nuclear electricity, which still represents almost the whole of its operations.

UTA is the French airline which links France to its former colonies and to some of its distant territories : Africa, Caribbean Islands, New Caledonia, etc. It is now competing with foreign airline companies on unprotected routes, but has built its success on the protected routes granted by government regulation.

From the point of view simply of their total value added for France, and investments for their shareholders, they are extremely valuable corporations. However, the sheltered businesses among them do not have the potential to create, through direct production or sub-supply, the increasingly higher value added traded goods and services that are required for a developed nation's increase in standard of living. They generate few exports, and when these companies have become international, it is through a series of geographical diversifications in operations which are not integrated in a common system of production and marketing. Multinationals in sheltered businesses therefore generate relatively less spin-off benefits for their home country than their counterparts in traded sectors.

(d) Too few high-tech corporations
It is most striking and worrying for a developed country like France to rely on only a small group of four Star companies operating in advanced technologies : Sanofi and Roussel-Uclaf in pharmaceuticals, Thomson-Brandt and Matra in electronics.

These four Stars face the challenge of exploiting their export potential on a world dimension. As traded businesses with high value added, they represent the largest return for the nation. Directly, they raise the level of knowledge and skills in R & D, marketing, customer service, etc. ; and indirectly, they generate spin-off business for component manufacturers (semiconductors for Thomson-Brandt or active chemical ingredients for Roussel) and service suppliers. They are all however of more recent origin than their foreign competitors. Partly as a result they have not gained the same market shares and accumulated the same cash and technical reserves. Their future is still at risk as competition in high-tech businesses intensifies and scale effects increase.

Sanofi and Roussel-Uclaf are the second and third French pharmaceutical corporations ranking behind the health care division of the nationalised group Rhône-Poulenc but with better profitability records. Sanofi is a conglomerate of more than twenty companies acquired by Elf-Aquitaine during the last 15 years, but is still at present far behind the fully internationally trading US, Swiss, German and British pharmaceutical corporations. Roussel-Uclaf is now partly owned by Hoechst and can use Hoechst's international distribution network to increase its exports. In an industry which does not export as much as its foreign rivals, Roussel-Uclaf remains a rare exception. France, however, still lacks world leadership positions such as those enjoyed by Ciba, Sandoz, Hoechst, Bayer, Glaxo or Beecham, just to mention some of the European rivals.

Thomson-Brandt, the fully owned subsidiary of the recently nationalized Thomson group, has followed an acquisition strategy throughout Europe to reach the scale economies necessary at all levels - R & D, advertising and production - to survive in the very competitive consumer electronics business. In colour TV, Thomson now matches the best Japanese products in design, quality and manufacturing technology, but not Japanese costs or overall component scale. It is still behind Japan in product and feature innovation generally, and has not yet become a full producer in the growing businesses of video cassette recorders and compact disc players.

Matra is one of the main defence and space government contractors for electronics and a very dynamic and innovative firm in advanced technologies linked to government contracts such as missiles and satellites formed in the 1960s by a dynamic entrepreneur S. Floirat. It has also diversified into machine tools (Manhurin), and car dashboard instruments (Jaeger) with less success and is now trying to unload these loss making operations. Its joint ventures with Harris in semi-conductors, and with Data Point and Norsk Data in minicomputers, are just getting off the ground. In military and space electronics Matra is far behind US leaders such as Hughes, Raytheon or RCA.

We can see that France has no Star in any of the large manufacturing businesses which form the backbone for sustained increase in the standard of living of advanced economies : automotive, machinery, electronics and computers, aircraft, chemicals and electrical engineering. The only Stars of that kind are foreign multinationals based in France like IBM. In foreign countries, when these corporations are Stars, like IBM and Mercedes, they make an unparallelled contribution to the increase in value added per person both directly and through demand generated for sub-suppliers. As world leaders in open competition for manufactured goods, they fund the development of increasing high-wage, high-skill national employment in goods and services in the continuous cycle of innovation and production. They are the major levers by which resources are moved to higher value added activity.

In France, unfortunately, the Stars in food, cosmetics or sheltered businesses cannot generate as much return for the country. The main objective is therefore to improve the positions of Bets in high value added manufacturing businesses.

## The Bets

French 'Bets' are real question marks for the future of the country, in high growth advanced technologies such as computers, electronics, aerospace or nuclear.

In computers, the French owned CII-HB (now Bull) is the result of two decades of unsuccessful attempts at creating a national champion to compete with US industry. CII was created in 1967 to carry out the government Plan Calcul (see below in part III) by merging three small companies. At the same time, Bull, the best French company and a European leader until the early 1960s, was allowed to fall under US control, first by General Electric and subsequently by Honeywell. The increasingly overwhelming leader IBM - whose French operations include manufacturing and research - gained market share during the same period. The internal battle between French producers diverted precious resources at a time when scale economies could only be obtained through international associations.

French industry has failed in computers for the opposite reasons which made it succeed in oil and oil related businesses.

- Government policies and initiatives have always been badly conceived strategically, ill-managed and constantly changing. The Ministry of Industry has poured money in various forms but with no clear objective. Policies have been nationalistic and inconsistent with world market requirements (see part III).

100

- Well-managed corporations can resist bad politics, but successive management teams have never been able to bring the mergers together. Product line proliferation, research duplication, lack of customer service have all progressively tarnished Bull's reputation and frightened away the best engineers and managers. The fight between conflicting parent companies (Thomson and CGE) during a whole decade and the disruption caused by internal politics have prevented the establishment of credibility, legitimacy and leadership. In the recent period, the association with Honeywell has not been fully exploited and Bull is now surrounded by US leaders well established in Europe and European competitors well linked to US or Japanese companies.

In foreign countries, IBM competitors have chosen one of two routes : either they marketed "compatible" hardware and focused their efforts on marketing and application software, or they exploited special niches (very large CPUs, minicomputers, process control, microcomputers, etc.) often in cooperation with others. The US of course still has a dozen aggressive competitors to IBM which are all larger than Bull (including Apple which is less than ten years old). In Europe, several companies have shown much stronger positions in one area (Nixdorf, Olivetti, Norskdata) or have entered new international cooperation agreements which make them less vulnerable (Siemens, Philips, ICL). Bull has persisted too long in its choice of remaining a full line, independent, main frame supplier and has suffered heavy losses until 1984. Its new management team has made special efforts to streamline the product line, rationalise production, restore customer service and link up with stronger partners, but financial results for 1985 are barely above break-even. .

The aerospace industry can be evaluated differently. It faces overwhelming US competitors who are supported by large scale government contracts (for the defence and space programmes), and who can exploit the largest domestic market for commercial aviation. French companies had to overcome even larger obstacles than in computers. The two airframe manufacturers - Aérospatiale and Dassault - and

101

the main engine producer - SNECMA - have played more skilfully on government support and have managed competitive levers in a more efficient manner than those in computers.

- Government contracts and R&D support have been consistent since World War II, and have been managed with continuity. Government agencies - Defence and Space - have always pursued a careful balance of technical performance for domestic needs leading to innovation, and the objective to export as much as possible.
- Management has been able to apply consistent policies on product lines, export marketing and R&D. Technical innovation and international distribution and service have resulted in leading positions in business segments such as small and medium size helicopters (Alouette, Puma), business jets (Falcon) or jet fighters (Mirage). This in turn has generated leadership positions for suppliers, like Turbomeca in helicopter turbines, or SFENA, Crouzet and Thomson in avionics.
- The structure of the industry has been concentrated early, to avoid unnecessary domestic competition but two groups have been maintained to ensure healthy stimulation. In the early 1960s, Sud-Aviation and Nord-Aviation have been merged into Aerospatiale for commercial aircraft, helicopters and missiles, and Breguet and Dassault were later merged into one entity for military aircraft and business jets. These mergers have been better managed than those in computers.
- Domestic mergers and government support have not been an obstacle to international alliances in order to reach scale economies in R&D, manufacturing, or access to foreign markets. SNECMA has successfully developed the CFM 56 jet engine with GE; and Aérospatiale has launched the Airbus and Ariane cooperations with European partners, after an initial failure with the Concorde.

French aerospace companies can therefore be seen as surviving contenders in a difficult race with some significant chances to stay in the pack. At the world level, French

102

aerospace industry ranks number 3 behind the US and the British, but has stronger positions than the UK in some areas (like helicopters) and is catching up in jet engines through the GE-SNECMA joint venture. They still need public money and government contracts to develop and invest but contribute successfully to high value added exports and employment, and serve as a spearhead for other businesses. As we will see below, smaller sub-suppliers and component manufacturers have benefited from the spin-offs of the larger aerospace companies.

In electronics, the largest French company is Thomson-CSF, mainly engaged in defence and medical electronics. Thomson has been one of the main defence contractors and has built the largest R&D capability of French industry. It has won a world reputation for products such as high performance cathode ray tubes, or radar equipment. It has also exploited its technical excellence to capture export markets, particularly in the Arab countries and South America , helped by French diplomacy and other defence sales. Thomson has not yet been able however to become a fully competitive electronic company in open markets. Its medical business suffers from heavy losses and lags in terms of innovation (scanners), and its recent aggressive investments in semiconductors are still far from matching those of its larger European competitors (Philips, Siemens), not to speak of its US and Japanese rivals. As the main electronic concern in a country which has had high ambitions in new technologies, Thomson has found itself engaged too heavily in a too broad spectrum of businesses from telephone transmission to avionics and consumer electronics (Thomson-Brandt described above) to armaments. Since 1982, the new management of the now nationalized firm has divested from hazardous diverisifications done in the past : the telephone business has been sold to CGE (see below) and the computer business to Bull. Totally heterogeneous financial services, advertising and engineering have been sold. The group is still subscale in each one of its divisions, in terms of R&D, component and distribution and has found very few international partners except for integrated circuits (OKI) and consumer electronics (JVC). Despite recent management improvements, Thomson is far from having the skills in

103

marketing and distribution, and the international presence of its Japanese, US or even European rivals. It remains too weak financially to carry risky high-technology ventures on its own, and needs state support for R&D and initial losses in new businesses.

Finally **in nuclear**, Cogema and Framatome are trying to build positions in export markets based on their experience with the world largest nuclear power plant build up of the decade. Cogema might have the best chance of the two in becoming a profitable operator of the nuclear fuel cycle. It has a world scale plant of waste treatment in La Hague which has captured a significant share of the Japanese and US markets, and is developing new technologies. Framatome is the only engineering contractor for all nuclear plants ordered by EDF but is just starting now to secure export orders in China and Egypt, and might have to face a drastic diversification to survive at its present size.

In summary, France's portfolio of companies still contains many knowledge-intensive Bets in key manufacturing businesses, (like computers and aircraft). This represents one of the most important challenges of the coming decade to really compete as an advanced industrial nation. The problem is that private shareholders cannot sustain a long competitive battle in high growth technologies and that the State resources are taken up by large bail-outs in hard hit mature companies, which have not been managed properly.

**The Drains**

The sources of Drain for France as well as for private investors are too many and too large. They can be broken down into three categories :

(a) Mature industries, perfectly adapted to high wage economies but suffering from lower growth rates and increased competition, and which have not adopted the right strategies : this is the most disturbing case of the automotive industry (Peugeot and Renault), but is also the case of the chemical and steel industries, as in many other European countries.

104

Figure 33

## THE ROLE OF THE AUTOMOTIVE INDUSTRY IN NATIONAL EXPORTS

| | 1980 Exports Bill US $ | % of total National Exports |
|---|---|---|
| **FRANCE** | | |
| RENAULT (n. 1 exporter) | 8,0 | 7,5 |
| PEUGEOT (n. 2) | 7,8 | 7,0 |
| TOTAL | 15,8 | 14,5 |
| **GERMANY** | | |
| VW (n. 1) | 10,9 | 6,0 |
| D. BENZ (n. 4) | 8,8 | 4,5 |
| TOTAL | 19,7 | 10,5 |
| **UK** | | |
| B.L. (n. 4) | 2,1 | 1,8 |
| **USA** | | |
| GM (n. 2) | 5,3 | 2,5 |
| FORD (n. 4) | 3,4 | 1,5 |
| TOTAL | 8,7 | 4,0 |
| **JAPAN** | | |
| NISSAN (n. 1) | 7,2 | 5,5 |
| TOYOTA (n. 2) | 6,2 | 5,0 |
| TOTAL | 13,4 | 10,5 |
| **SWEDEN** | | |
| VOLVO (n. 1) | 2,7 | 8,7 |
| SAAB (n. 4) | 1,2 | 4,3 |
| TOTAL | 3,9 | 13,0 |

Source : Telesis analysis

(b) Traditionally low wage-rate and unskilled businesses which have not diversified or invested in automation or new products. This category comprises some large textile firms and all the large shipyards.

(c) Raw material based industries which have become uncompetitive owing to new, lower-cost natural endowments in foreign countries : coal mines.

(a) Mature industries

The first category is unfortunately the largest and the most critical for France future standard of living.

The fundamental role played by the automobile industry in the French economy is well recognised. A recent report commissionned by the government (rapport Dalle) notes that the industry employs close to one million people including sub-suppliers and outside contractors; it generates directly around 100 billion francs in exports (Figure 33). Hundreds of companies depend on the ability of two large groups -Peugeot and Renault - to overcome their present competitive difficulties. The French car makers were Stars until the early to mid 1970s. Their competitive decline illustrates some of the structural obstacles which French industry faces in keeping afloat in high value added sectors of manufacturing.

After two consistent decades of market share gains in most major European countries, both Peugeot and Renault have lost share at home and in export markets. Foreign penetration of the French car market has increased from 25 per cent in 1973 to more than 40 per cent in 1985 despite quotas on Japanese cars, at a time when exports have only grown moderately. This is due to a number of complex reasons, including delays in new product introductions (the top-selling R5 was more than ten years old when it was replaced in early 1985), customer disenchantment with quality and reliability, and failures to capture the lucrative high-end segments. French makers have been outcompeted on those dimensions by other European companies, such as Mercedes, BMW, Audi and Volvo in the specialty segments and VW and Fiat in the volume segments. French management and engineering departments have focused more on technology (where French industry is at parity and sometimes leading)

106

than on a consistent integration between product design, production processes, factory layouts and personnel motivation to improve quality at affordable prices.

Production costs have increased faster than those of other European competitors and are definitely higher than those of Japanese cars sold in Europe. This has been partly due to higher inflation rates but the roots of the problem are more fundamental. In trying to reach better scale economies, the French car industry has been obsessed with overall volume rather than appropriate scale for each cost element. In its process of mergers (Peugeot-Citroën in 1975), acquisitions (Peugeot-Chrysler in 1978) and volume building (the 2 million cars mark set by Renault in 1973), the car manufacturers have not given enough attention to more important elements influencing cost position such as :

- component standardization across models and across variants, which allows longer run length, better assembly process and lower inventories. Renault has more versions of gearboxes, engines, and dashboards than all other volume producers. This has in turn fragmented runs for component suppliers which are seldom competitive on world markets (the situation of Valeo and Chausson is very critical as illustrated on the figure) ;
- the management of a stable, high quality and efficient network of sub-suppliers. French producers have not paid the same attention to their sub-contractors as Japanese or German rivals have. It is only recently that Renault and Peugeot are making special efforts to include them in their product planning and quality control procedures and to support them with long lead times and technical assistance ;
- process automation at all stages, and not only at the final assembly process. Even if Renault and Peugeot have kept abreast of technological developments in robotics, and flexible machining systems, the whole production system has not been realigned as consistently as in German or Swedish factories. Again reflecting French cultural bias, too much attention has been paid to technical performance and

not enough to integrated production engineering : lines are not in balance, inventories are too high, on-line faults are too frequent, etc.

Distribution strategies have also failed to protect market shares and customer satisfaction. The disastrous merger of Peugeot and Chrysler (Simca) dealer networks in France has opened new slots for foreign competitors. In many European markets, French industry has not yet the same strengths in dealers' financial resources and spare parts logistics as other international brands.

The progress made by Volvo in the last decade (specialty segments) or the recent turnaround of Fiat (volume segments) indicate that there is no inevitability and that the French car industry can restore its competitiveness. But the road is difficult. Management failures have led to a widespread confidence crisis in the workforce. Irresponsible union leadership in some plants (like Poissy or Aulnay) has compounded social unrest, and could lead to a situation similar to that in the worst British times. On the other hand, French industry still possesses the technical capabilities, brand image, and market shares necessary to increase return and value added per person. Three conditions are necessary :

- it is management's prime responsibility to restore quality and product reputation at the same time as it brings cost down to competitive levels ;
- the unions (and particularly the dominant communist-led CGT) should accept unavoidable employment reductions, including some lay-offs as has been the case of all other volume producers. Their recent attitude at Renault does not give high hopes, but their credibility has fallen very low as illustrated by the Citroën conflicts ;
- government should find the appropriate financial instruments (cheap loans or tax reductions) to allow the companies to continue to invest without suffering from a negative leverage effect in the short term. This support should not be dependent on additional constraints (particularly in terms of employment).

The automobile industry will have a crucial role to play in all advanced economies for many years to come. It still generates the largest employment and exports of all manufacturing sectors, particularly when sub-contractors and component suppliers of all kinds are included. It will represent one of the largest markets for major technological innovations in electronics, materials and energy. No country of the rank, ambition and size of France can sustain its development with a troubled car industry. This is the number 1 challenge of French industry today.

The French chemical industry has never been competitive - except in a few areas like agrochemicals or some specialty products - with its much older and stronger rivals in Germany, the UK, Switzerland and of course the US. The long historical lag in R&D has never been compensated by marketing or production specialization. Until recently the structure of the industry has remained fragmented, with no clear specialization and much less international presence. The history of mergers, acquisitions and divestitures in chemicals is probably the most complex and least productive of all sectors in France and has involved all actors in French society : the large established private groups of the postwar period like St Gobain, Pechiney and Rhône-Poulenc, the government-owned feedstock producers like Charbonnages de France, Elf and CFP, the banks and the State itself. The end result is fairly poor and the blame is to be borne collectively. The competitive problems of French chemical companies stem from a combination of natural handicaps and management failures.

The French handicaps lie with the lack of natural resources which once served as feedstock to chemical commodities, and with a historical lack of research and engineering experience. France has always suffered from little or uncompetitive feedstock compared with German, US or British coal, or US oil and gas. The coal-based chemical industry, which has developed in the North and in the East and is now in the CDF-Chimie portfolio, is not competitive. Petroleum materials on the other hand began to be refined in France a good 5 to 10 years after Germany or the Uk, when the first petrochemical platforms were installed in Lyon. France has always been behind the tremendous technical resources of the US, German or British industry, where many of the modern organic chemicals have originated. Still in 1979 France has 12 times fewer engineers and scientists in chemical research than the US, and three times less than Germany or the UK. French engineering schools in chemistry and chemical engineering are very few and small by international standards ; they do not attract the best students, and it is very rare to find a chemical engineer at the top of corporations as in Germany and Switzerland.

Several management failures have compounded the lag in product and process innovation. First companies have covered too broad an area of businesses through upstream and downstream integration and by purchasing foreign licences and setting up joint ventures. This has allowed French industry to catch up quickly after the war in high-tech, high-growth businesses like Rhône-Poulenc silicones, and synthetic fibres. This has been done however with a fragmented corporate structure and mostly for the domestic market. The subsequent mergers and acquisitions have resulted in a juxtaposition of incompatible product lines and technologies, sub-scale plants at home, and little international distribution.

The second management failure has been a lack of attention to building a strong application engineering and industrial marketing capability. The chemical industry is segmented into thousands of businesses which vary with the characteristics of the end-user. In specialty chemicals, fine chemicals pharmaceuticals or agrochemicals it is possible to focus successfully and grow on world markets with specific applications. There are dozens of such specialized leaders in scalants, pigments, dyes, emulsions, etc. but very few are French. Rhône-Poulenc silicon mastics and rare earths, Kuhlman's leather dyes and CECA (SNEA) active carbons are rare examples. Pharmaceutical companies have generally too broad a product line with few world leading positions despite many inventions. In pesticides and insecticides, Rhône-Poulenc has a few innovative products and significant exports but remains small compared with the world giants like Hoechst, Ciba, Bayer or Pfizer.

The third management failure has been a lack of efficiency in manufacturing and capacity planning. By focusing too much on the domestic market, and in order to catch up quickly, French corporations have invested too quickly and in duplication in too many locations in the 1960s, and have not reduced obsolete capacity or shut down high cost platforms soon enough. French chemical plants remain too often sub-scale, and not optimized to utilize efficiently by-products and co-products. Each company has developed its own network of product flows and the mergers have complicated rather than rationalized these decisions. The former IG Farben in Germany - on the contrary - had the power to optimize the major investment decisions at a much higher level of scale and by-products economies. After the war, IG Farben was split into three major companies, Bayer, Hoechst and BASF, along logical lines of specialization and around large-scale manufacturing complexes (the Bayer site in Leverkusen for example). The French State itself has encouraged too much sub-scale and redundant capacity building in the 1960s, by providing cheap capital to everyone, pushing new projects to regional targets like Lorraine and the Marseille Region, and creating two new publicly owned companies in addition to the already excessive number of producers : CDF-Chimie (1965) and SNEA (1966).

The recent nationalizations of 1981 have put the only two remaining large private groups - Rhône-Poulenc and PCUK - into the public domain which now accounts for most of the industry. The financial situation in 1981-83 was such - particularly in petrochemicals and plastics - that the State had to allocate several billion francs in the form of equity or participating loans. The positive result of the nationalizations has been to categorize the main companies better by broad business area. Rhône-Poulenc is now recognized as the main 'specialty producer' and as such has received the pharmaceuticals and agrochemicals operations of PCUK. SNEA has been asked to take full responsibility for petrochemicals and plastics, owing to its oil business and cash flows, and is in the process of rationalizing plants from Rhône-Poulenc (CHLOE), PCUK and ATO-Chimie, as well as its own. Finally CDF-Chimie is regrouping the paints and fertilizers businesses. French chemical companies are however still far from being generally competitive with their foreign rivals. Rhône-Poulenc managed to make a profit of close to 1 billion francs in 1984, after several years' losses. This was due however to higher prices in dollars and it should be said that its British and German competitors have been two or three times more profitable. CDF-Chimie is still making

111

considerable losses (600 million francs in 1984) which leaves little hope for average years. SNEA has some reasonably profitable businesses in specialty, pharmaceuticals and cosmetics but will continue to barely break even on its heavy chemicals operations, despite recent rationalizations.

The steel companies are on both sides of the value-added median, Usinor being higher and Sacilor lower. The steel industry also illustrates some of the same management failures, although in a much more difficult market and competitive environment, compounded with counter-productive interference from public policy. Management has failed on several issues and has performed more poorly than some of its European colleagues in the face of rising Japanese competition, market maturity and overcapacity.

First of all, French companies have not redeployed their assets early enough, and never completely, from high-cost inland historical locations (Lorraine, le Creusot, and Valenciennes) to lower-cost plants near deep water ports. When modern capacity of the latter kind was built in Dunkerque and Fos in the late 1960s, obsolete capacity was kept in operation, thereby raising average costs and threatening corporate financial balance. The whole of French society - conservatives and socialists, unions and management -failed to recognize the need for redundancies, and to bear the political risk of closing down old plants. The government massively increased its financial support from the early 1970s on, with little pressure for capacity reduction and industry rationalization. It is only with the last government plan of 1984 that cross arrangements on product specializations and new investments between the two main groups Usinor and Sacilor have seriously started, particularly in special steels.

Industry-wide production rationalizations have been considerably stalled by old rivalries among the historical 'maîtres de forge' which have persisted even after their companies had been de facto nationalized by the Barre government in 1978. The fragmentation of resources and duplication of new investments which are now leading to the closing of modern facilities (like in Fos) have never been really addressed - as in the case of chemicals - by successive goverments which have preferred passively to bail out inefficient managements with no quid pro quo. The mergers of the Lorraine and North companies in Sacilor and Usinor respectively in the late 1960s came too late and had little impact for the following decade. Furthermore, this left important companies like Ugine (PUK) or Metallurgique de Normandie (Schneider) in even more isolated and vulnerable positions, suffering from unfair treatment from the State.

The management of the French steel industry also failed to recognize several important technological trends in its allocations of resources, such as the growing advantages of electric arc furnaces and mini-mills, which the Italian Bresciani have exploited, or the galvanization process for the automotive market which the Swedish and German industries have much better developed.

The non-ferrous metals companies are in a somewhat better position. They have often been technological innovators or at least efficient followers, like Pechiney in aluminium and Cogema in uranium. They have generally invested worldwide either to secure raw material sources (Cogema in Niger and Australia, Pechiney in Guinea, le Nickel in New Caledonia) or to exploit cheap sources of the power which constitutes a large portion of the processing costs (Pechiney in Greece and Canada). These companies can, however, be in different financial situations owing to very cyclical market and price trends in the world.

(b) Low wage-rate businesses
In the second category of Drains - French companies attacked by lower-wage rate countries (such as in textiles and shipyards) - the response of French industry has been in many cases too slow.

The shipyards have been kept alive by the State for three decades, without clear objectives or pressures for rationalization. The fragmentation of the industry in the three main ports (Dunkerque, St Nazaire and La Ciotat), plus numerous smaller yards in other regions, has been a permanent obstacle to capacity and employment reductions. As in the case of the steel industry, this has also slowed down new investment in automation. The recent mergers in 1982 leading to two main groups - Normed and Chantiers de l'Atlantique - can pave the way to a better coordinated rationalization.

113

The situations of the main textile companies are very contrasting, although none is flourishing like competitors in Italy, Germany or the US. Some like DMC, Prouvost or Lainière de Roubaix are now making serious efforts at product specialization, after years of uncontrolled diversification. Boussac, however, once the wealthiest French textile company, and virtually State financed after its bankrupcy in 1981, has been unable to adopt a clear strategy owing to constant turmoil in management, until a recent legal settlement in early 1985.

### (c) Raw material based businesses

In the third category, Charbonnages de France is the only significant company (with Potasses d'Alsace) to exploit natural resources outside agriculture. Coal extracted in France (in the North and Lorraine regions) has been higher-cost than US or Australian coal shipped to the home market for more than two decades. Employment has been reduced from 300,000 in the postwar period to 30,000 today, with only one major strike (in 1962). Compared to the British situation it represents a fairly well managed - although costly - transition. A strong commitment from both the management and the State to replace a declining industry by new jobs has allowed the company to progressively close its most costly mines. This process was temporarily stopped in 1981 but has been initiated again more recently.

**The Havens**

Profitable businesses with lower value added per person than the OECD average tend to be sheltered in part or in total from international competition. They are often brilliant enterprises founded by a dynamic postwar generation in construction (F. Bouygues, the Chauffour family of Dumez) or distribution (Promodes, Darty). For older established firms in construction or distribution, a natural selection process within France has sorted out the best managed companies from the others : Grands Travaux de Marseille and SCREG in construction have done better than SGE, Fougerolle, Campenon Bernard or Spie-Batignolles. Printemps and Casino in distribution have outperformed Galeries Lafayette and Magasins Réunis. CFAO in trading has done better than

Figure 34

## INTERNATIONAL PERFORMANCES
## OF THE MAIN FRENCH CONSTRUCTION COMPANIES

| | Foreign sales 1982 Billions FF | Foreign sales growth 1979-82 (% per year) |
|---|---|---|
| SCREG-COLAS | 9,0 | 20 |
| SPIE-BATIGNOLLES | 7,8 | 27 |
| GTM-ENTREPOSE | 7,0 | 25 |
| DUMEZ | 7,0 | 50 |
| BOUYGUES | 5,2 | 68 |
| SGE-SAINRAPT | 5,0 | 26 |
| SAE | 4,0 | 100 |
| FOUGEROLLE | 3,7 | 45 |
| C. BERNARD | 2,1 | 28 |
| **TOTAL** | **50,8** | **28** |

Source : Annual reports, DAEI, Telesis interviews

115

SCOA. Compagnie Générale des Eaux is more profitable than Lyonnaise des Eaux in water distribution and local services. In sheltered businesses some lose, some win, but the net result for France is neutral : no sustainable employment is lost or created and the balance of payments is marginally affected by competitive failures and successes.

The only exception in this category is the world presence which the large French engineering contractors have gained over the last ten years : a dozen companies have won an international reputation in large public works, particularly in Arab countries, America and Africa. Foreign sales for the nine largest groups represented a total of 51 billion francs in 1983 and increased by 28 per cent per year over the three years 1979-82 (Figure 34). Those revenues coming from foreign markets give rise to only a minority percentage of exports, as an increasing portion of the value added is made by local contractors or local workers.

**The borderline cases**
Of course, the world does not divide up into four quadrants, but is rather a continuum on both axes and a number of companies are therefore on boundary lines.

Some significant complex-factor manufacturing businesses involved in high technology or medium technology areas have yet to improve their competitive position to become truly Star performers : Alsthom (in railway and power generation equipment) or CIT-Alcatel (in telecommunications and office equipment) are both members of .the large CGE Group. They still rely too heavily on State purchases and artificial prices to be truly considered as world competitive. The same holds true for Jeumont-Schneider (in railway and power equipment).

Merlin-Gérin (Empain-Schneider Group) on the other hand is becoming a true world-competitive producer of medium and high voltage equipment and is diversifying in process control equipment. Together with Télémécanique (industrial switchgear), Legrand (low voltage household gear) and Leroy-Somer (small electric motors), these four electrical engineering firms are still medium-sized companies, but developing well, owing to a clear strategy of product innovation and cost leadership in well-defined business

116

segments. They represent a healthy layer of companies, born in the "provinces" but much more international than many Paris-based companies. They follow a path of world dominance in smaller segments. Such has been the case of Bic, which has diversified from writing instruments to surf boards and lighters with the same success in low production costs, world distribution and brand awareness. Unfortunately, there are not enough of them to compensate for the decline or the difficulties of the larger groups.

The large groups on the border lines, Compagnie Générale d'Electricité (CGE) and Saint-Gobain, are two excellent representatives of the French industrial establishment. They were formed by a series of mergers and acquisitions in the 1960s and early 1970s, often among unrelated businesses, with the objective of reaching the status, size and often prestige of a multinational. They have been managed by the 'cream' of France's elite system, Ingénieurs du Corps des Mines (Polytechnique) and Inspecteurs des Finances (ENA). They have maintained close relationships with the State technostructure, which has given them privileged access to government contracts (as in the case of telephone and railways) and a favourable social profile. Their prospects and strategic position are however very different.

CGE is responsible for many high-tech businesses where France has the ambition to become a world contender : digital telecommunications, high speed trains, electric turbines, office automation. In none of them can it be considered as a leader outside protected home markets. Like Thomson - its past arch rival in many industries - CGE been involved too superficially too in many businesses to become truly international in any one of them. Its competitors are generally much stronger financially, investing much more in R & D and more international : Siemens, ASEA, General Electric, Hitachi, Toshiba among others. In the past, CGE has failed in computers and been kept out of nuclear power. It remains to be seen if it can summon enough resources and internationalize quickly enough to manage high-tech businesses successfully.

Saint-Gobain is the result of one of the few successfully managed mergers of French industry, between Pont-à-Mousson (iron pipes and mechanical engineering) and

Saint Gobain (glass and construction). Although some of its leadership positions have been seriously eroded by new competitors, Saint Gobain still generates satisfactory cash flows and seeks to invest in faster growth businesses.

All those borderline companies have the potential to become Stars, if they make the correct strategic decisions and are managed with consistency in the next decade.

## Successes in small business

In every country mythology typically clouds any discussion of the performance and the true contribution of small and medium-sized companies to the national economy. The Birch study in the US widely publicized the fact, for example, that new jobs were exclusively created by small firms. This overlooks two aspects which put the role of small business in perspective. First, those jobs were created mostly in the sheltered sectors (restaurants, cleaning, etc.), when they can only reach larger numbers in a vast autonomous market like the US. Second, the jobs created by small firms are for a good part the spin-offs of the growth and competitive positions of the larger firms for which they act as suppliers, services, subcontractors, etc.

The performance of French small business is ambiguous : on the one hand it shows a very healthy level of business creation and growth, particularly during the 1960s. On the other hand, only a minority of the postwar business creations have been in traded activities. Figure 35 shows the most prominent successes among French medium-sized companies by ranking their growth rates and profitability. More than half of those are in sheltered or protected markets : distribution, food and beverages, advertising and media. The pattern is strikingly similar to the one observed in large industry. Six of those companies have enjoyed growth rates of 30 per cent or above ; only one company operates in open markets. Many postwar entrepreneurs in sheltered business are now ranked among the most successful capitalists of modern France : Roger Bellon, founder of Sodexho (French catering leader), MM. Dubrule et Pelisson, founders of Novotel and now heads of Accor (French largest hotel and restaurant chain), Serge Kampf, the founder of Cap Gemini Sogeti (second largest European computer service firm) M.

Figure 35

## MEDIUM SIZE CORPORATE SUCCESSES IN FRANCE
### Top 30 growth rates

| SHELTERED OR PROTECTED MARKETS | Growth in % (1976-81 sales growth per year) | 1981 Employees |
|---|---|---|
| CASTORAMA (Distribution) | 60 | 3.200 |
| EUROCOM (Advertising) | 59 | 1.862 |
| TRAVAUX D'HYDRAULIQUE (Construction) | 50 | NA |
| NOVOTEL (Hotels) | 40 | 15.486 |
| VINIPRIX* (Distribution) | 35 | 4.338 |
| SAINRAPT & BRICE (Construction) | 30 | 12.020 |
| CEP (Publishing) | 22 | 2.387 |
| DARTY* (Distribution) | 22 | 4.425 |
| FRANCE GLACES FINDUS - Nestlé (Frozen food) | 18 | 3.134 |
| RHIN RHONE (Diversified services) | 17 | 2.964 |
| VERMANDOISE* (Miscellaneous) | 17 | 866 |
| GRANDS MOULINS DE PARIS (Food) | 16 | 2.650 |
| FRAISSINET (Construction) | 14 | 419 |
| PRIMAGAZ (Distribution) | 14 | 2.170 |
| ORTIZ* (Frozen food) | 14 | 4.919 |
| ALSACIENNE DE SUPERMARCHE (Distribution) | 14 | 4.171 |
| EUROPE 1. (Media) | 13 | 854 |
| AIR INTER* (Airlines) | 13 | 5.710 |

| INTERNATIONALLY OPEN MARKETS | | | 1981 Exports (%) |
|---|---|---|---|
| TAITTINGER (Champagne) | 54 | 3.272 | NA |
| CHARLES HEIDSICK-HENRIOT (Champagne) | 22 | 187 | NA |
| CROUZET (Electronics) | 21 | 8.822 | 51 |
| POULAIN (Confectionary) | 19 | 2.259 | 12 |
| FROMAGERIES BEL (Cheese) | 19 | 7.301 | 44 |
| SOURIAU* (Electronics) | 18 | 3.300 | 47 |
| VEUVE CLIQUOT PONSARDIN (Champagne) | 17 | 598 | 74 |
| ARJOMARI-PRIOUX (Paper) | 14 | 3.692 | 30 |
| JAEGER (Automotive components) | 13 | 8.384 | NA |
| GENERALE DE FONDERIE (Foundry) | 13 | 11.354 | 25 |
| TRAPIL (Pipeline engineering) | 13 | 1.032 | NA |
| SFIM* (Avionics) | 13 | 2.500 | 66 |

### Top 30 profitability

| SHELTERED OR PROTECTED MARKETS | Return in % (1981 return on net worth) | 1981 Employees |
|---|---|---|
| DARTY* (Distribution) | 50 | 4.425 |
| AIR INTER* (Airlines) | 31 | 5.710 |
| VERMANDOISE* (Sugar) | 30 | 866 |
| SAINT LOUIS BOUCHON (Food) | 26 | 4.812 |
| VINIPRIX* (Distribution) | 25 | 4.338 |
| UNICOPA (Distribution) | 23 | 1.847 |
| FRANCAISE DE SUCRERIE (Sugar) | 21 | 902 |
| O.C.P. (Pharmaceutical distribution) | 21 | 4.755 |
| COMPAGNIE FINANCIERE SUCRE & DENREE (Food) | 20 | 2.500 |
| CEDEST (Distribution) | 18 | 914 |
| FINANCIERE ETERNIT (Construction materials) | 18 | 5.171 |
| GENERALE COOPERATIVE & CONSOMMATION (Dist.) | 17 | 3.858 |
| GROUPE MAISONS FAMILIALES (Construction) | 16 | 2.971 |
| ORTIZ* (Frozen food) | 16 | 4.919 |
| GERLAND (Plastic & misc.) | 16 | 4.200 |

| INTERNATIONALLY OPEN MARKETS | | | 1981 Exports (%) |
|---|---|---|---|
| SOURIAU* (Electronics) | 30 | 3.300 | 47 |
| SFIM* (Avionics) | 28 | 2.500 | 66 |
| DAMART SERVIPOST (Textiles) | 26 | 1.410 | 20 |
| TURBOMECA (Helicopter turbines) | 25 | 4.330 | 65 |
| INTERTECHNIQUE (Computers) | 24 | 1.717 | 26 |
| MARNIER LAPOSTOLLE (Liquors) | 22 | 436 | 85 |
| EPEDA BERTRAND FAURE (Auto components) | 22 | NA | NA |
| FACOM (Hand tools) | 21 | 1.455 | 20 |
| ROQUETTE (Chemicals) | 19 | — | NA |
| LA SEIGNEURIE (Paints) | 17 | 1.210 | NA |
| DELMAS VIELJEUX (Transportation) | 16 | 2.146 | NA |
| POCLAIN (Hydraulic cranes) | 16 | 7.243 | 53 |
| CECA (Chemicals) | 16 | 2.290 | 67 |
| ENERTEC (Engineering) | 16 | 4.189 | NA |
| ESSILOR (Optical products) | 15 | 7.788 | 60 |

* Companies listed in both growth and profitability top 30
Source : Telesis Analysis from annual reports

119

Bleustein-Blanchet, founder of Publicis, and MM. Roux and Seguela, founder of the third largest advertising agency in France, J.C. Decaux who invented the concept of 'Abribus'. All of these business inventors have grown into successful managers of profitable and well run firms of medium size. Many of them have recently taken their company public and can be considered as the most recent layers of wealth generated from business in France. As more cash is generated by their base business these companies diversify in similar businesses in other countries and become international. They do not however become fully traded, as their competitors remain local firms in each market, and their activities give rise to only limited exports.

In the traded sector, Figure 36 shows the top 50 French companies which can be evaluated as leaders in their business. The focus of French traditional strongholds is quite striking : food and beverages, cosmetics and fashion, construction and engineering have been fertile ground for new companies as well as for the large established ones. The relatively small presence of technology based companies is obvious. French successes in electronics, computers, specialty chemicals or pharmaceuticals can be counted on one hand. France does not have the equivalent of Nixdorf, Novo (Denmark), Tetrapack or Alpha-Laval (Sweden), not to speak of all the US postwar business creations : DEC, Data General or Apple. Nor does it possess the equivalent of Swiss and German machinery and engineering companies.

In traded sectors apart from food, cosmetics and fashion, there is no clear pattern in French new business creation. Companies listed on Figure 36 have been founded on original business concepts invented and/or developed by strong and charismatic leaders : Trigano's popular vacation concept (Club Mediterranée), Bic's disposable plastic consumer items, Merieux's vaccines, Salomon's new ski bindings and ski boot shapes, Damart's chlorofiber for underwear, Slidowski's revolutionary use of turbine engines for helicopters (Turbomeca), Cristallerie d'Arques low-cost 'mechanical cristal', etc. All of these companies have generally managed to remain the leaders that they are, by expanding their markets worldwide, investing in modern production facilities, and continuing product refinements. They are the best

Figure 36

## FRANCE SMALL AND MEDIUM SIZE COMPANIES
## 50 TOP LEADERSHIP POSITIONS (1984 data)

| COMPANY | Business leadership | Sales Billion FF | % Export | Return % on equity |
|---|---|---|---|---|
| **FOOD AND BEVERAGES** | | | | |
| ORTIZ-MIKO* | Frozen food & ice creams | 3,5 | NA | NA |
| REMY MARTIN | Cognac | 3,0 | NA | 15 |
| MARTELL | Cognac | 1,9 | 97 | 15 |
| CLAEYS-LUCK | Seeds | 1,5 | 50 | NA |
| COINTREAU | Liquor | 1,5 | 76 | NA |
| VEUVE CLIQUOT | Champagne | 0,9 | 75 | 11 |
| COURVOISIER | Liquor | 0,7 | 90 | 3 |
| DUCROS* | Aromatics | 0,7 | 40 | 11 |
| MARNIER LAPOSTOLLE | Liquor | 0,6 | 88 | 25 |
| BENEDICTINE | Liquor | 0,3 | 90 | 16 |
| **OTHER CONSUMER GOODS** | | | | |
| CRISTALLERIE D'ARQUES (1982) | Mecanical glass articles | 3,1 | 71 | 37 |
| ESSILOR* | Optical lenses | 2,9 | 67 | 21 |
| MERIEUX* | Vaccines | 1,9 | 55 | 14 |
| SALOMON | Ski binding & shoes | 1,7 | 89 | 40 |
| FICHET-BAUCHE | Security equipment | 1,4 | 42 | 4 |
| DAMART SERVIPOST* | Tribo-electric underwear | 1,4 | 25 | 25 |
| ROSSIGNOL* | Skis | 1,1 | 78 | 16 |
| PORON* | Children's wear | 1,0 | 51 | 5 |
| DELBARD* | Rose grower | 0,8 | 0 | 4 |
| ADG (15 months)* | Camping gaz cans | 0,8 | 55 | 3 |
| ZODIAC* | Pneumatic boats & other soft material | 0,8 | 46 | 23 |
| PETIT BATEAU* | Underwears | 0,6 | 35 | 8 |
| TEISSEIRE | Sirups | 0,6 | 6 | 21 |
| MAJORETTE* | Car toys | 0,5 | 59 | 20 |
| BENETEAU | Sail boats | 0,4 | 65 | 24 |
| GUY DEGRENNE* | Silverware | 0,3 | 10 | 13 |
| JALATTE* | Safety shoes | 0,3 | 45 | 10 |
| **ENGINEERING & SERVICES** | | | | |
| CLUB MEDITERRANEE* | Vacation villages | 5,1 | NA | 13 |
| KIS* | Instant services | 3,3 | 88 | NA |
| CAP-GEMINI-SOGETI* | Computer software | 1,8 | 57 | 41 |
| COMEX* | Subsea mainten. & repair | 1,3 | 95 | −81 |
| DORIS* | Off-shore struct. engin. | 1,1 | NA | 9 |
| CCMC* | Computer services | 0,8 | 3 | 25 |
| SLIGOS* | Computer services | 0,7 | 0,5 | 11 |
| **COSMETICS & FASHION ARTICLES** | | | | |
| ADIDAS* | Sport shoes & sportswear | 2,3 | 52 | NA |
| CHANNEL-BOURJOIS | Perfumes | 1,5 | 60 | NA |
| LOUIS VUITTON | Leather luggage & articles | 1,1 | 72 | 59 |
| CHRISTIAN DIOR | Fashion | 0,6 | 80 | NA |
| HERMES | Perfumes, leather articles, fashion | 0,4 | 50 | NA |
| **TECHNOLOGY AND INDUSTRIAL GOODS** | | | | |
| POCLAIN* | Hydraulic excavators | 2,9 | 53 | − 16 |
| BERTRAND FAURE* | Auto seats & rigid luggage | 2,7 | NA | 20 |
| S. DASSAULT ELECTRONIQUE* | Avionics & terminals | 2,4 | 54 | 36 |
| TURBOMECA* | Helicopter turbines | 2,0 | 67 | 12 |
| COFLEXIP * | Flexible pipes for oil fields | 2,2 | 95 | 20 |
| SFENA* | Avionics | 1,2 | 17 | −19 |
| SFIM* | Avionics | 1,1 | 22 | 10 |
| INTERTECHNIQUE* | Mini-computers | 1,0 | NA | 26 |
| FACOM* | Hand tools | 0,9 | 20 | 17 |
| BENSON* | Graphic display periph. | 0,7 | 40 | NA |
| BOLLORE | Specialty paper | 0,4 | 81 | 19 |

*Postwar creation*
*Source : Telesis analysis from annual reports and interviews*

examples of what business leadership can do and of how competitive advantage is achieved and maintained. They are, however, too few really to compensate for the weaknesses of large industry.

## Conclusions

From this quick overview, we can discern France's main strengths and weaknesses, and the nature of the competitive challenge for the years ahead, particularly if one compares the situation with that of the most advanced industrial nations.

- The most brilliant corporate successes of French industry are concentrated in oil (and oil services), food and sheltered businesses. These companies typically generate less benefits for the nation in terms of exports, skill development and indirect employment than Stars in complex-factor manufacturing businesses in other countries, such as the German automotive and chemical companies or the US aircraft and computer companies. As in the UK, the top performers do not automatically bring the highest return for the country.

- A dominant proportion of new entrepreneurs, new skilled managers, and fresh capital has been attracted to sheltered or semi-sheltered businesses which offer in all countries higher returns but have generally lower value added per person and less indirect effects.

- Most high-tech (or even medium-tech) companies in France are still in fragile competitive positions and only a handful are self-sustainable. The French tradition of technical invention and State support in aircraft and military hardware has not yet been translated into autonomous business strengths. Computers, telecommunications and other electronics firms are facing very difficult competitive situations. Some medium sized companies can become real Stars but they are too few, and owing to their recent creation (1950s and early 1960s), none of them can match the large foreign technology-based multinationals.

- Most worryingly the car companies, which together generate around one million jobs directly and indirectly, have dramatically deteriorated and are jeopardizing other sectors of industry. The turnaround of the automotive industry - still a spearhead for all advanced economies - is probably the number one priority for the country. It has the potential to become the Star which it was in the 1960s, but fundamental changes in management and social relations have to take place.
- Too many companies, some of them very large, are still on borderlines. They all have the potential to become more profitable and generate higher value added per person, when compared to foreign competitors. This is again a challenge to management. More than other industrialized countries, France must pursue the process of closing excess capacity, employment reduction and modernization, particularly in mature industries like basic chemicals or steel. This is a condition for freeing capital and human resources to develop more promising businesses. This is a challenge to management but also to the society at large.

It is against a difficult background of increased international competition and lower growth, that French management must find the means of establishing and sustaining more business leadership positions.

## 3. FRENCH CORPORATE STRATEGIES : ESTABLISHING AND MAINTAINING A LEADING BUSINESS POSITION

France's lack of competitive companies of significant size in high value added traded businesses is first explained by common management and strategic deficiencies. These failures can be better understood when evaluated against a general framework of corporate competition. When success is not primarily based on the exploitation of natural endowments or cheap labour - neither being in great supply in France - it must result from a combination of investment decisions, skills, and management practices. In those businesses subject to competition from countries paying high wages - which we have called complex-factor businesses in part I - analysis, experience and creativity become critical.

Competitive success in complex-factor businesses depends on the particular economics of a given business and on the characteristics and growth rates of different parts of the market. Competition is complex because of the many factors that must be considered in order to gain strategic advantage over competitors : purchasing, manufacturing, marketing, pricing, distribution, R&D, product design, personnel or financial management.

Nevertheless, there are guidelines to competitive success, as well as techniques to analyse the series of dynamic interactions that constitute the international competitive market place. Through a combination of experience and analysis, managers can develop an understanding of the nature of competition in the markets they serve and can devise corporate strategies to improve the competitive position of the firm. Government officials and all leaders in society who hope to address the key economic issue facing the country - the relative decline in French competitive productivity - must understand the elements of successful strategic planning for the firm and appreciate how these strategies must change as conditions for a world economy shift.

This section is not a management textbook. We will therefore not offer here a detailed description of our model of corporate strategy, but will only summarize the main points[2].

The role of a corporation is to utilize its resources - human and capital - in order to maximize 'wealth' for its investors, over a long period of time. Of course, a defensible and sustainable return to the investor cannot be obtained without bringing satisfaction to both the employees and the customers. In this process, the corporate leadership must seek two goals :
- to establish and maintain a competitive position in any given business where the firm operates, against existing and new competitors ;
- to manage the corporate portfolio of businesses, and the corporate resources - human and financial - so as to maximize the consolidated returns across businesses.

## Business leadership
Leadership in a given business can be obtained by securing a defensible advantage over competitors in any of the three following domains, or through a superior combination among them :
- lower cost (cost advantage),
- higher price (price premium),
- lower capital employed.

### (a) Cost advantage
In most businesses some competitors have lower total costs than others, even with equal conditions in labour and raw material prices. The fact that their costs differ for performing essentially the same activities can be explained, at least in part, by the "experience curve". Costs differ among competitors, and for a single competitor between points in time, because the costs of producing and selling a unit of

---

2
The model which we use in our practice is more fully explained in, for example, Telesis, A review of Irish industrial policy, National Economic and Social Council Dublin, 1982, pp. 41-82 and B. Déchery and alia, Les mécanismes fondamentaux de la compétitivité, Editions Hommes et Techniques, Paris, 1980.

product decline with accumulated experience. A corollary is that the larger a company's share of business, the faster it can accumulate experience therefore decreasing costs faster than its competitors. If market-share leadership is sustained, that cost advantage can be maintained. Because of this, there is a link between the two key goals of growth and productivity improvement. When growth cannot be attained at home, it must be sought in foreign markets. This is why the Stars described in the previous chapter are all multinational companies.

The advantages of obtaining a lower cost position relative to others in the same business are obvious. At equal selling price, the lower-cost competitor is able to earn a greater return, reinvest more in the business and grow faster than others, thereby continuing to accumulate additional volume and realizing further cost reductions relative to others as demonstrated by Bic in ball point pens against Biro and Reynolds. The higher return can also enable the low-cost competitor to expand into new business areas, as shown by Moët-Hennessy, BSN or Elf. A low-cost position can also allow a competitor to sell at a lower price than others when necessary, while still remaining at least as profitable as they are. A low-cost competitor is therefore better able to withstand cyclical downturns in the market than are higher-cost producers. In trucks, Volvo and Daimler Benz are still profitable when Renault and British Leyland are losing money.

A high market share certainly only provides the opportunity for attaining a low-cost position. It does not guarantee it. Unless appropriate investments are made to take advantage of the possibilities for rationalization that the increased volume affords, a dominant market position may not yield further advantages in cost. Berliet, which once was a European leader in trucks, lost out to Daimler-Benz because of failure to invest in customer service and product design. Competitive success is a function of the company's ability to improve its cost relative to others, and to maintain the advantage once it is achieved. In this sense, competitive cost advantage is similar to the leading position in a race. The leader must continually work to maintain the lead. Moreover, it is the total cost that is relevant, not merely factor costs. Cost of raw materials, manufacturing value added, research and development, transportation, distribution, and service must all be considered. A geographically distant competitor, for example, may still be the low-cost supplier of a product if its higher transport costs can be offset by economies realized from a larger–scale, highly automated manufacturing process, as proven by Japanese exports in steel, cars or colour TVs.

(b) Price premium

In addition to or together with cost advantages, in certain businesses it is possible to attain a sustainable price premium over competitors. This can occur through better quality or performance in products, better after–sales service and stronger distributor coverage, or through the creation of a brand franchise.

Product design leadership can sometimes result in products that are more reliable or that perform better than those offered by competitors, or that have special features. On occasion, though not always, consumers are prepared to pay a price premium for this extra quality or performance. In these cases, such as Volvo and BMW cars or Sony color TVs, if the price premium exceeds the costs of implementing the extra quality of performance, then a competitive advantage can be gained.

Sometimes consumers are willing to pay a price premium if the distribution network is more convenient or the after–sales service is more reliable. Rather than travel to the larger city 50 miles away, they will pay extra to buy in their own town. Also, rather than rely on a distant service depot, they would prefer to pay a premium and have service more easily available. A company that has invested to establish a more widespread distribution or service support network, like Salomon ski bindings or DMC knitting yarn, may therefore be able to command a price premium. Again, the price premium is a strategic competitive advantage only when it more than offsets the extra costs of establishing the more elaborate distribution network.

Companies can also sustain a price premium by outspending competitors in advertising or promotion schemes or by gaining wider 'shelfspace' access than competitors in retail outlets. Customers may seek out and pay more for the

127

brand name like Perrier mineral water or Lacoste shirts. Again, this is a strategic advantage only when the price premium exceeds the extra costs of the promotional activity.

The extra return from price premiums can be put to the same strategic use as that obtained from being the low-cost producer in a business: reinvestment to sustain leadership.

### (c) Higher capital turnover

Finally a lower utilization of capital for the same level of revenue results in a higher return to the investor, with no difference in operating margin. In the distribution business for example, Carrefour has been able to generate a permanent surplus in working capital by turning over its inventories much quicker than traditional department stores while all its customers were paying cash. Similarly Club Méditerranée has a very efficient way of reducing its capital needs by requesting advance payments from its customers, changing cash for company payment instruments at the beginning of vacation, and leasing land instead of purchasing. Innovative methods can also be found in tapping the capital markets : some companies like St Gobain or Renault have been pioneers in various new instruments like convertible debentures, ECU-bonds, participating notes and certificates which have lowered their cost of capital.

## A model of corporate competition

True competitive advantages are not artificial and short-lived, like the temporary utilization of 'black economy' cheap labour or temporary price umbrellas in times of short supply. Rather they stem from the consistent implementation of carefully devised strategies. To do so, companies can exploit three main competitive levers :
- technology lead,
- scale economies,
- organizational effectiveness.

It is the identification and exploitation of these levers which form the essence of successful strategies. Figure 37 offers an overview of the various ways these levers can affect the different components of cost and added value in a given business. It is against this simplified model that we will

128

Figure 37

# A MODEL OF CORPORATE COMPETITION

## HOW THE THREE MAIN COMPETITIVE LEVERS CAN AFFECT COST, PRICE OR CAPITAL UTILIZATION

| COMPONENTS OF BUSINESS COST AND ADDED-VALUE | MAIN COMPETITIVE LEVERS | | |
|---|---|---|---|
| | Scale economies | Technology lead | Organizational effectiveness |
| PURCHASING | *Lower unit cost through :*<br>- volume discounts | *Lower unit cost through :*<br>- lower input due to proprietary process | *Lower unit cost through :*<br>- experienced buying, proprietary sources |
| MANUFACTURING | *Lower unit cost through :*<br>- overall plant scale<br>- machine scale<br>- run length | *Lower unit cost or higher unit price through proprietary technology :*<br>- higher quality<br>- less material usage<br>- more output<br>- less labour (automation) | *Lower unit cost or higher unit price through better production management :*<br>- capacity utilization<br>- labour productivity and quality (skills)<br>- material flow process<br>- mastering of process/machine<br>- quality control<br>- maintenance costs |
| MARKETING | *Lower unit cost through :*<br>- volume per brand | *Lower unit cost or higher unit price through :*<br>- proprietary packaging | *Lower unit cost or higher unit price through better :*<br>- brand management (image, premiums) |
| DISTRIBUTION | - volume per channel or region | - original logistics system | - training in customer service and organization of spare part logistics |
| APPLICATION ENGINEERING | - volume per application | - proprietary applications | - modularization know-how |
| RESEARCH & DEVELOPMENT | - volume per research area | - protected innovations | - creative management<br>- interdisciplinary teams<br>- international alliance policies |
| PRODUCT DESIGN | - volume per design | - proprietary designs | - product line management (timing introduction, pricing structure) and skill development |
| HUMAN RESOURCES | *Access to higher performance people through :*<br>- higher salaries<br>- better career tracks | *Higher output and quality through :*<br>- unique training techniques | *Higher output and quality through better :*<br>- motivation and human development |
| FINANCE | *Access to lower cost of capital through :*<br>- better use of international markets<br>- portfolio cash management | *Lower capital utilization through innovative methods :*<br>- computerization<br>- electronic fund transfer | *Lower capital utilization through better :*<br>- inventory and account receivable control<br>- knowledge of capital markets |

judge French management failures and successes. Our conviction is that not enough managers and policy makers in France understand and master the rules of the game in free market competition. This game is complex and constantly evolving.

The competitive levers interact with one another and change over time. For example, successful competition in the automobile business may be based on manufacturing scale advantages in key components (engines, transmissions), research and development technology (new model design) and distribution (sales, service, spare parts). It is the lack of attention to the interactions between all those factors which can best explain the declining market share of French automobile companies.

The basis for cost advantage and defensible barriers for a given business evolves over time. A currently reasonable strategy may later become obsolete. Failure to recognize changes as they occur can virtually ensure the loss of one's competitive position to other more perceptive competitors. It is this evolution that also offers opportunity for a new entrant or a high-cost competitor to overtake the industry leader.

In its entry into the North American cement market, Lafarge was able to utilize its production experience in dry process in Europe, to convert the less efficient wet process plants it bought in Canada and the US, and to gain cost advantage over established competitors. Technology and product design alone are not always sufficient. In telephone switching for example, CIT Alcatel was one of the world pioneers in digital time-based technology, and has started with a larger domestic market than most competitors. The firm however lacks the application engineering and marketing experience in world markets, and as a consequence has been losing market share and experience.

## Summary : competing in complex-factor businesses

Complex-factor businesses present the greatest challenge to managers and policy makers in developed countries. It is primarily in the success or failure of these businesses, which already represent France's majority of production and exports, that the future prosperity of the country will be won or lost. It is necessary to understand the cost structures of these businesses : the key levers for corporate strategy and economic policy occur where competitive cost differences are potentially greatest and where investment barriers make these differences sustainable over time. Success also requires anticipating changes in cost structure or investment barriers and capitalizing on them.

There are no direct relationships between aggregate levels of investment and competitive success in the economy as a whole, or in broad industries such as steel, automobiles, or semiconductors. Higher levels of investment can be useful to attain better productivity only if correct strategies are followed in order to gain a competitive advantage. Otherwise, there is a double loss, as more funds have been diverted from other uses, and yet competitive deterioration and the accompanying economic stagnation continue.

Over the last decade, the performance of many French companies in traded complex-factor businesses has been disappointing. In some cases, the methods by which French firms have organized and managed their businesses have resulted in poor strategic decisions. In other cases, poor decisions have resulted from a failure of analysis. In all cases, the outcome has been a loss of competitive productivity, resulting in the loss of business opportunities and profit for the companies, and the loss of employment, foreign exchange, and income for the nation.

As the international competitive environment has changed, so too have the principles of successful business management. Certain firms are better able to adapt than others. In general, French firms have not adapted to changing conditions well and quickly enough. In the following sections, we review the main failures which have contributed to declining competitive positions : failure to achieve scale, and inefficiencies of large industrial organizations.

## French industry's failure to achieve scale

French industry has too often been badly managed for exploiting scale economies. This is a major area of cost disadvantage against foreign competition and can be found in industries as different as trucks, petrochemicals, pharmaceuticals, steel, semiconductors or machine tools. In

many cases, management failures have been compounded by government policy mistakes. The roots of the problem are of two types :
- French management does not understand the subtle and complex effects of scale economies as well as its rivals in more successful industrialized economies. Moreover, French behaviour and traditions are obstacles to the full exploitation of scale effects ;
- France has not opened up to the world economy to the same extent that its main competitors have, and has therefore rarely been able to reach scale economies at an international level.

(a) Misunderstanding of scale economies and the obstacles of French traditions

French management and policy makers generally make two mistakes : they confuse the size of an organization with the true economies of scale, and they do not understand the relationships between scale and business cost. Those two misconceptions have been at the origin of many mistaken structural decisions, and still account for a large part of French industry's cost inefficiencies.

The first misconception originated in the mid-1960s, during the preparation of the fifth Plan when industrial leaders, bankers and government officials were trying to adapt to the new competitive challenge created by the Common Market. It was perceived at that time that French companies were not 'large enough' to match foreign rivals, or that French industry as a whole was too fragmented. Following this widely held diagnosis, subsequent tax incentives and direct government guidance (in case of State controlled markets), the most important process of corporate mergers and concentration developed in France throughout the early 1970s. This gave rise to a new class of large enterprises : some of them in related businesses, but many of them by agglomeration of largely unrelated businesses. In both cases, it was expected that pooling of resources would help the new champions to invest more and become more international. Twenty years after this process started, very few of those agglomerations have succeeded in achieving competitive results. BSN-Gervais Danone and Pernod-Ricard (both in food and beverages) and to a lesser extent Dassault-Breguet (aircraft) are among the few who offer satisfactory returns on invested capital, and are developing well. A few others have average performance and many are true disasters both for their investors and the country. Clearly, the objective of creating large organizations to match international competition was either misconceived or badly implemented, or both. Here are some reasons.

Scale generates economies when it allows a greater volume per identical operation (or unit produced), not when it simply adds apples and oranges in the same box. Combining the chemical businesses of Kuhlman, the steel operations of Ugine with the non-ferrous metal divisions of Pechiney (aluminium, copper and uranium) does not create more efficient plants, lower overheads or purchasing discounts on raw materials, but creates a complex conglomerate with unrelated businesses, tortuous decision processes and bureaucracy. The same can be said about almost all major concentrations into large conglomerates, decided in the late 1960s and early 1970s. The more successful exceptions like Saint Gobain or BSN (who ironically fought about takeover in 1968) have managed truly to diversify rather than simply add existing businesses. BSN has pursued a domestic portfolio shift from glass to food and beverages and has learned how to manage consumer products. Saint Gobain tapped the management and cash resources of Pont à Mousson, when the latter had decided to withdraw from steel and the former from chemicals, so that both parties had unused talents and financial capacity.

Except when those large corporate mergers were based on a sound assessment of resources and growth opportunities, they failed to produce synergies. Headquarters turned into rather passive holding companies, with little control over divisional strategies and performances. This mode of operation is not surprising when one knows that these concentrations were often pushed and arranged by external forces rather than by corporate management. The State and/or the banks were a very negative influence in this process. For various motives, ranging from prestige to self interest or personal career, they initiated some major deals (like Thomson-CSF or

Empain-Schneider) and set a model for others. Little strategic analysis was done before the mergers were arranged, and no one felt responsible for or committed to their successful outcome.

The second misconception applies to concentrations within the same industry. Large organizations do not generate scale economies per se. Instead, scale is a very subtle and complex concept which can apply to the various components of cost and added value which form a total business, from purchasing and manufacturing, to marketing and application engineering. The mergers between companies in related businesses were supposed to generate such economies. Again, and for various reasons, very few reorganizations have been successful. In general, French traditional mental structures and power centres have been obstacles to efficient scale businesses. We review some of these obstacles for the various kinds of scale effects found in business : manufacturing, administration, marketing and application engineering.

Manufacturing scale. There are many businesses in which manufacturing costs are the key area in which competitive advantage may be gained. Depending on the specific characteristics of these types of businesses, advantages may be realized from overall plant scale, machine scale or run length. French companies have not always recognized that each case is different, and that the effects of scale do not automatically follow a merger, but rather have to be correctly identified and systematically pursued by consistent management. This is why changes in corporate structures decided by banks or the government cannot produce efficiency if they are not conducted by a management which has a detailed knowledge of scale effects.

Overall plant scale can be a source of competitive advantage in some businesses because of the savings it allows in direct labor, manufacturing overheads and sometimes process development. Plant scale was the objective of many reorganizations in France, particularly in capital intensive industries such as steel, petrochemicals and plastics. They were, however, decided too late or incompletely executed and were therefore unable to improve French industry cost levels sufficiently at a time when foreign competition - Japanese

134

and German steel, German and US petrochemicals - was achieving scale twice or three times as large. Plant scale should also be carefully traded off with capacity utilization. French management and engineers have too often built technical marvels or monsters which could not run smoothly at full capacity. In other instances they have not scrapped old equipment, but merely created redundant capacity at times of slower demand. The steel industry remained very fragmented until the late 1960s, and the new scale plants like Dunkirk or Fos did not replace the older smaller mills, but rather resulted in excess capacity owing to intercompany and interregional rivalries. Furthermore, some steel companies, like Creusot-Loire, Ugine or SMN, were always left out of the sectoral concentrations, thereby making overall plant capacity optimization impossible. In the chemical commodities, no less than five companies - the two oil operators, two chemical companies and CdF Chimie (a branch of Charbonnages de France) - invested in the same period in sub-optimum plant, resulting in excess capacity and higher costs.State incentives for investment in underdeveloped regions were also at fault, when they induced companies to make some redundant plant investments.

Machine scale, as opposed to total plant scale, can have a similar effect in other businesses. For example, in various parts of the paper industry, wider and faster machines yield more paper per unit of labour and energy than do more standard machines. The fixed cost of a machine making Kraft liner paper can be $ 50 less per ton for a 300,000-ton machine than for a 150,000-ton machine. French companies have not always been able to invest in the optimum size of machines owing to a narrow geographical market base (lack of internationalization) or to a piecemeal approach to investment. Accounting systems are also misleading in France when they show that an obsolete piece of equipment fully depreciated can be more profitable than a new machine, despite much higher cash costs.

Finally, in some businesses, run length can be a critical determinant of manufacturing cost advantage. This is especially true if the time to set up the production machinery is very long. The lot size, or 'run length', of the product therefore becomes important; a longer run length allows costs incurred in the set-up phase to be spread over more units. Ball bearings produced in run lengths of 500,000 may have labour productivity that is 20 per cent higher than bearings produced in run lengths of 50,000. Besides lower set-up costs, longer run lengths can lower manufacturing costs in less direct ways, such as reducing the costs of quality control and generating a higher yield because of more uniform production. A longer run length can also facilitate more efficient materials flow, require less complex supervision, and result in less unused production time, all of which result in lower unit costs of production and a consequent competitive advantage relative to other producers.

Achieving proper run length requires a finely tuned, detailed knowledge of customer and product segments which results from a combination of market knowledge and experienced production management. French companies rarely integrate the two functions properly, especially in large organizations, and do not know how to allocate their product lines by plant, or machining line, and how to price by customer group. This relates back to a lack of cross-departmental communications, multifunctional careers and the style of autocratic 'vertical' organizations.

There is a complex relationship between scale and segmentation which can only be well mastered through a long experience of the business and systematic analysis. The large French companies have not been managed with enough rigour to accumulate this knowledge. Abrupt disruptions in corporate structures have too often resulted in the displacement of experienced people. French managers and engineers are also typically inclined to demonstrate brilliance and smartness by changing everything in their new jobs, even when they 'reinvent the wheel'. They tend to base their own success on technical invention and prowess (which they often achieve, as in the case of the Concorde), rather than on patient and more mundane cost reductions or product adaptations. A brilliant French engineer from Polytechnique would be dishonoured if he were to stay more than a few years in a plant. Quick turnover in management has prevented strict accountability for cost performance. This is particularly illustrated in the inefficiencies of managing overhead costs.

Scale and managing overhead costs. Surprising as it may seem, many major French companies do not know how much it costs them to produce and distribute most of their goods. They know the total costs of their operation but not the cost of producing one of their products relative to another, or the cost of serving one of their markets relative to another. The reason for this ignorance is the practice of allocating overhead costs both in factories and in distribution organizations, which demonstrates a lack of understanding of the relationships between scale and business segmentation. It is also a reflection of the lack of adequacy of accounting and control systems for production management.

In most businesses, a large number of different product varieties are manufactured in the same factory or sold and distributed through the same marketing and sales network. The accounting and industrial engineering efforts of most French companies measure the direct labour costs of producing these products precisely : worker's movements are measured down to seconds, and significant effort is often put into reducing these times. Similarly, much effort goes into negotiating wage contracts to the penny in order to keep direct labour costs low. Yet in most industries, overhead costs associated with manufacturing or marketing and distribution greatly exceed direct labour costs. Manufacturing overheads are usually between 150 and 250 per cent of direct labour costs in most plants. These typically include the costs of materials handling, inspection, internal transport, warehousing, set-up, changeover of machines, rework, technical service, maintenance, scrap, supervision, machine downtime, and quality control. Most companies allocate these overhead costs proportionally to all products based on direct labour hours. Similarly, marketing personnel, selling, distribution, warehousing, warranty, field service, and other marketing overheads, often larger than direct labour costs, are typically allocated on some average basis. This 'average costing' of overheads can create mistaken impressions of true profitability.

Such average costing by French companies allowed foreign competitors, focusing on long runs or mass distribution channels, to take over a significant share of the French market. This happened in glass products where

Guardian and PPG (US) have been allowed to build new scale plants in Europe, under the price umbrella held by Saint Gobain and BSN. The new competitors have entered the market by concentrating on high volume - direct sales segments like the automobile - and offering lower prices, less product variations and less service. Once a new competitor has successfully attacked the low cost segments, it disrupts the whole financial balance of the full range producer by pulling down its price levels, and reducing its capacity utilization. This has happened again and again in many segmented businesses of French industry, like electric motors, ball bearings, small farm equipment, machine tools and watches, and explains to a large extent Japanese import penetration.

French companies in a number of industries have tended to overcost the simpler ends of their product line sold to higher-volume customers by "averaging" them with manufacturing overheads from more complex products and extra distribution costs from smaller customers. Meanwhile, Japanese competitors have focused on sales to high-volume customers at the simple end of the product line. Consequently, they have achieved lower costs than the French firms. Believing that these simpler products sold to large customers were less profitable, the French firms have retreated from that end of the market. Blaming low Japanese wages and unfair trade practices, French managers have often spoken of ceding the low, 'cheap' end of the business to the Japanese or Koreans and have focused instead on the 'higher-value-added', 'higher-price-realization', or 'higher quality' end of the line, assuming that the foreigners will not be able to penetrate these products.

History has shown, in such businesses as motorcycles, radios, televisions, watches, cameras, and in various segments of industrial machinery, that once they have established a foothold at the 'lower end' of the line, Japanese competitors have often followed the retreating French firms all the way through the product line. French companies consider too quickly that they are better off focussing on so-called specialties and high-price items, without understanding the global interactions with other segments, and without really knowing how to justify and to defend a high-price position.

Marketing and distribution scale. A third way in which cost advantages can be gained is in the marketing and distribution areas. Typically, this occurs when there is a fragmented customer base, in which many small customers have significant requirements for information, after-sales service, and/or spare parts.

In these cases, a low cost position can be achieved by obtaining a high share of sales in a given geographical region. Share of sales within a region, rather than total world market share, is significant for two reasons : (1) economies of scale can be realized at the dealer level in the selling function and (2) after-sales services to customers can be provided at lower unit cost.

A high share of regional sales enables a dealer or distributor (whether a subsidiary or independent) to incur lower operating costs per unit sold than low-share competitors in the region. This stems from higher sales by each salesperson and the ability to spread advertising and marketing costs over a larger number of units. In addition, a higher share of regional sales can facilitate higher inventory turnover for a dealer, thereby lowering the dealer's working capital requirements per unit sold and increasing his profitability.

A high share of regional sales can also reduce a dealer's service costs per unit sold. It enables a dealer to open more service depots so that service people travel shorter distances to make each call. In turn, this permits the distributor to provide repairs or maintenance at lower cost; this can be passed on as a lower service price to the customer. At the same time, the customer has use of the product for a much higher porportion of the time.

This saving in sales and service costs per unit sold can be a source of competitive advantage to a producer. Lower costs can enable the producer to earn a return equal to that of smaller competitors while charging a lower price. This, in turn, may help the producer increase market share in a region, which again can help to further the competitive cost advantage by allowing the producer to open more service depots, reduce service costs, realize selling economies, and

139

therefore reduce prices. A virtuous cycle of cost reductions may ensue, to the continued advantage of the low-cost producer.

Marketing and distribution scale can affect overall profitability in another way. As a company's share of the local market increases, so does the number of products relying on the company's distribution system for service and spare parts. Service and parts may make up a key portion of both the manufacturer's and the dealer's sales and profits : 20 to 40 per cent of total sales for the manufacturer and 40 to 60 per cent of total profits. The dealer's service and parts business is an important marketing tool for replacement sales, as well as a profitable business in itself.

French companies have rarely understood the benefits of a high share in foreign markets. Instead of concentrating on a few key countries and providing local dealers with profitable franchise, they have exported randomly, by "coups" with little investment in customer service, advertising or product adaptation. As a result foreign business has been less profitable than for competitors and more vulnerable to new attacks.

Scale in applications engineering. Another means of gaining cost advantage in complex-factor businesses is through 'applications engineering'. Applications engineering costs are those incurred in tailoring basic equipment or software to the specific requirements of a customer. These costs are not generally classified as such in a company's accounting system but rather are mixed in with general marketing, selling, and engineering expenses.

In businesses where these costs are the key to competitive success, high market share per application provides the opportunity to gain competitive advantage. There are two steps necessary to improve one's cost position. First, it is necessary to correctly identify and focus on specific end-use applications that require customized products or systems and sophisticated selling processes. For example, one 'application' in the materials handling business is the computerization of conveying systems ; another 'application' might be a chemical cleaning formula for an industrial machine that is different from that required by other machines.

Having identified a particular application, the second step is to standardize modules of the product or system. Through standardizing modules, the engineering time needed for developing an individual system can be dramatically reduced at both the design and the selling stage. Standardization may take place in software packages, blueprints, chemical formulae, or pieces of hardware, depending on the precise nature of the particular business.

Applications engineering has become increasingly important as the technology of products has become more complex. The introduction of computer and microelectronic technologies into many businesses has increased the integration potential of products and customer needs and lowered the costs of customization. This development has created a proliferation of applications-based businesses in industries as diverse as chemicals, office equipment, and industrial machinery. There are very few French companies which have gained a leading position in this kind of businesses. Those who have done it like Merlin-Gérin or Télémécanique are independent medium sized firms rather than divisions of large groups.

Summary. By looking primarily at maximizing total sales for a given company, the French concentration process has overlooked the much more effective economies which could be derived at each cost level. The merger of two competitors into one does not produce greater volume per dealer, per application or per brand if detailed changes at all levels are not implemented : dealer selection, product pruning, plant closing, reallocations by machining line, component standardization, etc. These management measures are less spectacular than financial deals, but more lasting. The vast movement of mergers consecutive to the opening of the French economy to foreign competition in the 1960s failed to trigger these management measures. As a result of their failures, large French companies have recently restructured their business portfolios : conglomerates of unrelated businesses are divesting former acquisitions, and regroupings of related businesses are decentralizing.

The largest conglomerates formed in the 1960s and which were once a source of pride for the French elite have totally changed their profile in just three years : Pechiney has spun off its losing chemical operations which have been divided among Elf, Rhône-Poulenc and CDF-Chimie and has sold its special steels unit Ugine to Usinor. Thomson-CSF, which had diversified widely, is transferring its telephone operations to CIT-Alcatel, its computer companies to Bull, its lamp business to Philips, and selling a series of various smaller businesses ranging from banking to industrial machinery. In exchange for the telephone activities, CGE has sold its consumer appliances and military electronics businesses to Thomson. Saint-Gobain has sold its equity holding in Bull back to the State and its semiconductor diversification to Thomson and bought SGE (the largest construction company) from CGE as well as 20 per cent of Générale des Eaux. Rhône-Poulenc has divested from petrochemicals and thermoplastics (sold to Elf) and fertilizers to concentrate on pharmaceuticals, agrochemicals, specialty chemicals and fibres. Finally, Creusot-Loire has been dismembered after its bankruptcy and is being resold piece by piece, to various buyers more experienced in each respective business.

It is a most surprising paradox to observe that these major reallocations of business lines along better specializations and more consistent groupings have been facilitated by the 1982 nationalizations. Pechiney, for example, was barred from divesting its chemical branch (to Occidental Petroleum) by the Barre government before the reorganization of the whole chemical industry was triggered by the transfer of two of its major participants to the public sector. The telephone industry, which was extremely fragmented owing to the objective of the PTT to have several suppliers, was finally regrouped once Thomson and CGE - formely arch-rivals - came under the same shareholder. Because of its new responsibilities as a shareholder and also as a source of funds, the State was able to promote urgently needed exchanges of businesses and assets, which had been impossible under private ownership.

France's large corporations now have much more homogeneous business portfolios :
- CGE, the main French contender in telecommunications (CIT Alcatel) and office equipment, heavy electrical equipment (turbines, locomotives, transformers), still has however a heterogeneous shipyard activity ;
- Thomson is the only French firm left in consumer, military and medical electronics, and the main one in semiconductors ;
- Pechiney is now concentrating on non-ferrous metals in some areas of which it has leadership at world level ;
- Rhône-Poulenc in downstream chemicals and fibres ;
- Saint-Gobain in construction and materials for the construction and automobile industry.

It seems that the largest French companies can never adapt through internal forces like GM and Ford have done in the US or ICI in the UK. They have to be forced by the banks or the government to take these steps. Concentration into diversified conglomerates in the 1960s were largely a result of a government-inspired approach, implemented by the financial-technocratic establishment. Divestment and new specialization in the 1980s were in part made possible by the new role of the State as a shareholder. Management however played a much more significant role. This is a condition for making those new structures truly competitive. Another obstacle common to many French companies will have to be overcome, however, in order to reach better economies of scale.

(b) Failing to build true international operations
The concentration process described earlier has had a major chauvinistic bias : it w s aimed at regrouping French forces under the same flag to withstand foreign competition. As very few companies had international experience - in terms of product lines, distribution networks and production - the result was excess capacity at home and continuing deficiencies abroad. This is one of the main reasons for a continuing weak trade balance today.

The major concentrations undertaken in the 1960s and 1970s were restrictively French. Some of them were pushed by nationalistic governments or industrial leaders, against transnational solutions as in the computer, tyre and automotive industries. National focus has prevented further transnational restructuring from taking place, in other sectors such as steel or chemicals. Transnational corporations have been very rare : Hoechst-Roussel, Unic-Iveco, Thomson-Saba-Nordmende-Telefunken represent the rare examples of large organizations searching for scale over the border. Actually, more such links have been tried, but without success : Unidata, Fiat-Citroën, CFP-Veba, Kléber-Semperit have never flown. The role of public authorities which patronized or supported most of the French mergers in the late 1960s and 1970s may have strengthened their nationalistic bias, but the managers' inertia as regards looking for foreign alliances must not be underestimated.

A similar nationalistic bias is found for smaller companies : Lesieur in food, Sanofi and Rhône-Poulenc Santé in pharmaceuticals, Accor in restaurants and hotels, SGE in construction, or DMC in textiles, have all acquired other French competitors or related companies, whereas very few have acquired foreign companies. Générale Biscuit (in biscuits and snacks) and Hachette (in publishing) are rare exceptions. This chauvinistic attitude is mainly an issue of management because the State has had little influence on fragmented sectors of small companies such as the ones mentioned above.

Such a pattern may not be harmful when the markets are sheltered from international competition, either by economic barriers - as banking and insurance - or by the protection of public purchasing. In France for instance, the existence of a strong defence procurement in aircraft has allowed the formation of national champions. On that strong basis, they have then been able to open up to joint-ventures (as SNECMA with GE for engine or Aérosptiale with Airbus) or to develop world-scale businesses on their own (as SNIAS helicopters).

Conversely, in very competitive international markets, when mergers do not bring the required scale, they are no response to the business's needs French companies have not been very quick at securing foreign distribution networks,

144

Figure 38

# NATIONAL ECONOMIC BENEFITS OF INTERNATIONAL STRATEGIES

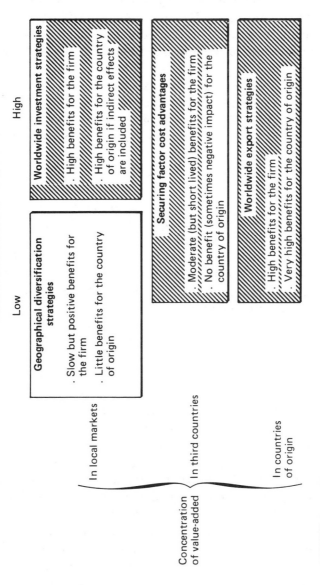

Share of local markets taken by multinationals

Low        High

**Geographical diversification strategies**

. Slow but positive benefits for the firm

. Little benefits for the country of origin

**Worldwide investment strategies**

. High benefits for the firm

. High benefits for the country of origin if indirect effects are included

**Securing factor cost advantages**

. Moderate (but short lived) benefits for the firm

. No benefit (sometimes negative impact) for the country of origin

**Worldwide export strategies**

. High benefits for the firm

. Very high benefits for the country of origin

In local markets

In third countries

In countries of origin

Concentration of value-added

///// Traded Businesses

*Source : Telesis study for the French Commissariat Général du Plan*

complementary product lines or new management teams from different countries. A firm of a medium-sized country like France rarely reaches the economies of scale required to compete on world markets, by staying a national champion.

The internationalization process differs widely between traded businesses and sheltered businesses (Figure 38). In traded businesses, international firms can chose between three broad models : worldwide investment strategies, securing factor cost advantages, or worldwide export strategies. In the first case, international firms invest abro d for most of their value added in order to secure a lower cost and more stable access to final markets. These firms manage an integrated network of plants and product development centres spread over the world and specialized by business line or even component, such as Ciba Geigy in chemicals, Philips in electronics or IBM in computers. The country of origin generally keeps the top management, R&D and marketing functions, it sets overall strategic directions and often manufactures key components (like active ingredients for the pharmaceutical firms). In this way these multinationals continue to generate a large flow of exports with a high value added per person. In the second case, firms invest where they can get the cheapest source of raw material, energy or even labour (although this is short lived). The latter category of firms generate of course an even greater flow of exports as illustrated by most Japanese companies. This strategy depends however on the ability to sustain a competitive cost for each export market and on open trade continuing. It generally requires sooner or later to invest abroad and replace some of the domestic value added as done now by Japanese auto or consumer electronics companies in the US. This is a difficult transition for firms which have long been accustomed to govern everything from one centre, to develop into a truly multipolar organization.

In sheltered businesses firms can internationalize by acquiring similar companies in foreign countries like Saint-Gobain's purchase of Certain Teed in the US, or by investing abroad to transplant a new business concept like Carrefour in Brazil. In all those instances, internationalization does not generate as much exports and value added for the country of origin as with the cases in the preceding paragraph.

Figure 39

# INTERNATIONAL STRATEGIES OF THE LARGE FRENCH CORPORATIONS

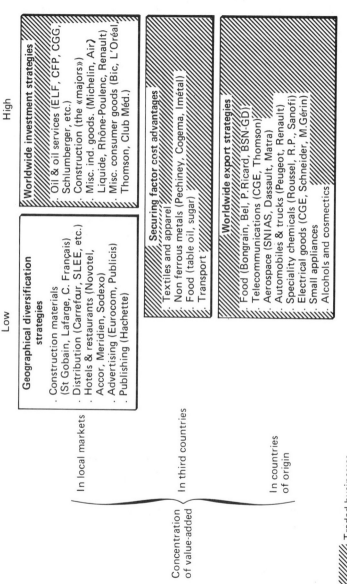

Share of local markets taken by multinationals

Low        High

**Geographical diversification strategies**

. Construction materials (St Gobain, Lafarge, C. Français)
. Distribution (Carrefour, SLEE, etc.)
. Hotels & restaurants (Novotel, Accor, Meridien, Sodexo)
. Advertising (Eurocom, Publicis)
. Publishing (Hachette)

**Worldwide investment strategies**

. Oil & oil services (ELF, CFP, CGG, Schlumberger, etc.)
. Construction (the «majors»)
. Misc. ind. goods. (Michelin, Air Liquide, Rhône-Poulenc, Renault)
. Misc. consumer goods (Bic, L'Oréal, Thomson, Club Méd.)

**Securing factor cost advantages**

. Textiles and apparel
. Non ferrous metals (Pechiney, Cogema, Imétal)
. Food (table oil, sugar)
. Transport

**Worldwide export strategies**

. Food (Bongrain, Bel, P. Ricard, BSN-GD)
. Telecommunications (CGE, Thomson)
. Aerospace (SNIAS, Dassault, Matra)
. Automobiles & trucks (Peugeot, Renault)
. Speciality chemicals (Roussel, R.P., Sanofi)
. Electrical goods (CGE, Schneider, M. Gérin)
. Small appliances
. Alcohols and cosmectics

Concentration of value-added

In local markets

In third countries

In countries of origin

///// Traded businesses

*Source : Telesis study for the French Commissariat Général du Plan*

147

Figures 38 to 40 illustrate the different benefits to the firm and to the country of origin of these four types of internationalization, and compare the pattern of the top 100 French companies to some of their most prominent European rivals.

Figure 38 attempts to assess schematically the range of economical spin-offs of the four types of internationalization, on the level of business as well as on the national level. French industry's successes and deficiencies in the world reflect the nature of the activities which have been subject to internationalization, and at the same time reflect the strategies employed in each activity. It is important to distinguish between the two cases illustrated in the figure.

In the first case (the shaded areas of Figure 38, which concern activities exposed to international competition) internationalization is at once necessary for the business's survival, and a source of the country's wealth. Foreign industrial and commercial investments serve to sustain the flow of exports, stabilize French employment, or increase the value added per person, for these activities. Successful internationalization is thus a double bonus for business and for the country.

Generally speaking, France still lacks real multinationals of this kind with global networks of investment establishments (as in the top right hand quadrant), above all in manufacturing activities (Figure 39). The international entrepreneur's spirit is more clearly revealed in the oil industry, public works and in banking. In each of these three sectors, and in an original way, France has been able to develop a real breeding-ground of creators or of managers drawing on solid technical traditions and able to give an international dimension to their businesses by producing abroad. In the manufacturing sector, on the other hand, investments have been more recent (the case of Air Liquide is among the exceptions) and more limited, quite often involving a single area of the world, such as the EEC or North America.

**Figure 40**

# INTERNATIONAL STRATEGIES – EUROPEAN LEADING COMPETITORS

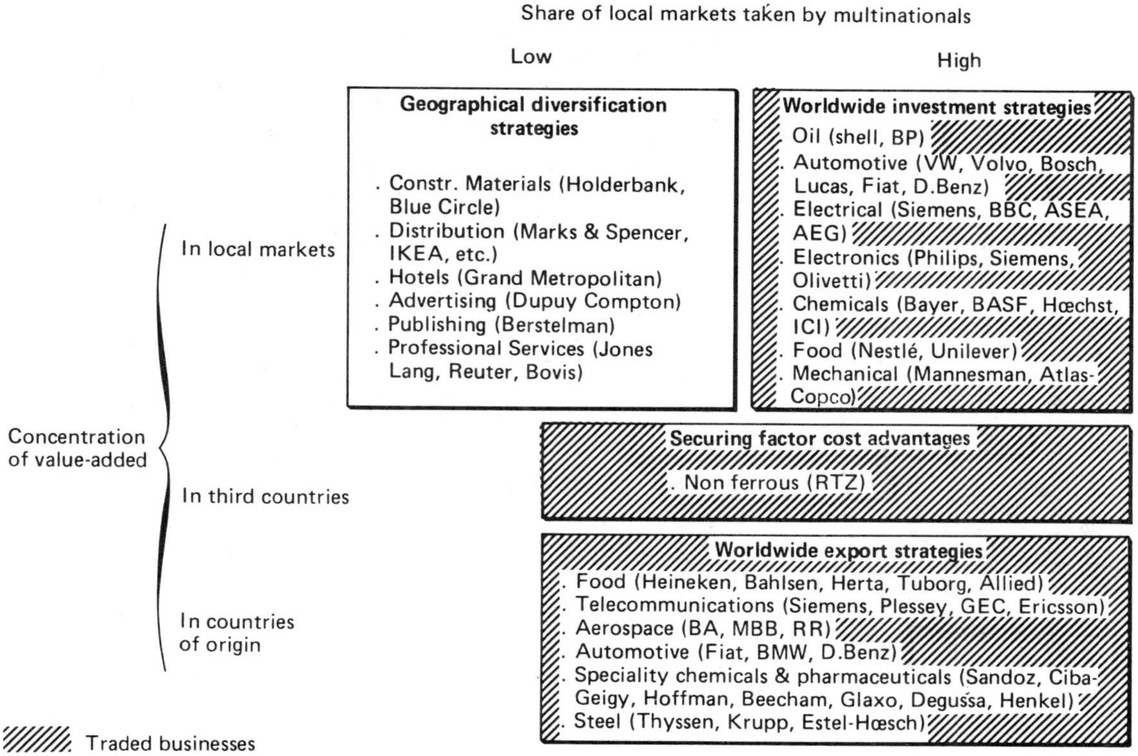

Share of local markets taken by multinationals

Low      High

**Worldwide investment strategies**
. Oil (shell, BP)
. Automotive (VW, Volvo, Bosch, Lucas, Fiat, D.Benz)
. Electrical (Siemens, BBC, ASEA, AEG)
. Electronics (Philips, Siemens, Olivetti)
. Chemicals (Bayer, BASF, Hœchst, ICI)
. Food (Nestlé, Unilever)
. Mechanical (Mannesman, Atlas-Copco)

**Geographical diversification strategies**
. Constr. Materials (Holderbank, Blue Circle)
. Distribution (Marks & Spencer, IKEA, etc.)
. Hotels (Grand Metropolitan)
. Advertising (Dupuy Compton)
. Publishing (Berstelman)
. Professional Services (Jones Lang, Reuter, Bovis)

**Securing factor cost advantages**
. Non ferrous (RTZ)

**Worldwide export strategies**
. Food (Heineken, Bahlsen, Herta, Tuborg, Allied)
. Telecommunications (Siemens, Plessey, GEC, Ericsson)
. Aerospace (BA, MBB, RR)
. Automotive (Fiat, BMW, D.Benz)
. Speciality chemicals & pharmaceuticals (Sandoz, Ciba-Geigy, Hoffman, Beecham, Glaxo, Degussa, Henkel)
. Steel (Thyssen, Krupp, Estel-Hœsch)

In local markets

In third countries

In countries of origin

Concentration of value-added

Traded businesses

*Source : Telesis study for the French Commissariat Général du Plan*

149

Businesses which have been able to carry out internationalization strategies in traded sectors **through direct investments abroad** are of three types :
- the oil and oil-related sector, which since the period between the wars, has become one of French industry's stars in the face of essentially American competitors, and has truly become international as seen in chapter 2 ;
- the building industry, public works, and civil engineering which for 15-odd years has been making a breakthrough into the large developing markets in the Middle East, Nigeria, South America and now Asia and South Asia ;
- Companies of diverse scales in different industrial sectors : Air Liquide or Rhone Poulenc, for over 50 years, Lafarge and BIC for 25 years, and Thomson-Brandt and Essilor for 10 years. This last group's internationalizations have often been accomplished by acquisitions of local companies rather than direct investment.

The absence here of businesses in manufacturing sectors which constitute a substantial part of the value added of industrialized countries is notable : auto and commercial vehicles industries, chemical, pharmaceutical, large electrical equipment, electronics, mechanical engineering industries, etc. Most of the European multinationals find themselves in this category and have thus contributed to gaining not only a solid competitive position for their respective countries, but also positive spin-offs in the form of high value added employment, stimulation of exportable equipment and engineering industries, as in West Germany, Switzerland and Sweden (Figure 40).

In the group of businesses whose main activity is exporting (at the bottom square of the figure) and which occupy a satisfactory part of the world market, French companies have often gained by France's diplomatic and military position (in the case of aeronautics, armaments and military electronics) or by the particular resources procured by French public markets (in the case of large equipment for the production and transmission of electricity, in railways and in telecommunications). The successes of 'global exporting'

150

independent of State support have been rarer (automobiles, some food businesses, fine chemicals). French businesses did not really consider exporting as an integral part of their strategy until after the opening of trade frontiers 25 years ago, much later than their North European competitors. They have not been able to catch up through sufficient commercial investments such as the constitution of a network of competitive distributors, after-sales service, product adaptation, and a world brand image as Japanese businesses have been able to do.

If French businesses adapted themselves better than was expected after the first shock of the Common Market in the 1960s, they were not, on the other hand, able to take the international changes of the 1970s. Their traditional industrial "jewels", such as the automobile, have faltered under the combined effects of Japanese competition and the globalization of industrial activities. France does not have enough widely implanted or widely exporting multinationals to allow it to overcome market downturns, and maintain a trade surplus or even balanced trade.

Businesses aiming for **global exports** - that is, attempting to establish their development out of their conquest of world markets - are more numerous and varied. Here we find French industry's great breakthroughs in exporting which have resulted from trade liberalization : the auto industry (Renault has been in the process of becoming a multinational with production establishments abroad for a few years only), fine chemicals, heavy electrical equipment, aeronautics, and, more recently, telecommunications (Figure 39 bottom quadrants).

Here also we notice serious gaps. French specialties, apart from perfume and alcohol, are exported less than is widely believed : little processed food (apart from cheeses), far fewer confectionary products and textiles than in other countries, etc. Moreover, export strategies are weaker than these of competitors in other European countries and Japan : market shares per country are lower, investments in after-sales service and distribution are insufficient, certain areas of the world are but little covered by French business (South America, Southeast Asia), etc.

151

French manufacturing industry, exposed to international competition, has drawn most of its foreign value added up to now from its exports. This kind of internationalization is hit head-on by Japanese rivals in many continuously growing sectors : automobiles, electrical equipment, machinery, fine chemicals, etc. Without parallel effort toward commercial investment and toward an increase of market shares in new countries, the successes of the last 20 years are at risk of turning out to be flimsy.

In the second case (non-shaded sections of Figure 38-40) the internationalization of business can be a good strategy, from the point of view of the company's growth and profitability, but it does not always create as marked a spin-off for the country. It is not a question, of course, of opposing foreign investments of this type which make up an integral part of free enterprise. But from the viewpoint of the national interest, it is more appropriate to give priority to the former types and to give them not only total liberty , but also wide access to key resources (capital, skills, technology).

Compared with the gaps and weaknesses of the above two categories, the two other types of internationalization have been widely achieved by French businesses :
- geographical diversification in 'sheltered' activities : Saint-Gobain (in neighbouring European countries, US and Brazil), Carrefour (in Brazil and Europe), (Lafarge in North America).;
- investments in gaining access to sources of raw materials and energy, by mining and metallurgical industries (Pechiney, Le Nickel, Cogema, Imetal, etc.)

The entire array of social forces (and especially the unions), must also realize the urgent necessity in an open economy to invest in foreign countries in order to assure the competitivity of businesses subject to international competition, and thus to reinforce employment in France and to generate exports of a greater value added per person. The reigning consensus of North European industrial countries and of Japan concerning the objectives and methods of internationalization is at once a proof of success for business and a factor of cohesion for the country.

**Summary**

French corporate structure still suffers from its legacy : an agricultural and colonial nation industrializing half a century later than its Northern neighbours ; a tradition of protection, monopolies, regulations and State initiative, and nationalistic behaviour. The postwar reconstruction was a success for most corporations because it fitted with those traditions : it was created on domestic needs, it used fairly centralized resource allocation mechanisms and it benefitted from a stable and protected trade environment, including the first ten years of the Common Market.

The recent decade is in marked contrast : what worked in a period of catching up, is not sufficient in times of head-on competition. Markets and competition are more and more international, the State's influence is waning and corporate success depends less on technical achievements and absolute levels of investments, and more on the mastering of global business dynamics. French corporate leaders have often been brilliant engineers and successful business creators. They prove less prepared to manage difficult transitions in complex organizations. What we have called complex-factor businesses are not driven by any single competitive leverage, but by the combination of intelligent strategies and effective management of all business functions : product development, manufacturing, marketing and customer service, etc. Managers become integrators. French corporate leaders are still too often experts.

France's portfolio of large corporations does not match yet its ambition to remain a great nation with influence on world affairs and one of the best standards of living. France has less true multinational Stars and more Drains than Germany, the US or Japan, particularly in the traded sectors which are of crucial importance for sustained wealth. France has relatively more successes in launching new Bets in advanced technology sectors, than most of its European neighbours. But how many of those can a medium-size country afford by itself ? As in Britain, many entrepreneurial talents, capital and corporate diversifications have been attracted by sheltered sectors like distribution, local consumer services and construction, thereby reducing the potential sources of exports.

In a complex economy open to trade, 'industrial policy' is the subtle combination of corporate strategies and public policies achieving a higher rate of wealth creation. The role of business is to take up the challenge of building competitive and growing companies in traded activities. The role of the State is to provide the infrastructure - physical and human ressources -, create the environment and the incentives, so that resources can be employed by the most productive corporations.

PART III   THE ROLE OF THE STATE

## 1. THE STATE : FRANCE's PRIME CAPITALIST

The State has pushed its intervention in business - and particularly in industry - further in France than in any other free market economy. The role of the modern French State in postwar reconstruction and the expansion of the 1960s has been very influential and pervasive. Following the precedents of the First World War period and the 1936 Front Populaire, successive governments of various ideologies have nationalized utilities, railways, airlines, radios and TV, the coal mines, almost the entire banking sector, the largest insurance companies and a quarter of the manufacturing sector including the whole or very significant portions of steel, shipbuilding, automobiles, oil, chemicals, aircraft, electronics and telecommunications. During the postwar period, the French State has created new markets, through its investments in infrastructure (telephone, nuclear energy, high speed trains and subways), in defence (nuclear submarines and carriers, fighter aircraft and missiles ) and in research and technology (Concorde, Plan Calcul, Ariane satellites). In markets where purchasing decisions are not made by the State but by millions of consumers, the French State has often regulated prices, distribution and foreign investments (as in the case of oil, pharmaceuticals or banking). The State has also continuously kept a tight rein on the thousands of decisions made by individual firms through a very complex apparatus of carrots and sticks : subsidies and favourable interest rates to strategic or ailing industries, export incentives, price controls, authorizations for foreign exchange and foreign investments, building permits, approvals for layoffs, etc. Finally, the State has always tried to influence directly the decisions of private firms by various means : through access to privileged public procurement, pressure through the banks, transfers of high-ranking civil servants to business, etc.

The methods used for direct and indirect State intervention in corporate decisions, and their effects on competitive position and growth, will be illustrated. The following chapters will stress the coexistence of a very strong

155

## LOUIS XI' INDUSTRIAL POLICY FOR THE TEXTILE INDUSTRIES
## EXCERPTS FROM A LETTER TO THE MERCHANTS OF LYON
### December 1466

*En décembre 1466, le Roi écrivit aux bourgeois de Lyon :«Nous avons été avertis que, à l'occasion de ce qu'il convient aller quérir et faire venir hors de notre royaume les draps d'or et de soie, est chacun an tiré d'icelui la somme de quatre à cinq mille écus d'or ou environ, qui est chose fort préjudiciable à nous et à la chose publique. Et pour ce que nous avons été avertis que ce serait chose bien conduisable et aisée de mettre sur l'art de faire lesdits draps d'or et de soie en notre royaume et spécialement en notre ville de Lyon, en laquelle au moyens d'aucuns particuliers ledit art, est, comme l'on dit, jà encommencé, nous, pour obvier à la grande vuidange d'or et d'argent que chacun an se fait de notre dit royaume à cause des dits draps d'or et de soie et des choses qui en dépendent, et considérant le très grand bien qui pourra venir audit fait de la chose publique et espécialement à notre dite ville de Lyon et à tous le pays d'environ (...) nous avons ordonné faire mettre sus icelui art de draps d'or et de soie pour être fait et exercé en notre dite ville de Lyon et pour cette cause y faire venir hommes et femmes expérimentés à ce faire. Et sommes avertis, considéré que c'est chose honorable et honnête, et à quoi se pourront occuper licitement hommes et femmes de tous états, que dix mille personnes, tant de ladite ville que des environs, et tant gens d'Eglise, nobles, femmes de religion que autres, qui à présent sont oiseux, y auront honnête et profitable occupation. Mais la chose ne peut être encommencée ni mise en train sans y faire aucune dépense. Pour laquelle cause (...) nous avons ordonné et mandé par nos lettres patentes mettre sus et imposer en ladite ville de Lyon, pour l'année qui commencera le premier jour de janvier prochain (1467), la somme de deux mille livres tournois, pour être convertie et employée en paiement et salaire qu'il conviendra donner aux dits ouvriers et ouvrières ...». Cependant, les bourgeois de Lyon n'étaient pas préparés comme l'était leur souverain à adopter de nouvelles méthodes, et, quelques années plus tard, Louis devrait prendre diverses mesures pour sauver son expérience.*

*Source : Paul Murray Kendall, <u>Louis XI</u> (Paris ; Fayard 1984)*

State apparatus and what remains nevertheless a predominantly market-based economy open to trade and international competition. The French State is not an enemy of the capitalist system, but rather its first supporter and its prime beneficiary. In fact, in France the State is the largest capitalist. This phenomenon has very old historical roots, and serious implications for the behaviour of French industry.

## Historical roots and French values

Common wisdom has always traced State economic intervention back to Colbert, who managed Louis XIV's finances for decades in the seventeenth century. In fact, two centuries earlier, Louis XI had envisaged the creation of a textile industry in Lyon specializing in gold and silk flags, in order to end the need for costly imports. He was willing to furnish the necessary capital for the industry, and was also aware that such an initiative would serve to create jobs in the region (see Annex 1).

In France, as opposed to England or the US, it was the State which created the nation. Strong fiefdoms with their economic, political and cultural identities existed before the king - who, until Louis XI, was the head only of the Ile-de-France. These strong regional identities continued to challenge the power of the State and to threaten the credibility of France against the other European nations. French history is a long succession of centralizations and rebellions, where the State finally won against all centrifugal forces : those of the provinces, of the trades, of the church, of the privileged. The various royal and republican regimes have used the brute force of the State - its taxes, its schools, its money, its prisons, its army - to unify and equalize what used to be (and still in many respects is) a very diverse and fragmented people. But this strong unification has caused many casualties on the way, one being private entrepreneurship.

It would have been most surprising if the direction of the economy had remained unaffected by the extent of State influence in French society. All powerful leaders have left their mark on the ways the French economy has developed. Royal 'manufactures' of tobacco, tapestries, and glass were created or developed by Colbert ; Louvois developed the 'arsenals' which are the predecessors of today's military production. Napoleon created the Banque de France, and Napoleon III is said to have been the first promoter of a 'national plan' for the machine tool industry.

More recently, the State has not appeared to step out of its role, when it created a chemical company (CDF-Chimie), an oil operator (Elf) or a computer enterprise (CII). Even with the current winds blowing towards a more liberal economy, most French people respect the State in its role as economic patron, and recent polls show that nationalizations are still popular. In fact, two fundamental beliefs of the French elite explain why the State - and not business - is seen as the legitimate source of economic leadership.

First, most politicians and civil servants - as well as many industrialists themselves and the media - doubt that French business is strong enough to compete successfully on its own against international rivals. Historically French merchants did not conquer the world as did the Italians in the fifteenth and sixteenth centuries, the Dutch in the seventeenth century or the English in the eighteenth and nineteenth centuries. France has long been one of the most densely populated and richest countries in the world, thanks to the extent of its domestic agricultural production. It needed to trade to a much smaller extent than all its neighbours in Europe. The industrial revolution came late and with slower results than in the UK, Germany or the US. Protectionism was and still is stronger than in any of these countries and is supported by political forces from all ideologies. It is natural, therefore, that most French leaders fear to lose out in an open game, where competitors have had far more practice. Many in France still think that the country would be richer if it were to close its borders. When opening borders to foreign trade is unavoidable the State is asked for support or compensation.

After two decades of industrial decline, the country awoke in 1945 with a new elite, conscious of the need to catch up with more modern nations. This has resulted in a typically French way of addressing economic challenges. Whereas Dr. Ludwig Erhard was totally confident in the market economy's capacity to rebuild German wealth, the

French enlarged the role of the State while at the same time mobilizing private initiative towards a patriotic objective. It was felt at that time that French business not only needed capital and a good infrastructure, but also strategic directions. Hence an 'indicative' planning system was developed by Jean Monnet under the leadership of General de Gaulle. Such a Plan was unheard of in any other western democracy.

De Gaulle himself stated in 1945 that 'the State must now assume directly the development of the great sources of energy (coal, electricity, oil) as well as the main transport systems (railways, sea, airlines). It must bring the production of steel up to its necessary level. It must control credit in order to channel the national savings to large investments.' The 1981 law which nationalized new sectors of the economy also stresses : 'Public enterprises have always invested more than the private sector. From 1974 to 1980, public investment increased by 91 per cent, whereas private investment decreased by 5 per cent.' Before it sank into heavy losses and was burdened by debt, Renault was seen as the champion of French enterprise : no private company could match its prestige in public opinion.

Whereas in the US one would find national champions, the destiny of which the country likes to be identified with - for instance General Motors in the 1950s, or IBM today - France has no such paragons. Germany also exhibits a more trustful relationship between business and the nation. As detailed in part II, France's profitable corporations, as a matter of fact, often do not meet the nation's technological or export criteria, the most brilliant entrepreneurs operating mostly in sheltered activities (which is not the case of the German Stars). These actual shortcomings of French companies are compounded with national traditions which do not value very highly the entrepreneurial image.

Second, the French people and a large number of their leaders do not believe wholeheartedly that business success will translate into a  better standard of living for the country as a whole. In fact, they often think that private interest goes against general interest. The State should therefore not only regulate but in many cases own, control and operate economic activity. These beliefs also have long established historical roots in a mixture of catholic influence,

159

agrarian values, and social privileges. The Roman Catholic Church has certainly played a role in attaching a negative moral stigma to the concepts of profit and interest. The sociologist Weber stressed the importance of the Protestant values of individual work and merit in the success of private enterprise in Anglo-Saxon and Germanic countries. But there is more to it than that ; catholic Italy is very profit-minded, while in Spain and France, profit is considered as shameful, or even as sinful.

The importance of agriculture in the French economy is just as crucial in explaining this disdain of private enterprise : the peasant lives on the soil with his family and his own work. His objective is to be independent and to accumulate reserves to avoid famines. He is by nature allergic to large organizations, hierarchies, and quick changes. Profit is a reserve which guarantees survival, and should not be shown or shared, or even utilized to produce new wealth. The merchant – and later the industrialist – lives on trade and interdependence. He needs others as customers, labourers and suppliers. He needs to invent continuously and adapt quickly. He can fit into larger organizations and gain leverage from other people's work. His profit is public, and it is a means to defend a position or to expand rather than a treasury to be kept intact. French and Spanish industries and trade have tortuously developed against agrarian societies ; English, German, Italian or Dutch industries have naturally stemmed out of merchant societies.

Finally France – like Spain – has always been a class society and still is more divided into classes than most industrial nations. Classes are here defined not in the marxist sense by their economic role, but in the classic sense, in terms of privileges given by birth. France's value system has been shaped around the prestige, culture, taste, brio, and panache of a totally inactive aristocracy. As opposed to Germany or Italy where the aristocracy has progressively yielded power and wealth to the bourgeoisie, and has naturally declined, French aristocracy has been too quickly and too violently thrown out of power to fade away. Some of its values have just been taken over by the new elites : the importance of style over substance, the attraction of the homo universalis over the expert, the prestige of a brilliant intelligence over hard work, the supremacy of thought over manual labour : these values have been an obstacle to the growth of a modern industrial economy.

## Public ownership

The values of a catholic, agrarian and aristocratic society are not particularly favourable to the natural development of profit-minded enterprises operating in open competition and interdependence. When private entrepreneurs were scarce the State became involved, often as a capitalist, sometimes as a conductor. The importance of public ownership as a 'moralising force' in business is the first consequence of French history.

The modern ideology of nationalization was shaped in the twentieth century and cuts across political parties. After the First World War which enlarged the role of the State, and the Versailles Treaty which gave public control over the mines of Potasses d'Alsace, a large span of ideologies contributed to the French nationalization process. Among the leftist leaders, the idea finally won over its detractors (socialists such as Jules Guesde or Jean Jaurès used to oppose the idea of 'Etat-Patron'). The Catholic Church evolved more or less in the same direction : the encyclical 'Quadragesimo Anno' stated that some goods should not be left in the hands of private owners, given their importance for the whole community. The leftist Front Populaire in 1936-37 launched a few nationalizations (armaments and railways, aircraft and Banque de France), followed a few years later by the conservative Vichy government (with control taken of two media groups HAVAS & SOFIRAD, and with the creation of Petroles d'Aquitaines in oil) and then at the end of the war, by the Resistance programme.

In 1945, major sectors of the economy were nationalized in an application of philosophies developed by the Resistance and de Gaulle during the war. By nationalizing the three major commercial banks and the major insurance companies, and creating whole new banks the State gained effective control of the capital markets. The electrical utilities were nationalized into a single corporation, i.e. Electricité de France (EDF), which was to play a major role in the development of French nuclear power.

161

Figure 41

## THE TWELVE INDUSTRIAL NATIONALISATIONS OF 1982

| COMPANY | MAIN SHAREHOLDER | Sales in 1981 Bill. FF. | Price paid by the State Bill. FF. | Business lines in 1981 |
|---|---|---|---|---|
| **NATIONALIZATIONS FOR SIZE AND POWER** | | | | |
| PECHINEY-UGINE KUHLMAN | CAISSE DES DEPOTS 5 % | 41 | 3 | *Aluminium & non ferrous metals, chemicals, Sp.steel* |
| RHONE-POULENC | St GOBAIN 8 % | 36 | 3 | *Chemicals, fibres, Pharmac.* |
| SAINT-GOBAIN | COMPAGNIE FINANCIERE DE SUEZ 17 % | 44 | 6 | *Glass, iron pipes, construc. materials & civil engineer.* |
| **NATIONALIZATIONS OF STRATEGIC SECTORS** | | | | |
| CGE | | 20 | 3 | *Electrical engineer. electron. telecom & shipbuilding* |
| THOMSON-BRANDT | OPFI-PARIBAS 9 % | 43 | 2 | *Consumer & defense electron. telecommunications* |
| CII—HB | St GOBAIN | 2 | 1 | *Computers* |
| CGCT | ITT 100 % | 2,5 | 0,25 | *Telecommunications* |
| MDBA | Marcel Dassault 78 % | 12 | N.A. | *Aircraft* |
| ROUSSEL-UCLAF | HOECHST 58 % | 6 | 0,5 | *Pharmaceuticals* |
| MATRA | Groupe Floirat 48 % | 6 | 0,7 | *Electronics* |
| **RESCUE NATIONALIZATIONS** | | | | |
| USINOR | | 25 | 11* | *Steel* |
| SACILOR | | 18 | 11,4* | *Steel* |

*\* debt consolidation in 1982 prices*
*Sources : Liaisons Financières 1980, Annual reports, Rapport Charzat*

In the manufacturing and mining sectors, however, nationalizations were more limited. The aeronautic firms had been nationalized in 1936 for defence purposes ; this initiative was extended in 1945 by the nationalization of the aircraft engine sector (SNECMA). The coal mines were unified into a single state-owned company, Charbonnages de France, and Renault was nationalized, for punitive reasons (Louis Renault had collaborated with the Nazis).

Not until the mid-1960s, when several public sector companies were created, did the state-owned industrial sector expand further. Before 1982, it had not become significantly larger than the state-owned sector of free market countries like Germany or Sweden and was smaller than those of the UK and Italy. The very diverse public creations done in the mid-1960s show however the prestige, preeminence and ambitions of the State as a capitalist during de Gaulle years.

When the Left came to power in 1981, a new wave of nationalizations was quickly voted in, to implement political programmes prepared in 1972. Accordingly, the thirty-odd banks with assets over 1 billion francs each and twelve large industrial groups shifted to the public sector. Those groups had been selected either for their sheer size and supposed power, or for their involvement in 'strategic' sectors such as defence or telecommunications. Curiously, the main nuclear engineering contractor - Schneider -remained private. Some companies very close to the State and to national defence managed to keep a large proportion of their capital in private hands (Dassault and Matra) while companies engaged in businesses with little relevance to national priorities like Saint Gobain or Rhône-Poulenc were wholly nationalized. Only a small portion of the 45 billion francs paid in 1982 would have been required if the new government had exclusively sought to gain new levers for its industrial policy (Figure 41).

In fact, the main reasons for nationalization were not dictated by industrial policy objectives but originated from the same ideology of French State 'purification'. At the beginning of the nationalization law was a quotation from General de Gaulle mentioning the need to 'suspend the interplay of these vast conjunctions and coalitions of interests which have weighed too much on the State and on the citizens'. Besides, the fact that the socialist-communist

majority required 100 per cent of the shares for the nation
- whereas 51 per cent would have provided total control -
emphasized the ideological nature of the process.

In return, nationalization brought legitimacy to the
State's support of enterprises. Some of the recently
nationalized companies were large beneficiaries of R&D and
military contracts (Thomson, CGE, CGCT, Bull). The large
deficits which appeared in 1982 in most of these companies
would not have been easily filled by the State, without the
nation's right - and duty - of ownership. In addition to easier
financing, the painful restructuring imposed on these new
public enterprises was made possible not only by the existence
of a single shareholder, but also by its legitimacy. In France,
a private owner would have certainly found it much more
difficult - if not impossible - to impose such changes on its
employees and bankers.

In summary, behind all the ideological rhetoric, public
ownership has played several roles :

- it has 'moralized' and legitimized the role of business
  enterprise in the nation, making its image more
  attractive to public opinion, the workers, unions and
  the media. This in turn has helped to overcome the
  old stigma on profit and the old fears of the market
  system. In this sense, the nationalizations of 1945
  have transformed Renault and the large commercial
  banks into prestigious and powerful organizations.
  Similarly the 1982 nationalizations have brought back
  goodwill to discredited or demoralized industrial
  groups like Pechiney or Rhône-Poulenc. This has
  helped difficult plant rationalizations including the
  lay-off or early retirement of thousands of
  redundant workers.

- it has allowed a democratic State to transfer large
  sums of money into industry while maintaining
  several of the rules of a market economy. What
  would have been called 'subsidy' with private
  ownership could be called 'equity contributions' to
  cash-starved companies like Usinor and Sacilor,
  Thomson, Bull and now Renault. In this sense
  taxpayers' money does not fall directly into private
  shareholders' pockets. This State financing has

allowed some companies to survive their management's mistakes, but it also permits others to take long-term risks that could not be otherwise financed.

The price paid for direct State intervention in terms of industrial competition is more difficult to assess, and varies considerably across sectors, and even companies (see in following chapters). What can be said at this point is that the nature of the State is very different from that in Anglo-Saxon countries : far from Adam Smith's vision, the State is a very active, sometimes militant, participant and cannot play the role of a neutral custodian of the rules of the game.

**State policies and industrial strategies**
The second consequence of French history for the role of the State is even more far-reaching than public ownership.

By taking direct responsibility and by seeking public recognition for business development, the State is always inclined to impose its own priorities and needs - rather than market needs - on corporations. A State cannot impose an 'industrial policy' in the market place as it can impose a defence policy or even a foreign policy on allies and enemies. By direct intervention in businesses, the State will therefore seek to derive industrial strategies and policies from its natural domain of competence. It is not too extreme to claim that France lacks an industrial policy, but rather has strong State policies with far-reaching industrial implications. State policies have indeed shaped modern industry over the last 40 years : they have been continuous themes of French politics through various regimes, and can be summarized in two objectives :
   - to modernize the country and the society ;
   - to restore France as an independent and influential nation.

(a) 'Modernization' is not a new motto invented by the young Prime Minister Laurent Fabius in 1984. It is a permanent and central theme of French political rhetoric : from de Gaulle's and Jean Monnet's First Plan in 1945, to Pierre Mendès-France's junta 'la République moderne', to Pompidou's and Giscard's objectives to bring France to the leading edge of modern times. Throughout the 40 postwar years, the State has used all the resources and powers that a democracy gives to its rulers, to speed up the modernization of the country and the society :

- it has encouraged and sometimes stimulated the shift from agriculture to industry, from rural areas to cities (see part I) ;
- it has built new infrastructure at a pace and magnitude unparalleled by other European countries, in order to compensate for the obsolescence of the prewar period. Massive public investments in highways, electric railways, new ports, modern telecommunications, hydro and nuclear energy have in turn given birth to a series of technological developments and growing companies ;
- it has financed large R & D programmes either through public procurement development contracts or through direct support of public R & D centres, like CEA in nuclear energy, CNES in space, CNET in telephone, IRIA in computers, IRCHA in chemicals, ONERA in aircraft, IFP in oil exploration and production, INSERM in medical sciences, Institut Pasteur in biotechnology, and INRA in agribusiness. The role of these large public techno-structures, mobilizing the brightest scientists of the country for economic leadership, is unique in any free market economy for civilian sectors of industry ;
- it has directly supported - and sometimes managed - new high-tech ventures including commercial applications : Caravelle, Concorde and Airbus in aircraft, Ariane and now Hermes in space, Plan Calcul and the creation of CII in computers, the atomic programme and the creation of Framatome in nuclear energy, the electric locomotives and the TGV in high speed trains, the SECAM technology in colour TV have all been State driven and State-financed, with mixed results, but always with large resources allocated ;
- it has reshaped the industrial and technological map of the country by promoting new universities, research institutes and attracting new industries in

166

regional centres which had been starved of economic growth : Toulouse in aerospace, Grenoble in electronics, Rennes in telecommunications, Lyon in petrochemicals, Nice in high-tech services, have become new clusters of development in a country where brainpower and investment used to be concentrated in Paris.

(b) Independence and influence - the second permanent objective of French governments - have had as great if not a greater impact on business strategies :

- military independence has been the key objective of French defence policy since de Gaulle came back to power in 1958, reaching its climax when France withdrew from NATO's military organization. His concept of a third independent nuclear defence capability between the US and the Soviet Union has not gained any new supporters in Europe but has at least gathered 85 per cent of domestic support - excluding only the communists. The socialists have now supported the Force de Frappe (French-operated nuclear weapons) for more than a decade, and Charles Hernu the Defence Minister from 1981 to 1985 was one of the most consistent and effective advocates of French military investments. The nuclear forces have required the mastering of a vast array of technologies and given birth to growing companies in many fields : missiles, the full line of military aircraft, nuclear powered submarines and carriers, electronic warfare, digital transmissions and satellites. Conventional weapons procurement has also supported the development of new helicopters, tanks, ships, and allowed French industry to gain technical preeminence in many fields.

Owing to the impossibility for Japan and Germany (France's two most serious industrial competitors in export markets outside the US) to equip themselves in many of these weapon systems, France has held a very lucrative position as the world's third military exporter behind the two superpowers. These successes in export markets have been due partly to France's defence policy, and partly to its foreign policy after 1962 as a western nation favourable to the independence and prosperity of the third world. Many countries - particularly Latin American and African - have chosen French suppliers as a good middle ground between the two superpowers. French companies like Dassault, Thomson, Matra, or Aerospatiale have aggressively seized this opportunity. They have been constantly helped by domestic procurement plans, public R&D, export credits and the efficient marketing support of the Délégation Générale à l'Armement (DGA), the Defence Ministry's procurement and industrial agency, with a very active international sales organization.

- Technological independence has been in many cases linked to defence objectives, and has determined the launch of several industrial initiatives. In the mid-1960s when the US decided on an embargo of large computers used for the Force de Frappe, de Gaulle asked the government to support a French product development effort, which later culminated in the creation of the public company CII (see below for a full account). The national "graphite-gaz" technology used to produce nuclear energy was supported for many years against more competitive US technologies, and it was only when de Gaulle resigned that President Pompidou could allow French industry to license the PWR from Westinghouse, but only on condition that it would be made in France after a few years and that it could be freely exported, which it now is.

- In other instances, however, the State has pushed its objective of independence on purely prestige grounds against the interest of industry. Many of these nationalistic technology developments have become white elephants, or at best have gained limited world markets. The Concorde, for example, which absorbed close to 25 billion francs over 10 years - 70 billion francs in 1985 prices - was pushed by government officials (the Civil Aviation Authority, DGAC, and

de Gaulle's Cabinet) while Sud-Aviation already had
at that time the blueprints of what would become
Airbus.
- Energy independence has been an objective of French
policy since the late 1920s, when the first regulation
of oil prices and oil distribution was passed, and the
Compagnie Française des Pétroles (CFP) was charged
with conducting a major exploration drive in order
to gain autonomy from the US and British 'seven
sisters'. After the war, the development of domestic
energy sources (coal, Saharan oil, Lacq natural gas
and hydro-electricity) and the control of oil
exploration were the two major directions of French
State policies, acting through publicly owned utilities,
oil companies and research centres. These sectors of
the economy have traditionally attracted the elite
among engineers and civil servants (ingénieurs du
Corps des Mines, for example) and have benefited
from massive financial support. It is the same strong
State support which has made possible the very rapid
nuclear power buildup in the 1970s and early 1980s.
France is now the country which derives the highest
proportion of electricity from nuclear power, with
very high rates of operating efficiency. This has
caused a mushrooming of industrial expansion among
suppliers of ships, engineering, construction, and raw
material processing.
- Finally the desire of French political leadership from
all parties to restore the country's past influence on
world affairs has largely determined French
industrial export strategies, what J.D. Lefranc calls
the 'archaic-imperialist' syndrome[1]. Like British
industry, French industry long remained satisfied
with its predominant positions in former colonies.
Soft loans and preferential credit have been oriented
towards those countries where France wanted to
have an influence. The fact that these markets were
not the growing parts of the world only became

---

1

Jean-Daniel Lefranc, Industrie, Le Péril Français, le Seuil, 1983

169

obvious when overall growth slowed in the mid-1970s. It was then too late to recapture share from entrenched competitors like Japanese or German companies.

Fortunately French foreign policy had a positive influence on industry in one area of major importance : the constitution of an open European market, first with the European Coal and Steel Community in 1952 and then with the formation of the EEC in 1958. French political leaders - the fourth Republic regimes, and de Gaulle after 1958 –decided with quite some courage and vision on what was the only chance for French industry's renewal. Without the opening up of trade barriers, French industry would have remained self-centred on a small domestic and quasi-colonial market, archaic and uncompetitive. If the Treaty of Rome had been signed 10 years later, French companies would have been swallowed by their much stronger German rivals, US subsidiaries in Europe and the recession of the 1970s.

For better and for worse, strong State policies have influenced and often determined business strategies. In doing so, France's political leaders have not even been in agreement on economic philosophy. There has, however, been wide support for the main objectives of the State's economic intervention, modernization through public investments, and national independence. This has given all leaders - from business, government and the unions - the feeling that corporate success could be and should be determined by the State.

This hierarchy of priorities is in marked contrast with Japan and Germany. After the Second World War both countries gave up their historical ambitions in foreign policy and were prevented from building large defence capabilities. The objective of reconstruction and modernization therefore mobilized all their energies and talents. For both peoples, economic survival and then increasing material wealth became the only means of national pride. The State became concerned about economic success per se, not as a means to support a defence industry or influence the world. A national strategy of developing competitive positions worldwide has consciously grown out of the constraints imposed on political leaders. Governments and business leaders were striving for the same objectives through different means. Whereas the UK and France had strong State policies with an undefined industrial strategy, Japan and Germany formed a clear industrial strategy supported by relevant - and not overwhelming - State policies.

Both Germany and Japan rely almost exclusively on corporations and business leaders to make investments, product developments or diversifications. They rarely try to influence and finance selected technologies, companies or even sectors directly. Rather they spur national resources - skills and capital - in positive directions by indirect incentives and encourage the permanent evolution from obsolete businesses to new areas.

This adaptation of German or Japanese leadership to the rules of a free market economy was not in the natural course of history. The German renewal of a central and powerful State initiated by Bismarck (who invented the first social security system) and culminating with the Nazis could have led to the same pattern of public intervention as in France. As the historical roots of the State were weaker, the tradition of merchants and capitalism more established, and German industry stronger than in France, the marriage of the 'social market economy' and the sense of a national strategy produced the postwar 'economic miracle'. In Japan, the State intervention which developed under the Meiji era and through the military regimes of the 1930s left more of an influence, despite a systematic attempt by the Americans to disband all remnants of the Japanese Empire. The State-business interface in Japan is far from the model described by Adam Smith. The Japanese State, however, has much more respect, confidence and knowledge of market forces than its French counterpart. MITI - to take the best known Japanese agency - rarely tries to go against competitive forces. Rather, the Japanese State has proved a master in channelling resources to the best leverage points and stimulating new investments at the right time to take advantage of new market trends.

In France, success in the market place is not a national objective of enough importance for political leadership and civil servants. Business decisions must always be a subset of 'higher' political objectives. This attitude can create outstanding unexpected breakthroughs, but the risk of wasting resources or simply failing against stronger competitors is much greater.

In summary, the French State has become the prime capitalist, 'nationalising' and mobilising the best resources of the country towards a higher-level objective than profit making and success in the market place. Private entrepreneurs - despite brilliant individual successes as seen in part II - have been too scarce or have come too late in modern history to prove that the sum of business successes was the basis for national prosperity. French enterprise has never been at the forefront of the successive industrial revolutions, and in turn has been overwhelmed by State initiatives and controls. Financial resources and human talents have often been attracted by State-driven ventures rather than by private business. While staying within the limits of what a State apparatus can do in a democracy of free individuals, the French State has gone the furthest in the west in distorting market rules, by becoming the key player in the French market economy. It will continue to play a key role, in managing the difficult transitions which the country will face, whoever is in power.

## 2. THE ORGANIZATION OF FRENCH INDUSTRIAL POLICIES

### Background

Unlike its European neighbours, France has a long tradition of direct government involvement in the economy, which has survived very different political regimes. This historical precedent, however, did not lead political leaders to formulate explicit policies for industry until the early 1960s. In the years just after World War II, the country's economic policy focused on changes in ownership, control, and broad economic planning. Industrial policy was not a subject of debate until the early 1960s. The debate on public ownership was described in the previous chapter. We will briefly summarize the two other issues of control and planning, and describe the historical background of industrial policy.

### Control

Efforts were made relatively early to introduce worker participation in decision-making within the French corporate structure. Workers' councils (Comités d'Entreprise) have decision powers on certain social issues (e.g., health, housing or vacations) and an advisory role in economic matters. However, these institutions were not further developed until 1968 and still fall short of the workers' control schemes in many European countries (such as Sweden, Germany or the Netherlands). In 1983 the 'Lois Auroux' gave more power and resources to workers' organizations, and introduced new schemes of participation and control in corporate decisions. It remains to be seen, however, whether the law can really change the historical pattern of management's classical hierarchy. French corporations - with a few brilliant exceptions - have not been as successful as their counterparts in Northern Europe, in generating internally a process of participation and motivation. Instead, all attempts to shift power to the workers have been imposed from the outside

Figure 42

## THE NATIONAL PLANNING SYSTEM IN FRANCE

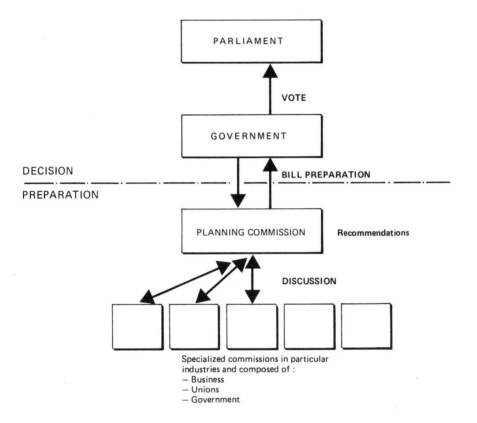

PARLIAMENT

VOTE

GOVERNMENT

DECISION
PREPARATION

BILL PREPARATION

PLANNING COMMISSION

Recommendations

DISCUSSION

Specialized commissions in particular
industries and composed of :
— Business
— Unions
— Government

174

- the State or the unions - and hence have been violently opposed by management. It will take several years before the 'Auroux laws' will really give rise to a new form of participative management, and a few decades before workers and managers do not consider each other as two antagonistic forces.

## Economic planning and history of industrial policy

After the war, France was unusual among Western European countries in adopting a formal indicative planning system for its economic policy. Each five-year Plan was prepared by a series of committees representing government, business and labour (Figure 42).

The Plan was viewed by its early supporters as the key element of a mixed economy. As long as the main problem was the postwar reconstruction of infrastructure, utilities and basic capital-intensive industries like steel, the Plan provided a useful framework for setting priorities and scheduling major investments for the country. During the First Plan (which began in 1948), two-thirds of total industrial investment was financed by publicly controlled funds. However, as the economy opened to international trade and the investment tradeoffs became more complex, the Plan became less useful for effective resource allocation. It was progressively replaced by other mechanisms, especially in the are of industrial policy.

From the end of World War II until 1958, little need was felt for an industrial policy in France. Competition·was primarily domestic, and industry was developing quickly from its low point following the war. In 1958, France entered the Common Market. Before that time, French tariffs were among the highest in Europe. Along with the opening to foreign trade, and especially to German competition, came a first wave of liberal economic policy measures inspired by the general philosophy of the Treaty of Rome. However, as the competitive pressure intensified and public support of technological development increased (as in the US), the French government became increasingly involved in industrial policy. This was closely related to the Gaullist ambition of restoring a highly respected State, modernizing the economy and gaining more influence in world economic matters. The decision in the early 1960s to establish a French nuclear çapability (the Force de Frappe) greatly influenced developments in military aircraft, electronics and nuclear energy. A US embargo on large, scientific computers led to the the continuing large defence and aircraft programmes.

Beginning in the early 1960s, the French Plans were designed to reflect an industrial policy, and to influence the pattern of investment among broadly defined sectors. The Fifth Plan (1965-70) aimed to promote three sectors - aircraft, computers and steel - and to encour ge the formation of large domestic companies in those same industries. Aérospatiale w s formed in aircraft, Usinor and Sacilor in steel and Thomson-Brandt in electronics, for ex mple. The government devised tax incentives to make mergers more attractive and took direct initiatives on some occasions. It was felt that corporate size in itself w s a crucial element of competitiveness and that mergers and acquisitions would increase the productivity of French industry. The Sixth Plan (1970-75) was the first to focus primarily on industrial growth. It tried to develop sectors with high export potential and higher 'value added', such as mechanical engineering, electronics and specialty chemicals.

The Plans, while using increasingly sophisticated econometric models, do not operate at a level of detail that is adequate for resource allocation decisions. More importantly, perhaps, the decision-making process has been increasingly criticized by the major trade unions as not democratic enough, and the last planning cycles have failed to be a vehicle for consensus in the area of industrial policy. The regionalization and decentralization of French administration undertaken in 1982 and 1983 and departing from centuries of centralization have added another layer of complexity to the planning process. Each of France's 22 regions is now invited to formulate its own development plan. It is too soon to predict the impact of this decentralization, but it is unlikely to restore confidence in the Plan.

All the French government's major industrial decisions have been made, and are made today more than ever before, outside the formal planning process of the Plan.

## Agencies involved in industrial policy

The French administration remains centralized and extremely influential in all areas of the economy. Responsibility for industrial policy, however, is fragmented among a dozen different agencies representing different philosophical traditions and interest groups, making the decision making process even more unpredictable, arcane and political. A particular industrial problem may be handled by number of different agencies. The most important of these and their respective areas of competence are shown in Figure 43.

The fact that the Ministry of Industry has had a new name, and a new Minister about every two years over the last twenty years, despite few new resources or responsibilities, illustrate its inadequacy.

In theory, the French Ministry of Industry, now combined with Foreign Trade and the PTT and called 'Ministry of Industrial Redeployment', has responsibility for formulating and implementing industrial policies. It is organized by branches of industry and has direct relationships with the major French corporations. It supervises the activities of the Nuclear Energy Agency (CEA), the Space Agency (CNES), and most of the nationalized companies in the manufacturing sector (excluding defence and aircraft) and in the energy field (petroleum, coal mines, Electricité de France, Gaz de France).

In practice, however, the Ministry of Industry has to work within the constraints imposed by the Ministry of Finance as well as other government departments responsible for key industries (Transport for civilian aircraft and shipbuilding, Post and Telephone, which remains a fairly autonomous agency and oversees all areas of telecommunications, Defence for military production, Health for pharmaceuticals nd Agriculture for food industries).

In addition, government research policy is made by a number of different agencies. The Defence Department finances three-quarters of the R&D grants to private companies ; the remaining quarter is divided among a research funding agency reporting to the Ministry of Industry, ANVAR and various smaller departments.

Figure 43

# INDUSTRIAL POLICY MAKING IN THE EXECUTIVE BRANCH (1985)

## AGENCIES AND AREAS OF COMPETENCE

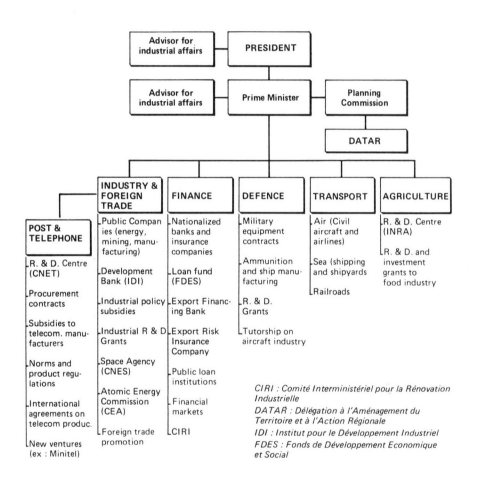

178

Regional policies are shared between a special agency - Délégation à l'Aménagement du Territoire et à l'Action Régionale (DATAR) - and the Ministry of Finance, which supervises grants and tax agreements for major projects. Grants below 10 million francs are authorized at the local level.

While the different agencies have some influence on industrial policy, the most important resource allocation decisions are still made by the Ministry of Economy and Finance, certainly the most powerful administration in France. It oversees the commercial banking system and the financial markets. All the major banks are nationalized and many medium- and long-term commercial banking functions are carried out by specific state-owned institutions : Crédit National in the industrial sector, and BFCE in export financing, for example. In addition, the central bank (Banque de France) can direct commercial credit selectively or refinance certain loans at favourable discount rates (export credit, for example). The Direction du Trésor (a sub-division of the Ministry of Economy) determines the timing of every important public issue (bond or equity) oversees the bank and insurance sectors, control foreign exchange movements and foreign investments in France, and allocates preferential loans to industry. This makes the 'Trésor' the single most powerfull agency in France and a breeding ground for the most influential civil servants and business executives.

The former Price Division of the Ministry of Economy and Finance administers the very heavy and intricate French system of price controls created in 1945 in war times and never dismantled since then. This gives the civil servants the right to administer prices in every sector of the economy, from wholesale margins to automobiles or restaurants. The methods can evolve and involve sometimes contractual agreements between companies or sector federations and the State on a several year basis. The same Ministry Division - now called Division of Consumers and Competition Policy - oversees consumer protection regulations and cartel and price fixing practices. The State has been less strict in those last two areas in France than in countries with a strong protestant ethic of fair competition like the UK, the US or Germany since the post war period.

179

In summary the combination of very powerfull, sometimes discretionary powers in almost all aspects of business - from prices and capital, to foreign exchanges and of course taxes and subsidies - has made the Ministry of Economy and Finance, the effective center of economic policy and the symbol of French 'State capitalism'. This has only increased in the recent years.

After the first oil shock, the government created four new funds to respond to increasing structural problems in industry. The first three are managed by the Direction du Trésor, the last one by the Minister of Industry :

. the CIASI (1975), to rescue small and medium sized companies that can become viable, has grown to around one and a half billion francs a year;

. the CIDISE (1978), to help growing businesses with special 'subordinated' loans with a few hundred millions francs a year ;

. the FSAI (1978), with a temporary mission of restructuring the North and the East of France away from steel and coal, has used around three billions francs over its life ;

. the FIM (1982), to finance 'modernization' investments at subsidized interest rates, has been able to use around six billion francs up to now.

In 1979, the Prime Minister, on the recommendation of the Minister of Industry, created a mechanism for coordinating the use of those funds and for making sure that businesses showing the most potential would be considered.A new interdepartmental committee - CODIS - was formed in 1978 to overcome this fragmentation and to bring together at a high level the policymaking functions of all key departments. It was also given power to decide on such measures as interest subsidies, tax credits, and export aids. CODIS comprised the Ministers of Finance, Industry and Foreign Trade under the chairmanship of the Prime Minister, but the day-to-day work was done by a task force headed by the Director of Industry and involving all the agencies concerned with industrial policy including Datar, Plan, Labour, etc. In 1981 it was still unclear whether this group would have succeeded in rationalizing French industrial policymaking, when the new left Government decided to disband it.

The economic planning agency (Commissariat du Plan) does not have direct authority for specific policies and serves more as a general consensus-forming group and a forum for new ideas to be developed and discussed.

This fragmentation in organization often hinders the flexibility and efficiency of French policymaking. Decisions can be slow to emerge on key issues. Unlike in Japan, the reason for this slowness is often political in-fighting among agencies rather than a careful consensus-forming process. As a result, policies once promulgated are often altered and inconsistently implemented.

Entire sectors of French industry have, however, stayed relatively immune from rivalries : aircraft, oil and off-shore, and nuclear, are examples. This is in part due to clear division of responsibilities, continuity in the executive branch and isolation from the normal organization of industrial policy (see chapter 4).

**Policies**

Four sets of policies have had the most influence on French industry. Each will be discussed in turn.

- Support of uncompetitive companies in low growth markets has been increasing; until very recently, there has been little concomitant rationalisation effort.
- Heavy investments have been made in a few major technological ventures, with some recent diversifications into clearly defined business segments.
- Regional development programmes have been limited and have had little positive impact on the restructuring of industry.
- There has been substantial financing of exports, especially in plant and machinery sold to developing and Eastern bloc countries.

(a) Support of uncompetitive and low growth sectors

The French government was directly involved in planning for
the postwar rebuilding of basic infrastructure and certain
industries were nationalized (aircraft, part of automobiles and
trucks). In this respect, France abandoned the liberal
tradition of non-intervention sooner than most other European
governments. As it turned out, however, the effect of
increasing competition from Japan and other developing
countries was felt primarily in other industries which were
privately owned (shipbuilding, steel and textiles). In general,
(and until recently) the government has offered early and
easy support to these industries (to shipbuilding in 1951, to
steel in 1966) without influencing the rationalization process,
or encouraging them to regroup around defensible positions.

In State-owned industries, curiously, government
control before 1982 has not usually been used to implement
an industrial policy. For example, the three State-owned
companies (Potasses d'Alsace, ONIA and CDF-Chimie) in the
fertilizer business gave the government effective control of
the sector. Instead of using that control to force the
companies to rationalize their production, the government has
let each manufacturer diversify into other businesses and
maintain sub-scale facilities. This has also been the case in
petrochemicals and oil refineries. The organization of
industrial policy in those fields has shown a lack of strategic
vision : most powers have remained with the Direction du
Trésor (with strong intervention from political personnel
around the President or the Prime Minister) and a small role
has been played by the Ministry of Industry.

The CIASI (now CIRI) : a selective approach to business
rescue. Because of the concentration of low wage-rate
businesses in certain areas, the increasing competition from
developing countries has affected some parts of France more
than others. An interministerial committee, the CIASI, was
established in 1975 to respond to this problem. It was to
focus on companies that were in financial trouble but that
could be expected to do well if properly restructured.

182

The CIASI (now called CIRI) is unusual in several ways : it cuts across existing agencies with entrenched positions, it exercises its leverage through the commercial banking system, and it tries to act as a catalyst furthering a consistent industrial restructuring.

The CIRI is coordinated by the Direction du Trésor and works closely with the business community and the banks to structure rationalization measures and put together financial packages to support them. The CIRI can use the low-interest funds of the FDES, but tries to exert leverage through its financial support with commercial credit and private equity. Over the past years, CIRI activities have been more important than the regional development schemes in terms of both expenditure and jobs created.

The CIRI had deliberately avoided the large sectoral problems (steel, shipbuilding) to focus on the more fragmented industries and smaller 'pockets' of unemployment (textiles in the Vosges, shoes in Bretagne, printing, machinery). In these situations, the cooperative mode of operation and the flexibility and power of an inter-agency body have enabled several areas successfully to restructure their local industry. The new CIRI however has been called upon more and more to solve the unemployment problems of the steel regions.

The CIRI's ten-year history can be seen in one way as a model of administrative efficiency and flexibility. Its small interdisciplinary team of top civil servants, financial analysts and engineers has accomplished many miraculous rescues, with hard work, determination, tough pragmatism and total political support. The institution, however, has become almost too successful and has raised too many unreasonable expectations. Furthermore, the CIRI does not have the time or the talent to reform fundamental strategies. It was created to respond to a crisis and cannot be viewed as a long-term approach to industri 1 restructuring.

(b) Promotion of growing sectors
The growing sectors have been supported through both government research policy and more direct action on corporate strategies.

Research policy. The form taken by French research policy has reflected two factors :
- after the war, the problem had been to build new capacity using available technology often bought from the US or Germany (steel and chemicals). In the 1960s, however, French businesses were competing on an international scale with growing foreign investments and a more difficult access to technology ;
- France, like many other European countries, was aware that the US federal government was playing an important role in the development of technology-intensive industries like aeronautics, electronics and nuclear power.

Efforts to promote French technological development began in the mid-to-late 1950s with the start of nuclear research. An interministerial committee was established to direct government R&D aid, and a special supporting agency, DGRST, reporting to the Prime Minister, was created to coordinate the activities of different departments.

In 1960, to give a clearer picture of the national public effort for R&D, the government instituted a centralized budgetary procedure, 'enveloppe recherche'. This budget always excluded such major expenditures as military and aircraft R&D for national security reasons: nevertheless, it shows that the spending level rose from 0.5 per cent of gross national product in 1958 to 2.6 per cent in 1967. Following the US model, the growth of French R&D expenditures occurred mainly in 'Big Science' projects like the Concorde, the Pl n Calcul, and the Force de Frappe. These were expected to contribute to the country's political independence and simultaneously improve the position of French industry. At the end of 1959, the government created the 'Concerted Actions' s a means to reorient traditional scientific institutions towards serving national needs. In 1962, the various 'Concerted Actions' in space were reorganized into the National Centre for Space Studies (CNES). Finally, military research policy was reorganized and centralized via the newly created Direction for Research and Testing (DRME).

These mechanisms served a clear policy objective : to embark French industry on major technological ventures in aerospace, computers and nuclear power. National self-sufficiency w s the main criterion rather than a business analysis of the competitive environment. The resources taken up by these large-scale technology programmes in the overall public funding of industrial R&D explain why the Ministry of Industry still has little power over strategic directions followed by French industry (Figure 44).

Successive governments have, however, tried to institute new schemes to diversify industrial policies and disseminate technology into smaller scale industries. In the late 1960s, the French government tried to refine its policies. France was the first European country to introduce a scheme of cooperation between business and government on R&D projects. The Aid to Development programme, introduced in 1965, subsidized the development cost of industrial projects. This assistance was to be repaid in the event of commercial success. An analogous 'pre-development' programme was also established, but funding h s been relatively insignificant. Two sectors were initially selected : heavy electrical equipment and machinery. This scheme served as a model for other European governments (the BMFT in Germany or STU in Sweden, and now the microelectronics programme in the UK or ES RIT at the European level).

In 1967, a special agency, ANVAR, w s created to offer support at the market introduction stage of the innovation process. The focus was to be on small firms or investors. Special tax advantages were given to newly created venture capital firms and risk credit could be provided to innovative firms. Thus, France developed a set of aid mechanisms to cover the entire innovation process, from basic to applied research, product development and market introduction (Figure 45). These programmes were developed as it became clear that the large scientific ventures were not leading to the expected improvements in business performance.

The focus of government support shifted to more clearly defined business segments where innovation could have a spill-over 'feeder' effect in other sectors of industry. In practice, the new Aid to Development procedure was mainly

Figure 44

## PUBLIC FUNDING OF INDUSTRIAL R. & D. IN FRANCE

| Area | Funding Agency | Government funds 1980 Budget (Bill. FF) | 1985 Budget (Bill. FF) |
|------|----------------|------------------|------------------|
| DEFENCE | DEFENCE MINISTRY | 11,3 | 21,7 |
| NUCLEAR | DEFENCE & INDUSTRY MINISTRIES (CEA) | 2,6 | 3,3 |
| SPACE | INDUSTRY MINISTRY (CNES) | 1,4 | 3,2 |
| TELECOMMUNICATIONS | PTT (CNET) & DEFENCE | 1,3 | 5,2 |
| AIRCRAFT | DEFENCE & TRANSPORTATION MINISTRIES | 0,8 | 5,0 |
| COMPUTERS | INDUSTRY MINISTRY | 0,4 | 2,8 |
| MARINE RESOURCES | INDUSTRY MINISTRY | 0,4 | 0,7 |
| NEW SOURCES OF ENERGY | INDUSTRY MINISTRY (AFME) | 0,3 | 0,4 |
| RAW MATERIALS MINING | INDUSTRY MINISTRY | 0,2 | 0,5 |
| BIOTECHNOLOGIES | INDUSTRY MINISTRY | — | 1,0 |
| INCENTIVES FOR VARIOUS INDUSTRIES | INDUSTRY MINISTRY | 1,5 | 1,5 |

**TOTAL : 20,2    45,3**

*Sources : Annexe Recherche 84/85, Budget documents, Telesis Analysis*

Figure 45

## FRENCH STATE FINANCIAL SUPPORT FOR INDUSTRIAL R. & D.
### AGENCIES AND MECANISMS

| STAGES OF INNOVATION | RECIPIENTS | | |
|---|---|---|---|
| | BUSINESS | Industry Cooperative Research Institutes | Public Research Institutes |
| Basic Research | Very infrequent support | Very infrequent support | Budget allocations at all Stages of financing for : |
| | Grants up to 50 per cent | Grants up to 50 per cent | — Nuclear (CEA) |
| Applied Research | Public procurement contracts include 5 to 10 per cent price premium for development costs (telecommunications, electronics, aircraft) «Etudes Libres» | | — Space (CNES) — Telecommunications (CNET) — Computers (IRIA) — Transports (IRT) — Chemicals (IRCHA) — Off-shore (CNEXO) — Oil (IFP) |
| Development | Loans & subsidies (ANVAR) Defence contracts Telephone contracts | Loans & subsidies (ANVAR) | — Agriculture (INRA) |
| Pre-Production | Loan guarantees (CNME) Assistance to small business (ANVAR) | Loan guarantees (CNME) ANVAR | |

*Sources : Telesis Analysis*

186

used to fund projects in machinery, electrical engineering and chemicals. As in Germany or the US, this support was concentrated on the large companies : 60 per cent of funds disbursed between 1965 and 1970 went to the top ten companies. Resources allocated to this effort, however, were limited in comparison to those committed to the large ventures in aircraft and computers. Funding at ANVAR has more than tripled since 1981 without reaching the levels of BMFT in Germany. The decision-making process of the development aids relies primarily on technical criteria and the sort of financial analysis typical of commercial banks. Less emphasis is put on the competitive environment and market prospects.

Direct influence on high-tech industries. Besides its funding of research, the French State has played a direct role in the start-up and growth of most new industries with a high-technology content. In publicly controlled markets, state-owned utilities such as EDF or PTT have determined product choices, industrial investments and even export strategies for their suppliers. In the absence of a respected Ministry of Industry they have shaped government policies, including control of foreign investments and price controls, as well as business strategies. The same holds true of course in all military businesses where the Defence Ministry acts as a source of R&D funds, a procurement agency and a "tutor" for whole sectors of industry (aircraft and space).

In open markets, the State has tried to exercise direct influence through dedicated agencies using various carrots and sticks. In computers, the Délégation à l'Informatique, created in 1966 and since disbanded, served as a source of funds for product development but also as a semi-official procurement agency for purchases made by the Administration and public bodies. In commercial aircraft, the Civil Aviation Authority (DGAC) has used its regulatory powers and its R&D budget to exercise a strong influence on the launching of new models. In oil exploration, the CEPM has used public funds to stimulate the R & D efforts of private engineering firms.

## (c) Regional development policy

Because of the concentration of industrial development in
Paris and the northern and eastern regions of the country,
regional development policies were first devised to control
domestic population movements and to reduce the congestion
of the cities. The first significant measures were taken in
1955, when the Fund for Economic and Social Development
(FDES) and regional development banks (SDR) were
established. Investment grants up to 20 per cent and tax
incentives were also made available. Additional mechanisms
were added in the early 1960s and a coordinating agency
(DATAR) was created in 1963 to carry out government
regional policies.

Significant changes were introduced in 1976 that had
the effect of increasing support to low-skilled labour-intensive
industries or uncompetitive companies with redundant work
forces :

- the investment grant was replaced by a subsidy based
  on the number of jobs created. This criterion works
  to the disavantage of more capital-intensive
  industries ;
- preference was given to investments made by small
  companies in small towns. These have tended to be in
  low-paid industries like clothing, shoes, wood-working
  or sheltered activities. Knowledge-intensive businesses
  are more likely to be located in larger towns,
  capital-intensive businesses in greenfield plants ;
- grants could be made to companies in difficulty as
  well as to those investing for expansion ;
- for investments under 10 million francs, the funding
  decision could be made at a local level. Clearly,
  local decision-makers have been subject to intense
  political pressure to rescue failing businesses.

Decisions rest almost entirely on the issue of short-
term employment prospects. Little consideration is given to
the long-term competitive position of the industry. Rescue
operations account for as much as 30 per cent of all grants
in certain regions (80 per cent when 'conversion' operations
are included). Whether these investments are effective in
securing long-term employment is doubtful. Regional tax
incentives do not favour capital-intensive businesses. While

German and Japanese tax incentives are based on investment cost and profitability, the French regional tax incentive is unrelated to corporate income tax or investment. Under the main mechanism, companies can apply for a five-year waiver of local property taxes. Funding for this mechanism has become even greater than for investment grants.

Government funding of regional programmes has more than doubled since the mid-1960s. Average annual budget-authorized grants (in 1977 FF) increased from 180 million francs in 1966-1967 to 450 million in the period 1970-1977. Investments are not chosen so as to promote industrial restructuring ; the more knowledge intensive industries (mechanical and electrical engineering and transport equipment) receive only 30 per cent of all regional funds, compared to 49 per cent in Germany. Indeed, a recent study done by the National Institute of Statistics showed that the French map of businesses subject to developing-country competition corresponded closely to the map of most-helped areas.

France (like many of its neighbours) faces a further problem in that large, troubled industries are concentrated in particular regions (steel in Lorraine, shipbuilding in Loire Atlantique, textiles in the Vosges). The problems these regions are facing now are beyond the scope of regional policies devised at a time when the problem was to 'distribute surpluses of industrial employment'. In an effort to promote new healthy companies through venture capital, several regions have created in the early 1980s new funds which invest equity under what should be market criteria. Those funds - IPO in the West, Participex in the South West etc. - are supplied by institutional investors and banks and generally managed by professional teams. They have also been imitated in the last five years by large companies with redundant work forces which felt that they had a special responsibility for creating new businesses in hard hit localities. The steel companies, Rhône-Poulenc, Saint-Gobain, Elf, BSN and CDF-Chimie have been the most active. Another innovation of regional policy has been to nominate strong personalities at the head of newly created administrative functions (like 'Commissaire à l'industrialisation') with the powers to attract new industries and develop new infrastructure. The recent nomination of Jacques Cherèque (former deputy leader of the CFDT labour union) at the head of the Lorraine redeployment effort with the high rank of Prefet may be the forerunner of a new form of cooperation between business, unions and the State in what is the most difficult challenge of the French economy.

(d) Export promotion

Shortly after the war, two companies were created to promote the financing of exports. The French Foreign Trade Bank (BFCE) provides a large part of the capital required for exports, especially long-term credit. In addition, the Banque de France refinances medium and long-term export credits extended by the commercial banks at a favourable discount rate (usually one per cent below market).

The Export Guarantee Company (COFACE), provides government guarantees for both regular commercial transactions (short-term guarantees) and special risks (political or economic). COFACE, in addition, administers special schemes to promote exports :

- a guarantee of marketing costs in new foreign markets,
- an exchange risk guarantee,
- an 'economic risk' guarantee which covers the difference between a normal rate of inflation (6.5 to 8 per cent) and the actual cost inflation incurred on capital goods orders which require more than one year to deliver,
- a guarantee for French investments abroad.

In addition, a state-owned Foreign Trade Centre (CFCE) offers companies information and consulting services on international markets and procedures, and organizes trade exhibitions abroad.

Investments abroad can be financed with the help of a State association, UFINEX. Investments in developing countries receive a favourable tax treatment (five-year tax deferral based on the cost of investment). Small companies that wish to export and develop abroad can obtain equity from a state-owned financing company (SOFININDEX). These last measures are not, however, funded as substantially as comparable programmes in Germany, nor has France developed any institutions analogous to the German DEG which organizes joint ventures with third world partners.

Overall, exports to new markets (developing countries, OPEC) and system sales (whole plants or complex machinery) have been considerably helped by the government. Economic risk guarantees (essentially direct subsidies) have increased substantially since the oil crisis, rising from an average of 600 million francs in 1972-76 to 1,150 million francs in 1975 and 2,100 million francs in 1976. Interest subsidies for long-term loans distributed by BFCE go mainly to capital-goods manufactures. They have increased substantially in the late 1970s. France uses 'mixed credits' arrangements to finance capital goods exports to developing countries, combining low-interest loans (3 per cent) under official aid and commercial credit. These mixed credits amount to more than three billion francs a year. Finally, between 2 and 3 billion francs a year of capital aid to developing countries was tied to import agreements by recipient countries of French made goods.

In summary, the organization of industrial policy in France stems from the objectives assigned to industry by the State : modernization and independence. Modernization is accomplished by means of direct involvement in new industries, new technologies or the rescue of ailing companies. Independence is pursued by strong and resourceful agencies such as Defence, PTT or EDF combining the roles of purchaser, regulator and fund provider. In the last forty years (and particularly since the early 1960s) the French State apparatus and its public 'satellites' - the State owned monopolies and the public research centres - have grown as powerful decision centres, taking their legitimacy from higher-level political objectives assigned to the country by its leaders.

Using its historical legitimacy and a renewed prestige when de Gaulle came back to power, the State has progressively adopted new means of exercising power in a modern economy without giving up the old ones. Hence the French State is in a unique position of controlling ownership,

191

price levels, imports and at the same time launching new technological ventures. The old ideology built on the distrust of trade and profit-making has not prevented the elite of the French State from looking ahead and setting ambitious goals for their country. Brilliant engineers and administrators, selected and trained in the top schools (all State-run) have often led successful policies against the odds, for example in oil, nuclear energy or aerospace, using all the instruments provided by a modern State apparatus. This power base and continuity in resource allocation has been a significant source of wealth creation for France.

But there has been a high cost. The sheer extent and the continuous ramification of State intervention in the economy have also led quite naturally to duplication, wasting of resources, rigidities and internal rivalries. Bureaucratic inefficiencies become more and more apparent and harmful, as the economy grows in complexity and opens up to the rest of the world. In some cases, State agencies have disappeared or become less important, as in the case of the Plan. In others, the old power strongholds are fighting for survival and most often succeed in gaining new roles, without a clear economic justification, as in the case of the PTT.

The structure of French agencies dealing with industrial policies reflects two centuries (and sometimes more) of accumulation of various layers of State intervention without major reshuffling or disappearance. The strongest power bases are either historically prestigious career paths (Mines, Treasury, Armement) or national priorities dating back to the early Gaullist period : EDF and CEA (Nuclear) or the PTT (telephone). Departments as important for overall consistency as the Direction Générale de l'Industrie, the DATAR (regional planning) or the Plan have been understaffed and underfinanced. This has only reinforced the two most serious flaws of the organization of industrial policy in France.

First, such organization does not make a clear division between departmental responsibilities and national responsibilities. The concentration of budgetary resources, technical expertise and regulatory or procurement roles in different, autonomous agencies often created conflict. It also makes it more difficult for government and parliament to

192

exercise control. Individual ministerial departments or State monopolies have a lot of freedom and little accountability, and can pursue policies in their own interest, and use power or resources with effects beyond their mandate. It has been difficult for the same reason to shift policy emphasis or budgets from one sector to the other.

Second, the State apparatus lacks a common economic philosophy. The fragmentation of an organization is not a problem when all parts aim in the same direction. It can then be a means of effective delegation of power. It becomes counter-productive, however, when the objectives are conflicting. Modernization and independence were mutually reinforcing concepts when the economy was catching up behind closed borders, but are now more and more often in conflict.

The pursuit of national independence in all fields - military, energy, technology -becomes unaffordable for a country the size of France, as the threshold of competitive scale rises. Resources have to be allocated more carefully and a choice must be made in many cases between prosperous interdependence and costly autonomy. French companies, on the other hand, need more and more international presence as the competition intensifies on a worldwide scale. The State apparatus has not yet adapted to the new competitive situation. It is still organized to conduct a Gaullist style policy in all sectors of the economy. The socialists have been only too happy to find all the tools of State influence and have even created new ones. But the strategic direction has not changed.

Many political leaders and civil servants have realized that the only goal of industrial policy is to create the conditions for national corporations to compete and grow more effectively than their rivals, and eventually stand on their own feet. They have not however modified the structure of state intervention accordingly.

Several factors make the adaptation of French industrial policy more difficult than in other countries. Corporations are not strong enough to take the lead or impose their views in most high-tech industries ; the State and its direct satellites continue to attract the elites. In 'strategic sectors' so many responsibilities have been taken

193

over by the State - from research to export credit, and from investment choices to product planning - that the return to free competition can only be a long educative process of trial and error, cautiously nurtured, rather than a brutal deregulation as in the US. Finally, given the financial weaknesses of French corporations and their needs in the years to come, the State will still have to fill needs which cannot be met by market mechanisms.

## 3. THE FINANCING OF INDUSTRY

In a free market economy, corporations finance their needs through a combination of three sources : internally generated cash flows, the financial markets (banks, stocks and bonds markets) and transfers from the State. In all industrial democracies the first two sources account for the vast majority of the cash needs. In France and Germany for example - which are often described as opposite examples of economic management philosophy - our analysis shows that they constitute between 70 per cent and 80 per cent of corporate needs. All European countries are in similar situations, despite differences in historical traditions and political rhetoric. The case of the US is not very different, with similar proportions of State transfers through space and defence spending. In Japan, it is difficult to separate transfers from the State and transfers through the banks.

The role of the State in the financing of industry extends, however, beyond its direct transfers. In all Western economies, the State has varying degrees of influence on internal cash flow levels and the financial markets. The constraints and costs imposed by the State on the overall financing of corporations largely determine industrial strategies and performance. In France, the role of the State has probably been more important than in any other free market economy.

### Traditional State control of corporate financing

It is difficult to trace the origins of the vicious circle of financial dependence in which French industry has been caught up since the early 1970s. In parts I and II we have described the gradual decline of French corporations' profitability. The lack of internal funds has been, of course, the main reason for the State's intervention. In turn, some State policies have kept industry at insufficient levels of cash generation.

Figure 46

## THE EVOLUTION OF FRENCH CORPORATE FINANCIAL PERFORMANCES
## ENTERPRISES FROM ALL SECTORS*

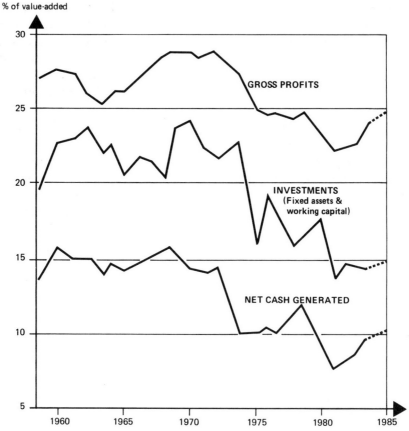

% of value-added

GROSS PROFITS

INVESTMENTS
(Fixed assets &
working capital)

NET CASH GENERATED

* Excluding State owned monopolies (Electricity, Railways, etc.)
Source : INSEE

196

Gross profitability of all companies together (not only industrial ones) has decreased from almost 30 per cent of value added in the 1960s to 22 per cent in 1981 and 24 per cent in 1983, and the level of net cash flows has been cut in half, from 16 per cent to 8 per cent (see Figure 46). Although the rate of investment has decreased – which in itself is of serious consequence for the future – companies have had to turn to outside capital. In 1982, internal cash flows financed only 37 per cent of total corporate investment and working capital, as opposed to 48 per cent in 1973 and approximately 70 per cent in the 1960s. The gap has been mostly filled by the banking system and to a smaller extent the stock market and the government itself. In all three sources of funds, the French State has always kept a high degree of influence.

The **French banking system** is probably in the unique situation among Western democracies of being almost entirely State-owned, highly regulated, and strongly cartelized. The result has been a rather costly and rigid credit distribution system, although some changes appear to be underway.

State ownership began in 1936 with the partial nationalization of the Banque de France, but was extended in 1945 and 1982. After the war, the four major commercial banks – two of them merged in the 1960s – were nationalized, and several specialized credit institutions were created, following several other European countries : Crédit National and CEPME for long-term loans to industry, CNME for government contractor financing, BFCE for export credit, Crédit Foncier for construction. In addition the quasi-public bank for agriculture (Crédit Agricole) diversified and expanded into what is now one of the largest banks in the world (in terms of deposits), partly thanks to special tax incentives and monopolies in certain areas. In 1967, the government allowed all commercial banks to become investment banks as well, which they did very significantly, eroding the traditional positions of Suez and Paribas, the two largest private investment banks. Given the size of the public sector, it was therefore both anachronistic and redundant for the Left to implement its old nationalization promises in 1982. More than thirty banks – most of them very small and several of them near bankruptcy - were drawn into what is now the largest State-owned banking system in the Western world.

In addition, the French State has always highly regulated almost all the major aspects of the banking business. Interest rates are set by the Central Bank which is not independent from the Treasury as it is in Germany or the US. The prices of most banking services are set by government decrees and new branch openings are subject to prior authorization from a State controlled commission. Until last year, the practice of credit rationing ('plafonnement du crédit') and other various levers had the effect of freezing market shares among the banks . Furthermore, the wide practice of interest rate subsidies by government organizations for loans used for national priorities like exports, regional development, etc., has limited allocation by the market to only half of the total credit distributed to the economy. The remainder is channelled through government-controlled mechanisms (agriculture, housing) and half of this is in the form of loans to industry.

Finally, the banks organized a powerful cartel for wage negotiations and discussions with the other sectors of the economy. The banking trade associations now also organize training and grant their own degrees.

The results of so much regulation and governmental control are ambiguous. French banks are among the largest and the best-established worldwide. Their total foreign assets, for example, rank third in the world, ahead of German and British banks. They have pionereed many new practices, from large project financing to eurocurrency management, including for example some aspects of the promotion of the ECU. This very dynamic internationalization appears, however, to be largely offset by weak competition and heavy constraints at home. Although international comparisons are difficult, recent studies (from the Commissariat du Plan for example) have shown that French banks are in general more costly to their customers than their foreign counterparts. The spread (which covers overhead and profits) between the cost of resources to the large 'network banks' and their cost of lending to corporate users is between 8 per cent and 9 per cent. If the inflation rate were to be reduced to 5 per cent in 1986, the bond markets could very easily be well below this spread, thus putting the French banking system into its most serious squeeze since the Second World War. The reasons for cost inefficiencies are now well known : branch overcapacity, lags in automation and redundant clerical staff, lack of specialization. However, little has been done so far to increase French banks' productivity.

**The stock and bond markets** have never played the role that they play in the US or the UK. French companies have little competitive source of risk capital from these markets. In 1981, the Paris stock exchange ranked a poor eleventh in the world in terms of domestic companies capitalization, and eighth in overall transactions (Figure 47). The value of publicly quoted companies represents a percentage of GDP seven times smaller than in the US or UK.

In 1978, legislation known as the Monory Act was introduced to stimulate both buyers and sellers in the capital market. Enterprises issuing new shares were exempted from payment of company tax on dividends for a number of years, and households were allowed to deduct from their taxable income a given amount of their new financial assets acquisition. Taxes also became heavier on income from financial investments other than securities. Net issues initially increased, but the legislation did more for increasing transactions than for a sustained level of new equity (Figure 48).

The stock and bond markets remain unattractive, in fact, because of their poor returns for investors. Dividend payouts are usually low in France, providing returns between 5 per cent and 8 per cent over the last two decades, well below the inflation rate. Appreciation of stock prices on the other hand has not compensated for low dividends. In 1982, the CAC index of the Paris Stock Exchange was only 15 per cent above the level of 1970, after having been 25 per cent below from 1974 to 1978. Besides little attractive supply of quoted stocks, there is less demand in France than in most other modern economies owing to the near-inexistence of privately managed pension funds. The centralization of retirement schemes by one organization, UNEDIC, has sterilized most of the available cash. The State-owned

Figure 47

# PARIS STOCK EXCHANGE RELATIVE POSITION
## INTERNATIONAL COMPARISONS

**DOMESTIC SHARES CAPITALIZATION (31.12.1981)**
(Bill. US $)

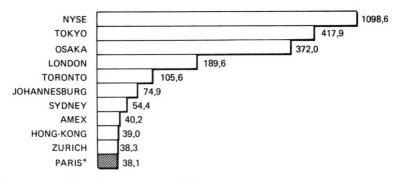

Note : Montreal not available — German markets excluded

**TRANSACTIONS OF ALL SHARES**
(1981 — Bill. US $)

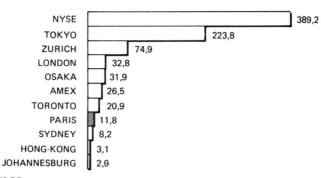

* $1 : 5,748 FF.
Source : McKinsey study

Figure 48

## PARIS STOCK EXCHANGE

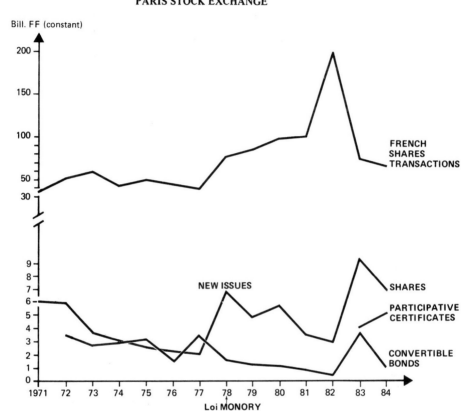

Bill. FF (constant)

Source : Telesis Analysis from Année Boursière

201

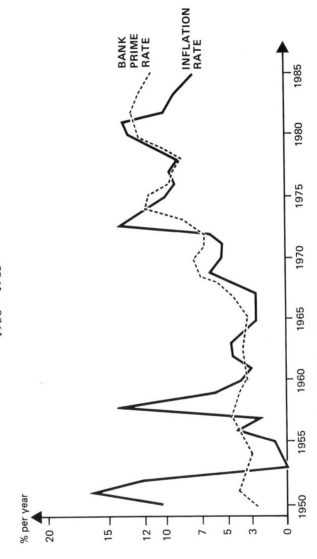

**Figure 49**

EVOLUTION OF REAL INTEREST RATES IN FRANCE
1950 – 1983

% per year

BANK
PRIME
RATE

INFLATION
RATE

*Source : Telesis Analysis from INSEE statistics*

202

channels for collecting savings at low cost and favourable fiscal conditions (Caisses d'Epargne collected by the Post Office, housing savings plans, treasury bonds) have also oriented domestic savings away from the markets.

The bond market has been much more active, even exploding in recent years, but this has been mainly due to the quick increase of public sector borrowing. The large public investments sustained throughout the 1970s, together with price controls maintained at low levels, have forced the State-owned utilities and monopolies, such as EDF or SNCF, to borrow heavily at home as well as abroad. The central government has itself dramatic lly increased its bond issues, particularly since the Left came to power. Public sector new bond issues almost doubled from 1981 to 1984 from 109 billion francs to 192 billion francs, while private sector bond issues were about five times sm ller. Interest rates have soared, also as a consequence of a weak franc against a strong dollar. The risk of 'crowding out' of private borrowings has been compensated by the flooding of the securities market with new cash coming from the former shareholders of nationalised companies, and from investors in the real estate market. The increasing needs of the public sector or a brutal privatisation of nationalized companies however will strain the small Paris securities market.

The financing of French corporations reflects the strengths and weaknesses of the country's economic development. Despite low returns nd the lack of risk capital channelled through market mechanisms, French industry kept its rate of investment at fairly high levels compared with its neighbours at least until the late 1970s. This has been possible through the heavy use of debt made available by the banking sector protected and sometimes directed by the State. The inefficiencies and high costs of a highly regulated banking sector have been partially offset by interest rate subsidies and favourable access to credit for investments meeting national priorities : exports, energy savings, automation and, more recently, employment creation. These low interest rates have been paid by the taxpayer and private savers in the form of low or even negative real interest rates (Figure 49). Implicit but systematic wealth transfers from the inactive population or uneducated savers to productive investments have allowed France to sustain its rapid expansion throughout the 1950s and 1960s, despite generally weak competitive positions in world markets. This, however, came to an end in the early 1970s, owing to several changes.

The two oil shocks and the subsequent slowdown in world trade have revealed the structural weaknesses of French industry and the risks to which its financial policies had exposed it. The changes in the financing of French industry make it impossible to get away with low profitability.

As explained in part II, the positive leverage effect which the use of debt can have on growth turned into a negative leverage when interest rates increased and rates of return decreased. Interest rates incre sed under the influence of growing public deficits and a weaker currency, and for the first time in postwar history, French corporations have had the unhappy surprise of finding themselves bearing positive real interest rates of several per cent for many years in succession. This dramatic rise in the cost of external capital - which too many managers had for too long regarded as costless - is compounded by the increasing difficulties which the banks face in coping with uncompetitive clients. Having been accustomed to easy times, and superficial analysis, they are now forced to take many 'first rate' loans as losses. Prestigious banks like Rothschild, Worms, Vernes or BUE would have been bankrupt if they had not been nationalized,and later rescued by larger banks or insurance companies.

The second change - even more worrying - is the decline of saving rates of private households since the early 1980s. Household savings have dropped from 18 per cent of income in the early 1970s down to 13 per cent in 1984, the lowest level since 1959. This severe drop in savings explains why the French are the only population in Europe not to have cut consumption despite a reduction in purchasing power. It is still difficult to say whether this is consequence of the sudden economic downturn or of fundamental changes in behavior, but the trend can only hurt the financial flexibility of corporations.

In summary, French business, which had paid little attention to its capitalists, is confronted with the mechanisms of a market economy. Owing to poor competitive positions, corporate profitability has fallen below the cost of capital, and the highly geared balance sheets cannot attract new investors.

The combination of low returns and a high cost of capital created in 1982 the worst financial squeeze for French industry of the last 15 years. Financial costs borne by corporations soared by 28 per cent in 1981 and 16 per cent in 1982. In 1983 the government had to declare a 'moratorium' for debt borrowed at rates over 12 per cent. Profitability has improved in the last three years and nominal rates are down but real interest rates remain high, owing to the long standing causes explained above. French corporations cannot continue to be financed  t a cost above return on investment. Fundamental changes are under way which seem to restore the market mechanisms in the allocation of capital and to stimulate the improvement of competitiveness. In the meanwhile, however, the State has to fill the gap more directly than before. If the corporate sector cannot ride any longer on the back of the uneducated saver (by borrowing), it will have to dig directly into the taxpayer's pocket, a difficult transition to make.

## Fundamental changes in preparation

The effects of Left and Right governments in France are always a paradox. In the financial domain, it is the conservatives who have continuously transferred wealth from their constituency (the ones who can save) to the 'productive forces'. It appears that the Left will do the opposite : restore market mechanisms and protect investors. The present administration is breaking new ground in two areas : creating attractive new financial products for the investor, and partially deregulating the banking sector.

Since 1981, a series of innovations have been introduced. A type of over-the-counter stock market, called 'second market', has been created which allows small and medium-sized companies to be listed on the various French stock exchanges, with reduced formalities and costs. More than sixty companies have been introduced to the Paris stock market in the last three years, whereas less than a handful of new securities were previously listed every year. This has made the Paris 'second market' a dynamic follower of the American Nasdaq and the British USM, and ahead of other European countries. In addition, taxation on capital gains has remained at a very favourable level (15 per cent on long term gains), while income tax rates have been increased for higher brackets.

Other forms of investment, on the other hand, have become less attractive : new forms of rent control and the end of anonymous transactions on gold have rechannelled savings into securities. The Paris Stock Exchange has never been so buoyant and the CAC index has increased from 100 in 1981 to 230 in mid-1985. Companies have massively increased their new issues of both shares and bonds, including nationalized companies allowed to float a variety of new financial instruments : non-voting share certificates, participating certificates (a mixed debt/equity intrument)and subordinated debentures. As a result the capitalization of debt has increased by 50 per cent between 1981 and 1985 and the capitalization of shares has almost doubled. New share issues have soared from a few billion francs in the 1970s to 12 billion francs in 1984 and 17 billion francs in 1985.

On the side of State control and regulation, the frozen world of French banking seems to be melting. More competition has been introduced among credit institutions which used to be monopolies or privileged (Crédit Agricole for example). Bank rationalization is being actively encouraged and some small non-viable banks have been taken over by more solid partners while others have regrouped their efforts. The very closed stockbroking profession- an old monopoly protected by regulation - has also been partially opened to competition. Finally, companies are now allowed to borrow directly and lend on the money markets without financial intermediaries.

These changes, which give more importance to market mechanisms in capital allocation, still leave industrial corporations with a serious financial gap.

**Increasing State support of industry's financial gap**

When all productive sectors are considered, French corporations have suffered from an increasingly severe financing deficit since the mid-1970s. Whereas in the 1960s, internal cash flows were sufficient to cover investments and increases in working capital, the borrowing requirements of all corporations is now widening from 23 billion francs in 1975 to 36 billion francs in 1979 and to 84 billion francs in 1982. The situation has improved in the last three years but is still worse than in 1979. As we have seen, injections of fresh equity through the market have been marginal until two years ago and corporations have had to turn to debt and State support. Transfers from the State amounted to 133 billion francs in 1982 of which 88 billion francs in operating subsidies, 16 billion francs in investment subsidies, 17 billion francs in equity to the public sector and 12 billion francs in interest rate subsidies. State transfers have increased at the very high rate of 24 per cent a year since 1974, in real terms. Although the traded sector of the economy - manufacturing, energy, trade and services - still represents less than half of these transfers, they have received most of the increase. Transfers to the manufacturing sector only, which used to be marginal, have doubled in real terms between 1979 and 1982. They now amount to 34 billion francs. When tax reductions, R&D contracts and subsidies to public centres to conduct industrial research are included, global State support to manufacturing industry is of the order of 70 billion francs. These transfers represent about 30 per cent of corporate investments in fixed assets and research and development, up from 21 per cent in the early 1970s. In comparison, the German government (Federal and local) has stabilized and even recently reduced its level of transfers to the manufacturing sector, to around 25 per cent (Figure 50).

One of the obvious reasons for this sharp increase in State transfers in France is the result of the recent nationalizations. Government is no longer a discretionary source of funds which can be shifted, but the sole shareholder facing massive deficits. The combined net income of all nationalized industrial companies (seven before 1982 and twelve after) went from 15.5 billion francs of profits in 1980, to 6.8 billion francs of losses in 1981 and 17.5 billion

**Figure 50**

## GOVERNMENT FINANCIAL TRANSFERS*
### Mining & manufacturing companies

% OF CORPORATE INVESTMENTS IN FIXED ASSETS AND R. & D.

|         | 1972-1979 | 1976 | 1977 | 1978 | 1979 | 1982 (Est.) |
|---------|-----------|------|------|------|------|-------------|
| FRANCE  | 21        | 25   | 25   | 25   | 27   | 30          |
| GERMANY | 27        | 24   | 26   | 27   | 27   | 25          |

* Includes all cash subsidies, interest rate subsidies, equity transfers to public companies, tax exemptions and R. & D. contracts

Sources : Telesis Analysis from Rapport au parlement sur les aides publiques à l'industrie, Annual reports of DGRST, FDES, CVCEP, CEA, CNES, CNET, Subvention bericht, BMFT programs, Fakten bericht, Annual reports of ERP, DEG, KFW

francs of losses in 1984 (Figure 51). The sudden change in profitability was the result of low world prices in commodities like chemicals and aluminium (4.8 billion francs of losses together), previous delays in plant rationalizations and workforce reductions (9 billion francs losses in steel for example), and a number of other more specific reasons which have little to do with the nationalizations themselves (see part II). In 1981 and 1982 all State-owned companies but two showed loss increases or profit decreases. Since 1983 there have been great improvements : seven, losing money in 1981, are profitable in 1985 ; five have increased their profitability ; and two have significantly reduced their losses. Unfortunately, one of the steel companies is losing more than before, despite numerous announcements of lay offs and plant shutdowns, and Renault had staggering record losses of 21.5 billion francs in 1984 and 1985 combined.

The strain put on the State budget by its own companies has been very severe : in the last four years, a total of almost 50 billion francs has been allocated to the publicly owned companies, with 40 per cent going to the two steel companies alone (Figure 52). This compares with a few billion francs a year before 1981, as most State-owned companies were self-financed. In addition to officially owned companies, the State is the sole creditor of a number of bankrupt companies which together need several billion francs a year in subsidies to survive. Either through the CIRI, or directly through departmental budgets, the State has found itself paying for the operating costs (wages and salaries) of the three largest shippyards and various companies like Boussac (Textiles), ARCT (textile machinery), La Chapelle Darblay (paper), Creusot-Loire (mechanical engineering), Ernault-Somua (machine tools) and various smaller ones.

More recently industry has become a subject of concern and a candidate for subsidies (and funding) from local and regional authorities. The regions can now be indirect shareholders in enterprises, through the recently created Instituts Régionaux de Participations ; they can contribute to the guarantee of locally distributed loans through the Fonds de Garantie Régionaux, and can even give direct subsidies.

Figure 51

# FINANCIAL PERFORMANCES OF THE STATE-OWNED INDUSTRIAL SECTOR

NET INCOME (Billion FF 1983)

| | 1980 | 1981 | 1984 | 1985 |
|---|---|---|---|---|
| **NATIONALIZATIONS BEFORE 1982** | | | | |
| ELF AQUITAINE | 8,00 | 4,50 | 6,00 | 5,20 |
| AIR FRANCE | 1,33 | -0,46 | 0,90 | 0,70 |
| SNIAS | 0,16 | 0,19 | 0,30 | 0,35 |
| SNECMA | 0,08 | -0,16 | 0,05 | NA |
| EMC | | -0,10 | 0,02 | 0,10 |
| CDF–CHIMIE | -0,60 | -1,27 | -0,64 | -0,70 |
| RENAULT | 0,80 | -0,74 | -11,50 | -10,0 |
| CGM | -0,50 | -0,49 | -0,29 | NA |
| **TOTAL** | 9,27 | 1,47 | -5,16 | NA |
| **NATIONALIZATIONS AFTER 1982** | | | | |
| RHONE-POULENC | -2,70 | -0,41 | 1,84 | 2,20 |
| CGE | 0,04 | 0,50 | 0,73 | 1,00 |
| SAINT GOBAIN | 1,20 | 0,55 | 0,55 | 0,70 |
| ROUSSEL-UCLAF | 0,18 | 0,16 | 0,42 | NA |
| DASSAULT | 0,43 | 0,36 | 0,40 | NA |
| THOMSON SA | 0,40 | -0,18 | 0,00 | 0,50 |
| MATRA | 0,30 | 0,20 | 0,06 | NA |
| CGCT | | -0,30 | -0,99 | -0,20 |
| BULL | 0,25 | -0,55 | -0,46 | 0,05 |
| PECHINEY | 0,80 | -3,10 | 0,55 | 0,75 |
| USINOR | -1,70 | -5,20 | -7,34 | -2,00 |
| SACILOR | -2,70 | -3,50 | -8,14 | -4,50 |
| **TOTAL** | 6,27 | -8,28 | -12,38 | NA |
| **TOTAL STATE-OWNED SECTOR** | 15,54 | -6,81 | -17,54 | NA |

*Source : Annual reports, Press communiqués*

Figure 52

## STATE EQUITY CONTRIBUTIONS TO NATIONALIZED COMPANIES
### Manufacturing sector
1982 – 1985 (Bill. FF. 1984)

| COMPANIES | 1982 | 1983 | 1984 | 1985 | TOTAL 1982-85 |
|---|---|---|---|---|---|
| **STEEL** | | | | | |
| SACILOR | 1,80 | 3,40 | 3,40 | 2,70 | 11,30 |
| USINOR | 1,40 | 2,80 | 2,10 | 2,70 | 9,00 |
| TOTAL | | | | | 20,30 |
| **CHEMICALS-PHARMACEUTICALS** | | | | | |
| CDF-CHIMIE | 0,50 | 0,30 | 1,00 | 0,66 | 2,46 |
| RHONE-POULENC | 1,30 | 0,30 | 0,30 | – | 1,90 |
| EMC | 0,10 | 0,05 | 0,20 | 0,14 | 0,49 |
| ROUSSEL-UCLAF | – | – | – | 0,04 | 0,04 |
| SECTOR RESTRUCTURING | – | 1,70 | 1,00 | 1,00 | 3,70 |
| TOTAL | | | | | 8,59 |
| **ELECTRONICS & TELECOMMUNICATIONS** | | | | | |
| BULL | – | 1,60 | 1,00 | 0,90 | 3,50 |
| THOMSON | 0,30 | 0,50 | 1,00 | 1,22 | 3,02 |
| CGCT | – | 0,40 | 0,30 | 0,40 | 1,10 |
| THOMSON-CGE | – | – | 0,70 | – | 0,70 |
| CGE | – | 0,15 | – | – | 0,15 |
| TOTAL | | | | | 8,47 |
| **AIRCRAFT** | | | | | |
| SNIAS & SNECMA | 0,25 | 0,16 | 0,21 | 0,90 | 1,52 |
| **AUTOMOTIVE** | | | | | |
| RENAULT | 1,20 | 1,00 | 1,20 | 2,80 | 6,20 |
| **MISCELLEANOUS** | | | | | |
| PECHINEY (non ferrous) | 2,30 | 0,70 | 0,15 | – | 3,15 |
| St GOBAIN (construction) | 0,20 | 0,30 | 0,15 | 0,14 | 0,79 |
| TOTAL | | | | | 3,94 |
| **TOTAL** | 9,35 | 13,36 | 12,71 | 13,60 | 49,02 |

Sources : Budget documents communicated to Parliament (planned contributions)

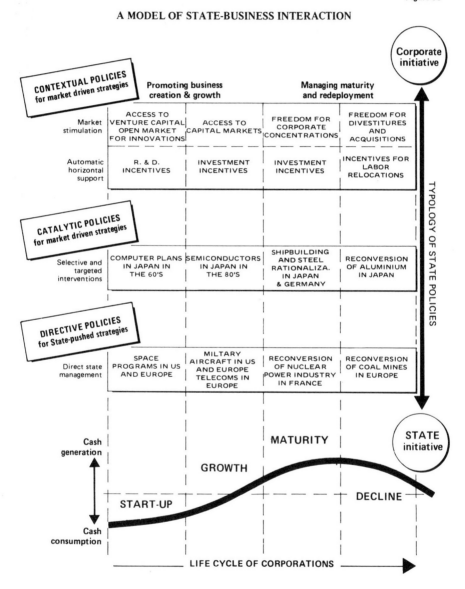

Figure 53

A MODEL OF STATE-BUSINESS INTERACTION

212

Through its various forms of shareholding and subsidies, the State is filling the gap left by private owners. The nationalizations have allowed private shareholders to leave a number of no longer profitable large companies, and to take advantage of their compensation - quite generously assessed - to invest in new stock market opportunities.

The net result is more funds for industry and a segmentation of financing methods. The State supports the large unprofitable companies which it has nationalized and a revived capital market finances private profitable ventures. Public authorities are therefore, as a whole, more and more involved in the nation's industry. More specifically, one wonders how this overall commitment has been translated into specific industrial objectives - i.e., into an industrial strategy. An analysis of public resource allocation over the last ten years suggests that the progressive enlargement of public intervention has not been matched with a balanced industrial strategy. Moreover, the concept of industrial policy is itself brought into question today much more than in the past decades, when the need for reconstruction, and then the nationalistic gaullist ideology, legitimized most of the State's efforts.

**A dangerous drifting of resource allocation**
    (a) The framework : a model for State-business cooperation (Figure 53)

Our approach is based on two dimensions : the pattern of State initiatives, and the life cycle of a corporation. Together they will allow us to segment different types of industrial policies and their relevance to various competitive situations.

The philosophies of public involvement in most industrialised countries can be characterized according to the nature of economic initiatives : the spectrum ranges from the most spontaneous to the totally planned, where the State itself becomes the entrepreneur.

If the development of successful companies is left to spontaneous market forces, public intervention will be limited to macro-economic and social policies. These typically include a favourable tax environment, the competition policy and liberty of decisions in all fields (prices, labour, foreign exchange) with the aim of creating a stimulating and competitive environment for entrepreneurial initiatives. In most industrialized countries, however, the State seeks to support corporate initiatives through 'horizontal measures' which do not differentiate between businesses, and with no strings attached. Government incentives are then devised to be as automatic and transparent as possible and to reinforce and accelerate private initiative rather than direct it. This horizontal support is organized around general objectives which can be agreed upon by most parts of society : R&D, exports, investments, sometimes employment. The State uses its tax and budgetary powers to steer resources in these directions, but with no claim to select sectors or companies.

These two forms of industrial policy ‹ macropolicies for market stimulation and horizontal support › can be called 'contextual', as they fundamentally rely on the decisions and resources of enterprises to create national wealth. It is the philosophy (at least officially) of most policy makers in the US, Germany, and more recently Japan and the UK. Smaller open economies - like Holland or Sweden ‹ have always adopted this economic philosophy and structured their State apparatus accordingly.

In other countries ‹ and indeed in 'strategic' sectors of the most liberal economies › the State has adopted 'targeted' policies with the ambition of directly influencing investment choices, and business strategies. In the case of selective interventions, the State has allocated public resources to sectors or companies, on direct judgement rather than general objectives. Defence and space research contracts, or subsidies to ailing companies are two interventions of the same nature. They both distort the natural process of market forces, either through the creation of a State-controlled market, or through the artificial resurrection of a losing competitor.

Government resources allocated to businesses need not be massive to play a role. The MITI in Japan does not have large budgets for either R&D or investment but it acts as a catalyst with the help of banks and large conglomerates and in many cases has chosen this mode of targeted intervention. This pattern of State initiative is found in varying degrees in all economies. It requires a different organization of industrial policy than that which can typically be handled by the traditional civil service. The worst outcome has resulted when governments were forced into this mode of intervention - mostly in crisis situations ᕦ without prior modification of the Administration. The recent history of liberal economies trapped in massive interventions, like Belgium and Holland, contrasts with the more successful experience of countries with more experience of 'preplanned' and targeted interventions, like Austria or even Singapore or Korea. There is often very little choice for a government confronted with the decline of its industry or the necessity to develop 'infant' industries but to learn new patterns of State initiative compatible with the rules of business competition.

The last mode, direct State management, implies that the State is one of the direct participants in business competition, and therefore loses its objectivity and neutrality towards the country's economic forces. Through nationalizations, or direct corporate creations, many European governments have chosen ᕦ particularly after the Second World War ᕦ to be directly responsible for wealth creation. France has gone probably further than any in that direction, as we have seen in chapter 1. This is not to say that direct State management is always incompatible with the rules of successful business competition. This is sometimes necessary in new industries which face uncertain markets and need massive resources for development, before any commercial result can be achieved (as in Space). It causes, however, many conflicts of interest and rigidities in resource allocation and may also be a high cost policy method. In all cases, direct State management should be seen as exceptional and temporary and the organization of State ventures should treat other companies fairly.

The challenge for any modern economy is to combine and nurture the various types of economic initiatives free from ideology. The more export oriented economies like Japan or Germany are also those where spontaneous market forces have coexisted with strong State policies, particularly in technology and sectoral reconversions. These countries have shown that the State is a complex player in today's world : sometimes the custodian of free and open competition for everyone, and sometimes an active participant in the long term development of the economy. The US government itself has been the originator of several key industrial transformations with its role in defence, space or energy. Politically divided societies like the UK or France have been less successful at making corporations and the State allies rather than enemies. Too often contextual policies and targeted policies have been seen as mutually exclusive and have been chosen on ideological grounds rather than on factual analysis.

Along the second dimension, the position of the company on its life cycle determines the nature of the external support it may require. At the take-off stage, there is no internal cash generation to compensate for R&D and marketing investments. The company will therefore need equity capital (venture capital) for investment, mostly in non-tangible assets. During the growth stage, cash consumption to finance working capital and fixed assets is at its highest, requiring long term funds. The maturity phase provides on the other hand  the maximum net cash generation, and therefore the financing of asset renewal or diversification, while the decline phase, well managed, should also  generate cash but this may be needed to finance social relocations.

This financial life cycle has clear implications for public policies : at the stage of start-up and growth, most companies need R&D funds, risk-capital, or tax incentives for re-investment, while from the maturity to the decline phase, companies will need funds for modernization, diversification, and/or social reconversion. The position of a corporation on its life cycle also determines its potential for creating value added. Start-up and growing companies create new sources of wealth and therefore new employment opportunities. They tend to rely, however, on external (often foreign) expertise and components as their experience base is still limited. Mature and even declining companies, on the other hand, lose value added as prices fall or markets slow down, but have typically built a large pool of internal expertise, and local subsuppliers, which depend on their survival, and regeneration.

Resource allocation trade-offs are therefore very complex. The net effect on skill levels, value added and exports should be carefully assessed, as well as their future

216

trends, and compared to the cash investments necessary to make a company competitive in its business. The best type of State intervention should be chosen, taking into consideration the solidity of corporate initiatives, the environment for risk taking and also the experience of government agencies in handling one type of policy rather than another.

In summary, Figure 53 decribes the segmentation of industrial policies. There is no single prescription of the best mode of State intervention for a whole country or a whole sector. What was good for Japan in computers in the 1960s did not succeed in France at the same time and was certainly irrelevant for the US. Market stimulation in telecommunications through deregulation cannot have the same impact for US industry serving a homogeneous market from a leadership position, and for European industry plagued already with fragmentation and heterogeneous product lines. This model demonstrates the subtleties of State-business interaction and advocates a well-timed, segmented approach for government policies, rather than ideological statements concerning free market vs. State intervention. The Japanese government has shown that State policies can be of a catalytic nature and use the best levers of market competition.

The allocation of public resources to industry in France will be described using the same model. For this analysis we have grouped together all forms of financial transfers to industrial companies (subsidies, tax rebates, R&D contracts, equity to public companies) and allocated the various sectors in the policy quadrants according to our best judgement as to the kind of intervention and the company's position. We have compared two periods : 1972-73, which represents the end of the de Gaulle - Pompidou policies and the last glorious years of French prosperity ; and 1983-84, which is the last period available and reflects the impact of both the changes in government policies and the shift in French industry's competitive position and growth rate.

(b) The shifts of French industrial policy in the last ten years (Figures 54 and 55)

Over time, the allocation of funds shows :

н an increased share for the mature and declining sectors, despite absolute stability in the funding of start-up and growing sectors, and continuity in targeted sectors ;

- a drift towards more support to targeted interventions under the pressure of changing economic circumstances.

At a sectoral level, the weight of the mature or declining sectors has increased notably, owing both to automatically allocated resources and to specific sectoral policies. Automatic tools designed to accompany economic development have been distorted to bear the cost of industrial and social relocations, or to sustain artificially the profitability of,or employment in, uncompetitive corporations (through subsidized loans). Former mechanisms have been diverted from their original purposes, and new ones have been created which have ambiguous and sometimes conflicting objectives : the same mechanism may subsidize robotics and job creation in the same business. As far as targeted policies are concerned, the growth sectors used to benefit the most from public funding in the early seventies, whereas ten years later the balance is equal between the growth and non-growth sectors ; the increased relative importance of non-growth sectors coincides with a stability н in absolute terms н in the funding of the major public technological ventures.

The choice of start-up and growth sectors supported by the State has not changed during the period, except for the automotive industry, which was fast-growing on its own in the early 1970s and is now. positioned in a maturity phase. Aeronautics, nuclear, space, computer, electronics and off-shore industries are still the core of the French national effort, both on the civil and military sides. The allocation of funds to these sectors shows great stability. The nationalizations of 1982 have strengthened the traditional close linkage between the State and the enterprises of these sectors : Thomson CSF, Matra, Bull in electronics, Dassault in aeronautics, CGE (and ITT-France) in telecommunications, are now part of the public sector. This reinforces the political

218

legitimacy of the massive State support. Furthermore, the recent successes in aeronautics (Airbus) and space (Ariane) show that the time scale of industrial programmes is necessarily the long run, and that no major shift can be expected. The socialists have totally endorsed the sectoral choices made before them.

Therefore, the relative decline in share of these sectors is only due to the growing proportion of mature and declining sectors benefiting from State transfers.

As a matter of fact, there is also a large continuity in the sectors supported : steel, shipyards and coal constitute the permanent trilogy. Continuous financial support has not alleviated their cash drain. France is not the only country in this situation, but the growth of State support in recent years " in steel and shipbuilding in particular "has been higher ·in France than in any other European country. In addition a number of other sectors are now calling for a similar kind of support because of structural difficulties : chemicals, fertilizers, aluminium, paper, textiles and most worryingly, the automotive industry, which used to be one of France's healthiest sectors. The State has a shareholder's stake in most of these sectors and none of these drains is likely to disappear fast, except perhaps in aluminium and chemicals owing to favourable world price and exchange rate levels. Domestic coal still limits oil imports and generates currency savings, and as such will continue to be subsidized. Forecasts for shipyards in 1984-85 anticipate an even larger State commitment. Steel cannot self-finance its huge needs for modernization and the cost of layoffs and early retirement. In the automotive industry, the State's role has evolved from that of a passive shareholder of one healthy and growing company (Renault) to that of fund provider of the whole industry (equity to Renault and cheap loans to Peugeot).

The increasing importance of declining and troubled sectors in the allocation of public funds illustrates the acuteness of the industrial crisis but also reveals the central issue of any industrial strategy : how to handle efficiently the shift of an industrial base from mature or declining activities to start-up or growing industries, or, in other words, how to achieve portfolio management on a national scale. In France, it seems that the technologies of the future benefit from

Figure 54

# ALLOCATION OF GOVERNMENT FUNDS TO INDUSTRY
## 1973 – 1974

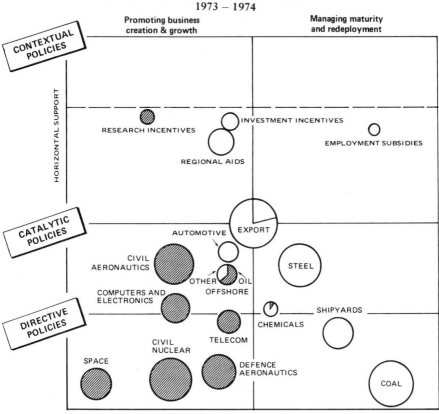

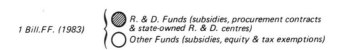

Sources : Telesis Analysis

Figure 55

# ALLOCATION OF GOVERNEMENT FUNDS TO INDUSTRY
## 1982 – 1983

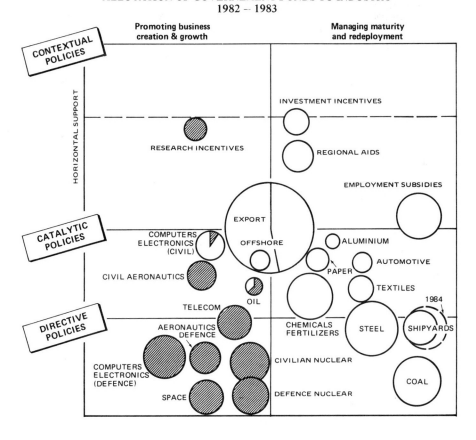

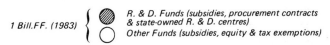

1 Bill.F.F. (1983)

R. & D. Funds (subsidies, procurement contracts & state-owned R. & D. centres)

Other Funds (subsidies, equity & tax exemptions)

Sources : Telesis Analysis

Figure 56

## GOVERNMENT SUPPORT FOR NEW TECHNOLOGIES

| | Government R. & D. funds | | |
|---|---|---|---|
| | Average annual (Mill. US $) | Period | TOTAL (Mill. US $) |
| **INFORMATION TECHNOLOGIES** | | | |
| VLSI/VHSIC | | | |
| — JAPAN | 66 | 1976-79 | 264 |
| — USA | 35 | 1980-85 | 210 |
| — GERMANY | 14 | 1977-83 | 100 |
| — FRANCE | 17 | 1977-82 | 100 |
| — UK | 23 | 1979-84 | 140 |
| SOFTWARE | | | |
| — JAPAN | 20 | 1971-84 | 278 |
| — GERMANY | 22 | 1981-83 | 66 |
| — UK (PLAN) | 23 | 1983-88 | 135 |
| CAD | | | |
| — JAPAN | 12 | 1975-81 | 85 |
| — GERMANY | 8 | 1980-82 | 23 |
| — UK (PLAN) | 4 | 1983-88 | 25 |
| 5th GENERATION COMPUTER | | | |
| — JAPAN | 33 | 1982-88 | 230 |
| — UK (PLAN) | 17 | 1983-88 | 100 |
| — GERMANY | | IN PREPARATION | |
| **BIOTECHNOLOGY** | | | |
| — USA | 57 | 1978-83 | 342 |
| — JAPAN | 14 | 1978-90 | 180 |
| — GERMANY | 27 | 1974-82 | 190 |
| — FRANCE | 30 | 1982-85 | 120 |
| — UK | 46 | 1983 | N.A. |
| **NEW MATERIALS** | | | |
| — USA | 136 | 1981-83 | 410 |
| — JAPAN | 11 | 1982-92 | 125 |
| — GERMANY | 10 | 1978-84 | 67 |
| **ENERGY** | | | |
| CONSERVATION & ALTERNATIVE SOURCES | | | |
| — USA | 2300 | 1981-83 | 7000 |
| — GERMANY | 199 | 1977-80 | 796 |
| — FRANCE | 147 | 1983 | — |
| — JAPAN | 64 | 1974-90 | 971 |
| — UK | 30 | 1976-79 | 90 |
| NUCLEAR | | | |
| — USA | 1900 | 1981-83 | 5700 |
| — JAPAN | 580 | 1975-80 | 3480 |
| — FRANCE | 528 | Budget 82 | — |
| — GERMANY | 449 | 1977-80 | 1796 |
| — UK | 249 | 1976-79 | 750 |

Sources : Telesis Analysis from
  US : AAAS, DOD, DOE, NSF, NIH
  JAPAN : MITI
  FRANCE : MRI, AIST
  GERMANY : BMFT
  UK : DOI

smaller public support than official pronouncements would make one believe. International comparisons show France's lag in R&D, and more generally the poor position of France in technologies of the future. Although the present government has halted the slowdown of the 1970s in terms of R&D expenditures, the objective of 2.5 per cent of GDP will not be achieved (expenditure will rather be 2 per cent). France does not compare favourably even with its European neighbours in a number of strategic fields, but especially in information technologies (Figure 56). The sum of researchers, scientists and engineers also lies below the rest. As for R&D expenditure in higher education, France lags behind Germany, and, like its European partners, has not followed the growth rate of the late 1970s of the US and Japan, which is an alarming indicator of future competitive strength.

Together with the increasing cost of targeted policies, the second major shift in resource allocation, which seems more tolerated than desired, concerns the explosion of the automatic subsidies, mainly for exports, employment and interest rate relief. This runaway expenditure is not the result of an aggressive and deliberate industrial policy but rather the outcome of uncontrollable mechanisms whose cost has dramatically soared with changing macroeconomic conditions.

First, the largest part (80 per cent) of the export policy cost is due to the interest rate differential between France's and the OECD's 'consensus' rate. It is therefore a means of offsetting an overall economic handicap more than a way of improving the basic competitiveness of a sector. In parallel, the sector which does profit the most from this system – construction and engineering – does so for the sake of the more global objective of promoting France's presence abroad (the positioning in the matrix in Figures 55 and 56 as a semi-automatic/semi-targeted policy is due to this sectoral bias). However, given the present market slowdown in large construction works (decrease in OPEC's revenues, insolvency of developing countries) the cost of export policy should at least be stabilized, after an average growth of 18 per cent a year in real terms in the last decade. In fact for the first time, in the summer of 1985, the consensus rate exceeded the French domestic interest rate.

Employment subsidies are also not primarily a tool of industrial policy. The amount which appears here does not include unemployment assistance but only the subsidies given to enterprises to reduce their cost of labour. The funds allocated to the textile industry, massively helped through that system, do not belong to the same quadrant of the matrix because the process was not automatic but related to short-term investment and employment commitments. These subsidies concern issues such as temporary unemployment, training contracts, the employment of youth, etc. They do not belong as such to industrial policy, except if they are integrated into a larger framework, setting the desired balance between the cost of labour and the cost of capital, or the relative intensity of these two factors in the long-run industrial structure. For instance, and as an illustrative caricature, the automotive industry would need now (has needed for many years already) low-cost capital rather than low-cost labour.

The third main component of the automatic subsidies concerns the relief of interest rates for medium or long term loans. Here again, although this kind of support is welcomed by business, the present heavy cost of the measure does not follow an explosive growth of investment ⅎ actually stagnant in manufacturing industry as a whole - but results from the differential between the market rate and expected return on investment. The causes of low profitability are not addressed, but its consequences alleviated. French industry has benefited for years from negative real interest rates. The brutal squeeze felt now brings the public authorities to subsidize extensively the cost of capital : between 1980 and 1983, the budget for such subsidies almost quintupled in real terms and 1984 also registered a sharp increase. A moratorium set in October 1982 allows also a re-financing of the long-term debts contracted earlier at a rate of more than 12 per cent.

These measures, as for exports and employment, mostly follow the global objective of supporting general activity levels rather than acting on industrial structures and competitive positions. Even if this definition of industrial policy were to be in theory a good one, it is clear that this kind of support has a decreasing impact on the national output, because of the increasing international exposure of the economy. Besides, as mentioned earlier, the State has a de facto stake in the present shift in industrial structure, given its direct responsibility both for the major industrial groups (in growing and in declining sectors), and for the scope of deindustrialization.

To summarize, until now, the State's industrial policy has mainly been a series of ad-hoc responses to political demands : the mechanisms designed in a period of prosperity have been maintained during the years of crisis. The cherished high-tech sectors have not been sacrified. The drains have been quite generously filled. However, the system (and more generally the entire welfare system of the 1960s and 1970s) is ready to explode. The drains may absorb the majority of public funds, and even jeopardize the large technological programmes, as already indicated by cutbacks in the 1985 budget to the technology based nationalized companies.

French industrial policy has not formulated priorities in fund allocation early and firmly enough to guide the basic shift in the structure of national value added. Paradoxically the need for a strong commitment comes at a time when the idea of an industrial policy is becoming more and more controversial.

In the 1950s and 1960s, the scope of reconstruction after the war, and then the Gaullist aura, legitimised to a large extent public intervention. In the 1970s, there was a relative consensus, not on industrial policy itself, but on the role of the State to offset the social consequences of the industrial decline of sectors or regions, mainly through rather generous unemployment compensation. The Left majority, which assumed power in 1981, came in with the ambitious objective of controlling a large part of the productive sector, the financial system, and the allocation of R & D resources. Emphasis was put on the means and on the symbols of such control more than on its objectives. Then, an increasing consciousness of the industrial crisis focussed the recent years on corporate strategies : the public industrial sector was extensively reshaped. Today, the financial constraints and the general political consensus for the stabilization and, if possible, the reduction of the share of State expenditure in GDP, tend to limit the scope of ambitions. Thus public

225

enterprises have been asked to return to profitability by 1986. Equity endowments have been stabilized ; in late 1984, the government asked that some loans with reduced interest rates be reimbursed before their maturity ; it has also taken higher dividends. For example, EDF, the electricity utility, will have to pay 8 per cent dividends in 1985 as opposed to its former 3 per cent or 5 per cent dividends.

Still, when a State is so heavily engaged in industry, it cannot rely on unplanned spin-offs from separate political decisions like defence or foreign policies. It must have a thorough understanding of the effects of its policies on business competition, and carefully address the obstacles and opportunities French companies face in markets.

When the State is the main customer or a least exercises effective control on product specifications and prices, it can influence corporate strategies in a 'targeted' approach. This is where Figures 54 and 55 show the historical focus of French governments in the promotion of new growth sectors through public procurement and State initiative. In open markets where the competitive battle lies in the hands of hundreds (or millions) of independent players the State can only act through free market forces.

## 4. THE RESULTS OF INDUSTRIAL POLICIES DRIVEN BY STATE PROCUREMENT

If 'industrial policy' has been a meaningful concept in France, it has mainly been in cases where the State had a high degree of control of market demand and could therefore tailor its interventions to its own needs. This control of the market can come from the fact that the products are purchased by public customers - such as military fighter aircraft - or that prices, standards and distribution are regulated by the State - such as for petroleum products in France. In those cases, the State can determine or strongly influence product characteristics, price levels, size and timing of demand, service requirements, etc. It can therefore choose the suppliers, exercise control on corporate decisions or engage in arms-length negotiations about R&D plans, investments, employment, or international cooperation. The corporations' strategic decisions are derived from the State's needs and have to comply with State criteria and objectives. This is the case, of course, of all major Western democracies in areas such as defence procurement or for many countries' public telecommunications networks. France, however, has effectively used the purchasing and regulatory power of the State in more sectors of industry than other 'free market' economies. It is also the only developed economy which has explicitly used public procurement to enforce industrial strategies in so many sectors, over an extended period of time. This has resulted in a powerful network of agencies, publicly-owned research institutes and quasi-industrial monopolies which we will briefly describe before we try to assess the effects on growth and competitive positions.

### The methods used
The French State has followed a conscious industrial policy derived from its procurement needs in five key areas : defence, telecommunications, nuclear energy, mass transport and space. Other smaller sectors include broadcasting and

medical equipment but the role of the State has been less decisive. In those five key sectors, policies have been formulated and implemented through the joint efforts of two or three powerful parties : a government procurement agency (or a publicly owned customer), one or two exclusive industrial suppliers and sometimes a separate public research institute (see Figures 58 and 59).

In the defence sectors, the procurement and industrial decisions have been concentrated in the powerful Délégation Générale à l'Armement (DGA) which is part of the Defence Ministry. DGA is both a procurement agency (for R & D and production contracts) and an industrial operator which directly supervises the State military 'arsenaux' producing ships, munitions, and road vehicles. It has also developed a very active and efficient international marketing staff (DAI) which sells French military hardware (whether private or public) to foreign countries, and trains foreign military staff. It acts as a 'tutor', a source of funds and a promoter for all French companies engaged in defence work. As such it has a Government 'commissioner' on the boards of private defence contractors, with power to examine internal accounts, pricing and profit margins. It has to authorize every foreign investment - or acquisition - in defence industries and plays an active role in promoting mergers and acquisitions among French companies. This was the case of airframe manufacturers in the early 1960s when the decision was taken to regroup Sud-Aviation and Nord-Aviation in SNIAS (Aérospatiale) and Dassault and Breguet in another group. It was the case more recently when SNECMA was asked to acquire SEP (Ariane's propulsion system developer) or when Aérospatiale and Crouzet were 'invited' to take over SFENA (in avionics). The DGA is in reality the agency setting strategic directions, moulding organizations and designating management for the aircraft and missile industries. Its degree of control over the electronic industry is weaker because of the higher proportion of civilian business and the countervailing influence of the PTT. DGA top officials come from the same schools as private industry executives : the 'Corps des Ingénieurs de l'Armement', 'Ecole navale' or 'Sup Aero' which serve as graduate engineering schools after Polytechnique. Many DGA civil servants go to industry after ten years of duty with the Government. Former DGA chiefs like Hughes de l'Estoile and André Martre, for example, are respectively number 2 at Dassault and number 1 at Aérospatiale. Many other ex-DGA executives now hold key engineering or management positions at Dassault, Turbomeca, etc.

Given the resources and power of DGA in setting the direction for French defence industries, the State has not felt a need to establish its own research organization. Defence procurement is also concerned with too many technologies and sectors of industry for it to be realistic to concentrate in one large institute the scientific resources necessary. DGA therefore contracts out research to companies, or other specialized public institutes like CEA (for nuclear weapons) or CNET (for military communication). This support explains the high level of in-house technical expertise reached by French industry in several defence applications. Thomson, for example, employs close to 4,000 engineers in R&D and has reached world levels of excellence in advanced technologies such as high resolution tubes, radar and mobile telecommunications, thanks to the continuous support of the defence budget and the sophisticated requirements of the French Armed Forces. As opposed to the US research system, however, universities are not beneficiaries of defence contracts. This is a major obstacle to cross-fertilization between the academic community and industry, and a reason for the gap existing in France between basic sciences and industrial applications.

In telecommunications, the key player is the Direction Générale des Télécommunications (DGT), a branch of the PTT. DGT has fairly similar powers to DGA. It is the sole operator and therefore the only customer for all the French network equipment (switches, transmission, satellites), as well as the regulatory body for all end-user equipment such as PBX, facsimile equipment, answering machines and telephone sets. It can, for example, set standards which effectively prevent imports and regulate domestic competition. As a monopolist operating company, DGT decides on the introduction of new products and services for consumers and businesses. DGT has gone further than DGA in its industrial role, by creating fully owned subsidiaries to develop, produce

Figure 58

INDUSTRIAL POLICY IN STATE–CONTROLLED MARKETS
A trilateral relationship

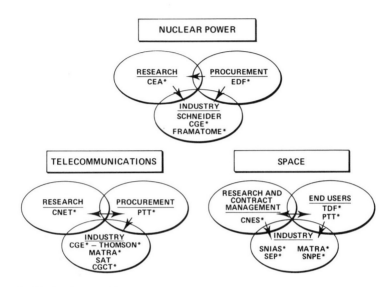

→ Direction of strongest influence

* State owned or State majority
controlled agencies and companies

230

Figure 59

## INDUSTRIAL POLICY IN STATE–CONTROLLED MARKETS
### A bilateral relationship

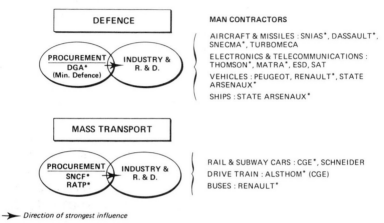

DEFENCE

PROCUREMENT DGA* (Min. Defence) → INDUSTRY & R. & D.

MAN CONTRACTORS

AIRCRAFT & MISSILES : SNIAS*, DASSAULT*, SNECMA*, TURBOMECA

ELECTRONICS & TELECOMMUNICATIONS : THOMSON*, MATRA*, ESD, SAT

VEHICLES : PEUGEOT, RENAULT*, STATE ARSENAUX*

SHIPS : STATE ARSENAUX*

MASS TRANSPORT

PROCUREMENT SNCF* RATP* → INDUSTRY & R. & D.

RAIL & SUBWAY CARS : CGE*, SCHNEIDER

DRIVE TRAIN : ALSTHOM* (CGE)

BUSES : RENAULT*

→ Direction of strongest influence

* State owned or State majority controlled agencies and companies

231

and market products and services. Its subsidiary, France-Câbles et Radio, for example, has sales of around one billion francs and is active in various businesses such as answering and pageing equipment, electronic mail, satellite transmission and telecopying. DGT can therefore be a direct competitor of its own suppliers. It operates its own testing facilities and funds a publicly owned research institute, CNET, with more than 2,000 engineers, active in all fields of telecommunications. The CNET can cooperate and/or compete with French telecommunication industry R&D centres.

The DGT is also the 'tutor' and promoter of the French telecommunications industry. In the mid-1970s, for example, it forced Ericsson to sell its French operations to Thomson in order to secure a second supplier beside CIT-Alcatel. It also prevented Thorn from acquiring Locatel, a rental organization. The DGT shapes the profiles of the major French firms active in the field by deciding on R&D contracts and industrial orders without real open competition : Alcatel-Thomson (CGE group) gets the lion's share (around 80 percent) with small pieces going to Thomson-Telephone (now controlled by CGE), Matra, SAT, TPI (Philips's French subsidiary) and other smaller firms. Like the DGA, the DGT has developed an international marketing organization (DAII) which seeks to promote French standards, equipment and services throughout the world, and operates branch offices in several countries. The symbiosis between DGT and industry is actively supported by cross-careers. DGT high ranking officials often come from the same schools (Polytechnique and Télécom) and go into industry after some time in the civil service.

In nuclear energy, all the decisions are made within a 'triangle' of influence. The monopolist national utility - EDF - is the sole customer and operator and therefore can decide on equipment specifications, safety standards, prices and profit margins for suppliers and quantities ordered. EDF is one of the most powerful organizations in postwar France, the second largest employer and capital spender after the PTT. It is EDF which embarked on an ambitious conversion from coal-fired to oil-fired power plants, to hydro-electricity, and, since the early 1970s, to nuclear power. It has also invested in one of the most efficient and modern transmission networks in the world, pioneering, for example, very high voltage lines and gas insulated circuit breakers. Unlike the PTT, EDF has never broken out of its charter as an operator. It has not developed its own research centres, engineering or industrial subsidiaries. These roles have been left to the two other groups of players.

For historical reasons (i.e. the A bomb programme) it is the Commissariat à l'Energie Atomique (CEA) which has been responsible for technology development. CEA is France's largest research centre (10,000 engineers and technicians) and conducts the military and civil nuclear programmes. It has attracted top scientists and engineers who have been able to give the country a full nuclear capability. In civil applications, the CEA has adapted and improved the PWR Westinghouse technology which has been exported to South Africa and South Korea and will be introduced in China, and perhaps in Israël and Egypt ; it has invented a new way to dispose of nuclear waste through 'vitrification' and is now one of the few institutes in the world successfully developing advanced fast-breeder reactors (e.g. Super Phoenix now in operation). The CEA has developed spin-off technologies in several other fields, including nuclear resonance medicine, robotics, sensors and computer software. In microelectronics, the CEA operates what is considered as the top French research institute in the field, the LETI in Grenoble, which has developed for example several MOS integrated circuits. This activity ¬ together with EFCIS, another CEA subsidiary producing integrated circuits (ICs) ¬ has recently been transferred to Thomson, a more logical parent. Besides being the most powerful research centre in France, CEA is also one of the largest industrial holding companies, with a diversified portfolio of businesses created or acquired over the last thirty years and with total sales of about 20 billion francs. This is a clear illustration of how State-driven capitalism has flourished in postwar France, and particularly in the Gaullist period. CEA controls COGEMA, the company responsible for raw material processing and uranium reprocessing, a rather successful operation which until 1981 was run by Maurice Besse, the new head of Renault. It is COGEMA which has invested in the Pierrelatte, Tricastin plants, and in one of the world's leading reprocessing plants in

La Hague. COGEMA is now an effective exporter of its processes and know-how, including to Japan. CEA and Creusot-Loire jointly owned the nuclear plant engineering firm FRAMATOME which has been reponsible for French industrial investments in the field, and is now seeking to establish new export markets.

The last partner group of the 'nuclear triangle' is of course industry itself, which now consists mainly of Schneider for vessel production (formerly Creusot-Loire) and CGE for the conventional part (Alsthom in turbines and generators). The civil engineering work has been contracted to a few large firms like Spie-Batignolles (Schneider) or Campenon- Bernard.

**In mass transport and space,** the role of State-run organizations has been as decisive, although the resources involved and the industrial spin-off at stake are not of the same magnitude.

The railway company - SNCF - is of course the key player for train technology and has indeed promoted French leadership very aggressively and consistently in this field, including record-breaking electric locomotives in the 1950s, modern signalling and control systems, and lately the TGV, France's high-speed train. The Paris-Lyon TGV, running on 400 km of new track and linking the two cities in two hours, has been a 10 billion francs investment programme, totally developed and financed by SNCF. It is now, after two years of operation, one of the most successful and profitable infrastructure investments in France.Two other links are now being planned or studied between Paris and Bordeaux, and between Paris, Brussels and Cologne. This investment programme is only matched in the Western world by Japan, and the two countries are indeed the two head-on contenders for leadership in export markets. The Paris subway operator - RATP - has played a similar role in technology development and infrastructure investments. The RER - greater Paris's high-speed subway - is one of the most modern and extensive networks of its kind in the world.

Both SNCF and RATP have stayed within the limits of their role as an operator : they have financed infrastructure, specified the systems, coordinated industrial sub-contracting, but have left R & D and production to industry. The only direct role they have effectively played is that of an exporter of systems and technologies, through their engineering subsidiaries SOFRERAIL (for SNCF) and SOFRETU (for RATP). French subway technology has been exported to a number of foreign cities like Montreal, Mexico, Caracas, Cairo and Lagos. This has in turn generated large civil engineering contracts for French firms. The TGV could be exported to some US regions and become a basis for a pan-European approach to modern surface transportation.

The space organization - CNES - is both a research facility for military and civil applications, a procurement agency acting for final customers (such as PTT or the Army) and an industrial coordinator. It was CNES which pushed the concept of a new European launcher - Ariane - after the failures of the former attempts at ELDO and ESRO. The French State has financed almost two-thirds of Ariane and CNES has been its main architect.

Other State organizations with procurement or regulatory functions which have played a role in industrial policy include the former ORTF (now TDF) in broadcast equipment and now in TV satellites, Gaz de France in pipelines and home appliances, and AFME (a recently formed agency) in energy saving and solar and geothermal energy. Despite their smaller resources, the pattern of behaviour and interface with industry is very similar.

## Success factors and weaknesses

The factors which have contributed to successful industrial development can also generate their own 'antidotes'. We will first review the cases which can be considered as sucesses, before turning to the pitfalls and dangers of industrial policies exclusively driven by State procurement, or relying too much on State initiatives.

The success factors are all related to the existence of a strong and resourceful procurement organization which can combine under the same umbrella the roles of a customer, technology developer and industrial planner. The main points of leverage which cannot be activated as well (or as quickly) by private shareholders and free market forces are of five kinds.

235

First, by being able to plan their capital expenditure in the long term (fifteen to twenty years for defence, ten years for nuclear or telecommunications), and to commit large financial resources, State procurement creates attractive market conditions for business. The cycles are more predictable than in free markets and the long term outlook allows for riskier investments. This has allowed, for example, French industry to gear up in nuclear plants or space rocket launchers, and indeed to catch up with established leaders in the US. No French company was resourceful enough to develop these systems without a guaranteed domestic market.

Second, the conditions of competition are more favourable. R&D and prototype contracts financed by the State generally bear the major risks, and prices are most often calculated on a 'cost plus' basis with guarantees for cost over-runs in initial phases. It would be unheard of for a French (or any country's) defence or telecommunications contractor to be losing money on domestic orders. In fact, the only high-tech companies which have been profitable in France are State contractors : Thomson-CSF (except for 1981-83), CGE, Framatome, Matra military division, SNECMA and Aérospatiale military businesses, Dassault. The civilian divisions of the same companies or other corporations not engaged in State procurement (like Bull) have most often suffered losses. This is what has attracted several captains of industry to these businesses : Ambroise Roux, the 'tycoon' who led CGE for almost fifteen years, picked telecommunications and tried to get into nuclear with an alternative technology to Baron Empain of Empain-Schneider, who gained control of the essential part of the nuclear industry, as well as much of the railway equipment industry.

Third, the State concern to have reliable and resourceful suppliers in strategic equipment has led to the formation of some of the largest conglomerates of French industry : Empain-Schneider, Thomson, CGE, Aérospatiale. These companies have been able to dominate their own sector on the domestic scene, often by mergers with former competitors. This results of course in more stable sales and earnings levels, and helps to avoid overcapacity.

236

Fourth, State procurement covers most of the advanced technologies. This has allowed the key French companies to invest early in R&D and indeed gain an early lead in technology (not always followed up commercially) : high resolution displays (Thomson), fast-breeder reactors (CEA), digital switching (Cit-Alcatel), very high-voltage switchgear (Merlin-Gerin), automatic pilots (SFENA).

Finally, a strong and lucrative domestic market is a good basis for aggressive exports, and may result in solid international competitive positions as demonstrated by Dassault in fighter aircraft, SNIAS in missiles and helicopters, or Thomson in radar transmissions.

**The dangers** of industrial policies driven by State procurement are, however, implicit in the confusion between the roles of customer and industrial planner. When the procurement organization becomes too powerful or too one-sided, resources can be wasted or industry misled.

The first danger is to misuse R&D resources and to focus the company on the exclusive needs of a single large customer. This can result in different standards or product features which work as barriers to early internationalization. On the other hand, competitors operating from small countries with no important public customer have usually adapted their products more quickly to export markets : Ericsson in telecommunications, Asea in locomotives, or BBC in electricity generation have gained a worldwide presence much earlier than their French counterparts. The misuse of R&D resources can lead to even greater problems, when the requirements imposed by a powerful State customer favour technical achievements at the expense of economic performance. France's engineering culture particularly lends itself to technical prowess or prestige. The filière 'graphite-gaz' for nuclear power, the SECAM colour TV or the Biarritz optic fiber and visiophone experiment are all costly misdirections of development talents, which never led to internationally competitive positions. Few companies in France have been farsighted and/or strong enough to impose **their** product concepts instead of being passively supported by their State clients. Merlin-Gerin in switchgear and Jeumont-Schneider in PBX have been independent enough from the power of EDF and the PTT, respectively, to become successful in exports with an autonomous product development. But in general, the search for technical performance at any cost has resulted in high prices paid by the domestic consumer, and a lack of competitive products abroad.

The second danger is the lack of experience and investment in long run standardized production processes, while State requirements are more for "one-off" customized deliveries. As a consequence of their strong technical values, French State clients tend constantly to modify specifications and sometimes technologies. Almost every nuclear plant designed by Framatome for EDF has led to important design modifications and Creusot-Loire has had difficulties in gaining experience from repeat orders. The French national satellite programmes (Telecom 1, TDF 1) have different contractors, and have been very high cost and technologically ambitious. Gradually the best engineers and scientists in French industry, whether at Thomson, CIT-Alcatel, CEA or Matra, have been geared towards unique sophistication rather than standardization. They aim at a product's theoretical performance rather than on zero default production runs, or low production costs.

The third danger of determining business strategy via State procurement is systematically to favour national over transnational solutions. Rather than seeking trans-European alliances or even international joint ventures, French companies have merged among themselves to achieve the scale required by State procurement (see part II). This nationalistic concentration movement has often been encouraged, sometimes initiated by the State, which was eager to deal with large and resourceful suppliers able to meet the highest technical standards as well as reasonable cost performance while keeping control over the domestic scene.

Over the last twenty years, this process has resulted, for example, in the formation of one military aircraft supplier through the merger of Dassault and Breguet, one engine supplier for aircraft (Snecma which regrouped the engine divisions of three companies), one public exchange manufacturer (CGE now controls the Thomson telephone division). The French private capitalist establishment divided into two camps in the early 1960s. One group, with A. Roux of CGE, P. Richard of Thomson, or Baron Empain of Schneider, sought to take advantage of expanding public markets and establish domestic quasi monopolies. It has, however, lost some strategic and financial independence by linking its fate to the State and has geared most of its new developments to the requirements of the domestic market. The other group, including Saint-Gobain, Pechiney or Rhône-Poulenc, divested from businesses where State influence was overwhelming or turned down opportunities to diversify in State controlled markets. Although the new wave of nationalizations in 1982 has apparently and ironically put these two groups back together into a single State-owned family, they still remain very different kinds of corporations by their degree of autonomy, internationalization and management style.

The fourth danger of industrial policies driven by State procurement concerns potential conflicts arising from the various government agencies involved. In France, the sources of power can be, for example, split between the purchasing agency, the Finance Ministry and the Ministry of Industry. The higher the degree of State control of markets, the greater are the risks of divergence between different political objectives. The procurement agency will try, in general, to maximize its technical influence (at the risk of higher costs) and will keep competing suppliers as a means of better bargaining. It will, however, have a narrow view of cross-industry and cross-technology synergies. The Treasury will watch short term cash flows and debt levels, and the Ministry of Industry will try to influence business strategies through pressure for acquisitions, mergers or international cooperation. Other departments can increase the confusion by imposing short-term objectives like regional job creation or the bailing out of lame ducks. The end result can be discontinuities in strategies and lack of credibility abroad.

Finally, State procurement can be misused when it becomes the only way to salvage or boost a specific industry. When the State confuses its role as a public purchaser or an operator with its responsibilities for general economic welfare, this can lead to a waste of resources. It is also the responsibility of the companies to avoid too much dependence. When the PTT realized a few years ago that their massive investment programme in new telephone infrastructure would come to saturation and leave the industry with excess jobs, they decided to embark on much more adventurous projects : consumer telecopy, Teletel, visiophones, fibre optic cabling to private homes. None of these ventures, of course, can be justified economically on its own merits (as the new telephone exchanges were), and only non-economic considerations such as job creation or national pride can explain the vast sums of public money already invested.

In conclusion, it can be said that the country never gains by having the State confuse its roles of purchaser and of promoter of economic development. On the other hand, State procurement should integrate the key factors for success in competitive business : products adapted for export, customer diversification, trade-offs between technical and economic performance, pricing levels based on competitors' costs. State procurement agencies and State-owned monopolies should be constantly confronting French products and prices with their international competitors. Their managers should be trained to make the trade-offs themselves which would then dictate product requirements.

The greatest corporate successes led or facilitated by State procurement policies, such as Dassault, Matra or Merlin-Gérin, are all based on a combination of strong players on both sides : public purchasers with an understanding of technology evolution and the needs of world markets, and business leaders developing their own views of competitive differentiation. The two sides should be able to educate each other. Furthermore, in a medium-sized country like France, the State should in particular realize that its degree of control on markets will diminish with the appearance of the following new trends :

- the scale of investment in R & D required to keep pace with the US and Japan is exceeding the scope of the French budget. This will mean European-wide cooperation, as has already been seen in fast breeder-reactors, space, helicopters, missiles and jet fighters ;

- the pressure for deregulation in sectors like telecommunications, airlines and television will mean the emergence of private customers, and private operators (and more competition possibly in the home market).

State procurement will not have the same impact on business success that it had in the last twenty years. France should, however, take advantage of its strong traditions in State-driven technologies, to lead or participate in European cooperations, in the way that has proved quite successful in the case of Ariane.

## 5. THE RESULTS OF INDUSTRIAL POLICIES IN FREE MARKET BUSINESSES

State industrial planning is much more difficult to conceive - and even more so to put in practice - in businesses where purchasing decisions are made by independent customers than in State-controlled markets. Economic performance is then the result of successful strategies and organization of individual corporations rather than a satisfactory relationship between one supplier and one customer. In France, however, the State has long declared an ambition to help and sometimes direct industry in the national interest.

The methods used for State intervention in businesses not driven by public procurement have been described in chapters 2 and 3. They encompass all policy levers that a democratic government operating in a free market economy can have : nationalization, direct and indirect financial assistance, carrots and sticks for top management and bankers to follow certain directions, etc. The sectors of industry chosen by (or imposed on) government have been described in chapter 3 and include both industries chosen for their growth potential or their spin-off effects on the rest of the economy (computers, electronics, civil aeronautics, machine tools), or because they represent large employment threatened by new competitors or market decline (coal, shipbuilding, steel, textiles and now automotive).

The history of French State intervention in setting strategies in businesses open to free competition is much less successful than in businesses driven by public procurement. The main reasons are that the State has tried to exercise the same degree of control on corporate decisions, in businesses where market forces cannot be mastered by political will. The only successful examples are the result of 'catalytic' policies rather than 'directive' policies.

**Limits and contradictions of State planning**

The management of a company - particularly a private one - generally operates under a clear mandate to maximize wealth for its shareholders over the long term. Of course, intelligent management also seeks to satisfy its employees and to be responsive to its community, but lines of responsibility and priorities are clearly defined and accepted. Governments in all democratic societies on the other hand are elected for limited periods of time, with broad mandates, and are subject to contradictory pressures. Although they are responsible for increasing the standard of living of their country, they are not equipped to make day-to-day business decisions which involve complex analysis, hard trade-offs and rapid changes. This is why industrial strategy at the national level can only be a broad and flexible framework for resource allocation and methods used can only be 'catalytic' rather than directive.

The French State has been operating from a more powerful and legitimate base than any of its counterparts (particularly since the Fifth Republic with a prestigious leader, Charles de Gaulle) and with stronger instruments in the hands of the executive branch than in any other democracy : a seven year renewable mandate for the President, the right to dissolve the Assemblée Nationale, tight control of the parliamentary agenda and procedures, etc. The French political regime had the opportunity to push State planning as far as it could go in free market economies. Indeed, these political conditions will probably never be met again in the foreseeable future. Yet, French sectoral industrial policy experience has revealed some obvious limits and contradictions in its ambitious objectives of imposing directions for targeted companies or even whole sectors. Broadly speaking, these have to do with four main weaknesses :

(a) lack of relevant information and analysis ;
(b) ambiguity of the State's role in free markets ;
(c) pressures against politically difficult decisions ;
(d) lack of continuity and accountability.

243

(a) The lack of an accurate, up-to-date and relevant flow of information on businesses is obvious in any government. It is, however, crucially needed when government has the ambition to set strategies. The French State – like its foreign counterparts – has little access to the data which allow a true assessment of competitive positions : detailed market shares by business segment, cost and value added structures, comparative data for key competitors (investments, cash flows, R & D, quality levels, etc.). A constant analysis of these parameters can only be conducted by those who manage the business. Higher levels of aggregation like industrial associations or the State can only rely on information supplied by the business level. Thus to secure this data, the State needs open and trustful channels of communication with business. French government organizations have been rather less successful than their counterparts in Japan or Germany, and have been poorly helped by trade associations. Some of these problems have to do with France's relative inability to cope with free market forces, others relate to the inherent limits of State policies in free market businesses and the excess of ambition which successive French governments have demonstrated.

The State in France does not even have essential corporate data which other countries trace in better ways : investments abroad, government financial transfers, profitability by sector, value added and employees broken down into detailed sub-sectors, etc. France suffers from the lack of stringent and accurate corporate accounting and reporting practices, and from industrial associations highly deficient in collecting sectoral trends. Furthermore, the State has a quasi-monopoly of statistical and economic studies, contrary to the practice in Germany, Japan or the US where private institutes and universities stimulate a public debate on structural issues.

The lack of good analysis on business strategy issues in France is a result of self-centered civil service behaviour but also of the poor understanding of real market mechanisms. Autarchy is often a characteristic of too-powerful bureaucrats. This is compounded in France by the widespread feeling among high level civil servants recruited from top elite 'grands corps' like Inspection des Finances or Corps des

Mines that they can quickly learn complex issues totally new to them and decide without too much help from practitioners. On top of this, traditional rivalries between various administrations and a sense of loyalty to the 'Corps' rather than the State at large have prevented good flows of communication between public sources of information. In three recent attempts to study various aspects of French industrial planning, commissioned by the Planning Agency, the authors discovered that the most-needed data were jealously kept by their owner and were not even available to other government departments : only the Customs Department and the Central Bank knew in detail about investments abroad (each with a different approach) and no one in the Treasury, Industry or Budget Departments could reconcile State transfers to the corporate sector, by specific company.

More worryingly, in France most government agencies involved in industrial planning fail to understand the nature of free markets and the basis for competitive advantage (see part II). The lack of thorough comprehension of business segmentation and scale economies explains, for example, why government bureaucrats have often promoted non-viable mergers or acquisitions between companies (see machine tools below). The logic of French State intervention is to pass political objectives, such as national independence or employment, on to financially respectable players, rather than to encourage new competitive business organizations.

(b) The ambiguity of State intervention lies not only with the confusion of responsibilities due to the size of the public sector, but also with the difficult choices that a government has to make in its public profile.

The sheer magnitude of France's industrial public sector - a third of total sales and exports and more than half of investments - poses immense problems of accountability, transparency and fairness. The management of nationalized companies is held responsible before elected politicians, themselves subject to changes in public opinion, priorities and agendas. In the past, the management of such companies as Renault or Elf-Aquitaine had been almost totally immune to direct political interventions. In fact, the authors have found in a study for the French Plan that the experience of French nationalizations before 1981 had been a remarkable and quite paradoxical case of strong corporate management and independent strategies[2]. The influence of public ownership was more implicit than explicit and acted in positive directions to achieve international expansion, risk-taking in new technologies, and workers' participation.

On the whole, and based on forty years of nationalizations, the State has not prevented structural adjustments (even when it meant the closing down of whole plants), and has even recently encouraged industry rationalizations : in petrochemicals and plastics (between PUK, Elf, ATO and CDF), in telephones (between Thomson, CIT-Alcatel, and CGCT), in aluminium (Pechiney), special steels or civil engineering. In all these cases, mergers and corporate portfolio remodelling have meant losses of jobs. This is now also true for Renault, the steel and shipyard companies.

State control of industrial companies has not prevented foreign investments as illustrated by the spectacular decision announced by President Mitterrand one week after his election to allow the US acquisition of Texas Gulf by Elf after the ban pronounced a year earlier by his predecessor against acquiring another US company. Since then many State-owned companies have invested abroad and/or divested at home, including CGE, Saint-Gobain and Rhône-Poulenc.

The lack of an effective capitalist tradition in France encourages the State to play an active role. This can have a very positive impact on the renewal of the elites, on the financing of risky ventures and on forging a consensus among social forces.

However, the recent dramatic shift of the borderline between private and public ownership, and the initial ideology of the Mitterrand government have changed the problem. After the nationalizations were passed in Parliament in 1982, the government had to nominate close to fifty chief executives in key sectors of the economy. This wave of nominations plus what could be called the 'spoils system' for the management of former publicly owned companies created

2

Les entreprises publiques du secteur concurrentiel, Telesis for the Commissariat Général du Plan, 1982.

a very visible leverage for political intervention in business decisions. In addition, the style of the Minister of Industry at that time - Jean Pierre Chevènement - leant towards heavy-handed government and so-called 'planning contracts' between the State and the nationalized companies, signed explicitly to formulate government expectations in three areas selected as national priorities : 'domestic market recapture', investing in new technologies and contributing to the unemployment problem. These explicit objectives have tended to work as additional constraints for management, even if rhetoric has been more important than real obstacles.

With Laurent Fabius as Minister of Industry in 1983 and moves towards a more pragmatic economic policy, nationalized companies were released from day-to-day bureaucratic intervention, but new constraints emerged. With pressure to show good results before the 1986 elections, the government set the return to profitability as the priority. This is certainly different from the initial objectives of the nationalizations, and could even prove to be detrimental in the long run, if management chooses to sacrifice future investment for political credibility. As the recent brutal dismissal of Renault's chief executive B. Hanon shows, there is no protected job in the public sector.

The management of publicly owned companies in a free market system also runs into problems of confidentiality and rapidity of decisions. It is difficult, for example, to keep acquisition or divesture processes secret, and even more so, to make these decisions quickly without antagonizing the State. Companies like Saint-Gobain, for example, have recently experienced problems of this type. The fact that all financial flows between shareholders and the companies are - and should be - made public, means that much information is given to competitors.

Finally the issue of fairness of State behaviour between its own companies and private companies (some of them being its competitors) is the trickiest. In recent years, private companies - and therefore their employees and communities as well as their shareholders - might have been mistreated in comparison with privileges given to public companies : easier and quicker State approvals ; access to public procurement, access to low-cost capital. Even if these practices have stopped, the State can prevent more effective competitors from reaping the full benefits of successful strategies by the mere fact that it feels obliged to subsidize non-viable entities which it owns. Why should privately-owned Jeumont Schneider compete with the heavily subsidized, loss making CGCT in the private exchange business, causing it to lose share and engage in price cutting ?

The State's role is ambiguous not only when it is the owner, but also when it directly favours one domestic competitor over another. In cases where there is only one domestic company facing international competitors, State intervention is only exposed to criticism and sometimes legal claims from international competitors and organizations such as the EC or GATT. There can even be cases of anti-dumping charges. But the problem is politically more difficult when the State is asked - or chooses - to assist one ailing company and therefore indirectly hurts the ones with better performance, which could have otherwise increased their market shares and/or their profit margins. The difficulties of Bull in computers and some viable machine tool companies (see case studies below) are an illustration of the vicious effects of a 'picking the winner' or 'bailing out the loser' philosophy.

(c) The pressures exercised on politically sensitive decisions can be a cause of slowness, inefficiency and sometimes misdirection.

The first kind of pressure comes from unions and local politicians who resist job reductions, and even more so plant closures. It is generally difficult for governments to foresee overcapacity, market slowdown or competitive shifts. It is even more difficult to find the opportunity areas which would compensate for lack of growth. Industrial restructuring can be planned in advance, but constant flows of communication have to be established between management and government at all levels.

The second difficulty lies with the bias against transnational solutions over national. Governments, particularly of large countries, are only accountable to their domestic constituencies, and in general will favour nationalistic planning. Past examples in the 1970s, such as the failure of Unidata, the forced divestiture of Ericsson in telephones, or the ban on Occidental Petroleum's bid for Pechiney's chemical operations are examples of the chauvinistic attitudes of all political leaders, including the ones who call themselves liberal.

(d) Finally, the lack of continuous and precise accountibility for past performance disrupts policies which could otherwise be more effective.

As shown in the case studies below, the strategic directions or methods used can shift abruptly following changes in Ministers or even high level government officials. The 'Plan Calcul' for example took a 180° turn with disastrous results on corporate financial performance, motivation and credibility abroad, when President Giscard d'Estaing took power (see below). The same occurred with the steel companies in 1981-82 when optimistic production targets delayed the plant closures and inter-company specializations which were planned.

Many of these shortcomings of State industrial policy can be overcome, as exemplified by MITI's successes in Japan and some successes in France. As illustrated in the following case studies, the best policies are the ones which use market levers, and do not go against them. To be effective, governments have to fight their own natural tendencies. They must learn how to rely on outside expertise and open up clear channels of communication with business. They must set precise deadlines, performance and cost measures, and people's responsibilities. They have to make unpopular decisions. Under these conditions 'State planning' becomes intelligent support of domestic competitors. This is also what should be learned from past failures and successes.

**Case studies of sectoral policies in free markets**
The impacts of the policies considered here have been quite different, despite similar competitive factors, and they illustrate the role of government tutorship, and its changing understanding of market forces. Off-shore equipment and the French computer industry had already a base to start from but were facing very dominant US competition (roughly an 80 per cent share of the world market in each case) ; the

government did not represent more than a quarter of the domestic market, which implied that any long-term success had to be based on private sector purchasing and export.

(a) The sectoral policy in computers 1966-80

The computer policy, traditionally called 'Plan Calcul', is almost a twenty year-old story. However, the competitive situation of the French computer industry is not very different now from what it was twenty years ago. The Plan Calcul actually reflects most of the mistakes which can prevent a national objective from being efficiently translated into corporate strategy.

The case study highlights in particular an overwhelming focus on 'national independence' which ran counter to the key success factors of the computer industry, and a failure to take advantage of the various technological breakthroughs which cleared the way for newcomers (mini and micro computers).

The first plans for an all-French computer industry were initiated around 1963-64 by the government. Two events accelerated political decisions. First, the US embargo on the large Control Data computer needed by the Force de Frappe nuclear buildup in the spring of 1963 convinced de Gaulle of the need for an independent French industry in large mainframes (at least for scientific and military purposes). Second, the French computer company Machines Bull, number 2 in Europe after IBM, began to need help both in terms of extra cash and in establishing an international marketing network.

In 1966, a report drawn up by the Commissariat du Plan exposed the three-fold rationale for creating an all-French computer industry :

- it would employ an increasingly large number of highly-trained personnel (in R&D, in marketing and production) ;
- it would result in productivity improvements and successes in many other industries, believing that a mastery in one area could be used to serve all others ;

- it would be a step towards technological independence, mainly from the US. Indeed, this last point was very important for President de Gaulle.

However, at that time, the government had failed to find a French partner for Machines Bull, and had allowed its sale in 1964 to General Electric of the US, although the firm had produced 25 per cent of the computers installed in France and was exporting 45 per cent of its production. It also had an excellent R & D staff and a very good reputation in the market place. Bull, which could have been the nucleus of a French computer industry, was to remain outside the Plan Calcul until 1976.

Therefore, instead of restructuring all French assets in computers into one large company as the UK has done with ICL or even Germany with Siemens (after the purchase of Telefunken's computer division) the French government was left only with smaller companies : SEA (near bankruptcy), CAE, SETI, and SNERI. These together were 15 times smaller than Bull, had product lines with three different licensors (SAS, GE and Packard-Bell), and had no export base to speak of. In addition, they were only marginally involved in the large mainframe business for which the Plan Calcul was conceived. These small, purely French-based companies were to be the base for the newly created national champion, Compagnie Internationale pour l'Informatique (CII), officially incorporated in December 1966. The Plan Calcul, a package of government programmes, incentives, purchasing and direct participation in the computer industry, set the direction of government programmes for ten years (1966-76).

Because CII was created for 'national independence' and 'technological lead', it was given the mission of developing an entirely new product line in medium and large CPUs to match the IBM 360-40 and 360-50 models. The new line, in addition to being incompatible with IBM's line, would also become incompatible with that of the two main founders CAE and SEA. The 360 series cost about $ 5 billion in development and market introduction and the challenge for CII was to work with at least three different technical origins (Bull, GE and SDS) and to come up with a technology of its own in three years, for the very modest sum of less than $ 200 million. Obviously, the cost of independence in fast-moving R & D businesses was not well appreciated in France in the mid-1960s. At the same time, the French government embarked on the Concorde programme and on an independent nuclear technology ('graphite-gaz').

The increasing involvement of the French government in the detail of the strategic choices of CII was in part due to the fact that it was never able to enlist strong support from the largest French electronic companies of that time : CSF, CGE and Schneider. None of them really wanted to risk large sums of money outside limited applications such as mini-computers for process control. The smaller companies (at that time) like Compagnie des Compteurs or Thomson were more optimistic about the computer industry but did not have the resources to continue their own development. Because of this general business conservatism and fragmentation of industrial resources, the government created its own agency - the Délégation à l'Informatique -to take responsibility for :

- controlling State aid to firms participating in the Plan Calcul ;
- private computer research through IRIA ;
- coordinating the purchasing and leasing of computers in all State agencies which had to have permission for all new equipment.

Originally, the Délégation was to leave business strategies and management to the private shareholders of CII. In practice, CII private shareholders never agreed on anything except to put as little money as possible into it. Between 1966 and 1976 the two main shareholders CGE and Thomson put 160 million francs into large computers as opposed to the 5 billion francs put in by the government. CGE and Thomson have always been arch rivals in the field of electronics and electrical equipment : thus it was like sponsoring a joint venture between Xerox and IBM in 'office of the future' equipment ! The government had to fill this vacuum, and in effect the Délégation à l'Informatique actually determined, together with the general manager of CII, the product line choices.

In parallel, on the Machines Bull-Honeywell side, the association was not exploited to its utmost. Honeywell was a 'small' American, and the Honeywell-Bull association did not

252

do much to improve scale effects. Worse, instead of allocating the various product lines among themselves, France started a brand new series, incompatible both with the existing lines and with Honeywell's software.

By 1974, thanks to the massive infusion of 2.5 billion francs (1975 FF) from the government and a preferential purchasing policy, CII had reached 14 per cent of the French market (a 5.5 per cent share of Europe), half of which was in the protected State market. This penetration, however, was not against IBM-France but against Honeywell-Bull, a mutually detrimental competition. Exports were mainly to socialist countries where France's independent foreign policy helped it to compete with the US : USSR, Cuba, China, North Korea. Licences were sold in Romania and in Hungary. By the end of 1974, CII reached a level of sales of 1.2 billion francs but still needed State subsidies to survive and had a very limited marketing organization outside France.

The policies of the two following years, although underwritten by the recently elected liberal President Giscard d'Estaing, who did not feel tied by any initiative taken under the Gaullist period, and despite an apparent undoing of the Plan Calcul, did not succeed any better in understanding the rules of the game in that industry.

In two years, the new government totally reversed the course of public policy in the computer industry and further increased confusion and waste of resources :

- the agency in charge of conducting the Plan Calcul, the Delegation à l'Informatique, was eliminated in October 1974 ;
- in November 1974, preliminary talks started very confidentially with Honeywell in order to merge Honeywell, Bull and CII. At the same time, France reaffirmed its commitment to UNIDATA.

UNIDATA was a European project, with Dutch (Philips), German (Siemens) and French (CII) partners, with the support of the BMFT in Germany. However, none of the French participants in CII felt strongly enough about CII's potential or committed enough to make the European venture. Siemens computer division was twice the size of CII and the French government was afraid of being dominated. A partnership between a merged Siemens-Telefunken and a merged CII-Bull in 1972 would have been much more balanced and had a better chance for survival than a three-way, loose association between three insecure partners.

Eventually, in February 1975, the main points of the Honeywell-Bull/CII merger were agreed upon but it was not until May that they were made public. The final agreement was signed in December, four days after UNIDATA had been dissolved. The new company CII-HB was 53 per cent controlled by a French holding company Machines Bull - itself divided between the State (17 per cent) and CGE (83 per cent).

The 'liberal' French government poured the largest resources ever into the computer industry since the beginning of the Plan Calcul :
- 1,200 million francs in cash subsidies (1976-80) ;
- the covering of 1976 losses amounting to 685 million francs ;
  - 4 billion francs in guaranteed purchases of computers, paid in cash by a government bank (CNME) over four years ;
  - the cost of changing programmes from CII to HB systems for these new end-users in the State organizations.

Mini-computer operations were regrouped with Thomson and Télémécanique into a new company, SEMS, which was expected to receive 120 million francs in grants and R&D loans.

Finally, when the Socialists were elected in 1981, the computer industry was in poor shape. IBM-France remained the largest employer, taxpayer and trade balance contributor in the French computer industry. CII-Honeywell-Bull, (the end product of the Plan Calcul) was expected to stand on its feet by 1980, yet when preferential government contracts were phased out, it continued to need some form of assistance (either R&D grants or others) in order to resist IBM and US mini-computer companies at both ends of its product line. It had a lower share of the European market than the top three French companies had in 1963 or 1966.

As to large computers, one should mention that while the nuclear Force de Frappe finally managed to use a Control Data computer leased by SEMA, a French software company, CII was very successful in developing the large computers needed by the military.

In mini-computers, SEMS (controlled by Thomson) had regrouped all French activities previously held by CII, Télémécanique and Thomson. It faced very serious difficulties in terms of both market share and cash losses in a field where new US companies had done extremely well. It must be noted that, except for Nixdorf, no European company managed to take advantage of the mini-computer breakthrough, whereas newcomers such as DEC, Wang, and HP had great success.

In micro-computers, the French industry also missed the key parameter, which is the need for a very wide range of programs (software) which in turn requires a world-wide presence.

In peripheral equipment and terminals, French industry had done better, with some world-wide positions, for example in graphic design (Benson). But before 1976, this part of the industry received very little attention from the Plan Calcul. It was only in 1976 that the Ministry of Industry signed a planning agreement with five companies to help them grow and export.

In semiconductors, the government never really formulated any large scale programme before 1978. The only company which resulted from the Plan Calcul (COSEM, then SESCOSEM) remained very small and it was only in 1979-80 that some coordinated effort between private industry and government resulted in a few investments, mostly based on US technology with US partners (National Semiconductors and Harris).

In software, French industry was number 2 in the world with the two European leaders being French. But this was in large local business, where economies of scale are not as important and export potential limited. The software industry has developed without any significant government involvement (25 million francs between 1967 and 1971 vs 800 million francs for hardware).

For these poor results, the government has spent more than 5 billion francs between 1966 and 1980, about 10 billion francs in real terms (1980 francs). This is ten times more than the amount spent in off-shore and three times larger than the French contribution to the Airbus programme.

The main issues that the successive governments addressed unsuccessfully, i.e. those of scale, and of alliances, are still on the agenda, but the margin for action is even smaller.

(b) The recent machine tool plan 1981-85

The French machine-tool industry has never had a major presence at the world level, nor represented a major domestic sector in terms of share of GDP or jobs (26,000 jobs in 1975). However, it has benefited for years, and especially in the last decade, from a number of supportive public policies, because of its strategic position in promoting technical innovation throughout the rest of industry. Besides, the whole sector experienced a technical breakthrough in the 1970s - numerical controls (NC) -which drastically modified competitive rules in the business, making way for newcomers. Today, however, after a series of fiscal alleviations to favour investment (in 1966, 1968, 1975, 1980), the launching as early as 1972 of direct subsidies for the purchase of NC machine tools by small and medium-sized companies, and the setting of thorough sectoral plans ( in 1975 and particularly in 1981), the French machine-tool industry has not definitively overcome its crisis, although it has considerably shrunk : 26,000 jobs and 5 per cent of world production in 1975, vs 18,000 and 2.7 per cent in 1982. The trade balance is deteriorating : in 1975, exports were 96 per cent of imports, 68 per cent in 1982. This means, for instance, that any revitalization of industrial investment in France implies first an increased trade deficit.

We shall focus here on the last sectoral plan - that of 1981 : by far the most ambitious and costly (about 4 billion francs over 3 years). This illustrates one of the most prominent policies of the recent government.

The context of that plan was the almost complete failure of French producers to seize the opportunities created by numerical control. Since the 1970s, the machine-

256

tool industry's activity has changed radically. Companies have had to shift from in-house production to design and assembly of components bought outside. The industrial cost structure reflects that shift : whereas more than 70 per cent of the manufacturing cost was due to in-house added costs, this ratio now applies to the purchases made externally, in particular electronic components. This change allowed newcomers, and especially the Japanese, backed by their very strong electronics industry, to break into the field. They have been able to address the high volume market segments, where they have gained in a few years a 50 per cent world market share. In parallel, the traditional machine tool manufacturers encountered difficulties, apart from those, like Germany and Switzerland, which had been more focused on specialty segments. That was not the case of Britain, nor of France (except in a few segments related to the French nuclear, automotive and aeronautics industries), nor the US, where specialties were only marginal.

After a few years only, the world competition evolved roughly as follows : both the US and Germany accepted a 'natural selection' and organized the grouping of former independent companies around large poles; Italy tried to adjust to the Japanese model through small companies dealing with design and assembly; the UK let its machine tool industry almost die out ; and France launched a very voluntarist sectoral plan, with the ambition of modifying the competitive structure of this declining sector, as well as sustaining the overall level of demand.

On the market side, the plan provided subsidies through 'MECA', a mechanism to favour the purchase of sophisticated equipment (500 million francs in subsidies for 1982-85), and set up a new leasing corporation. It also funded a renewal of the machine tools of the Ministry of National Education for 1.2 billion francs over 3 years, and subsidized the purchase of French machine tools by industry (1.2 billion francs subsidized loans in 1981).

On the supply side, the plan forecasted a quadrupling of NC machine tools and a doubling of heavy machines (the other segments ⋈ conventional and specialty machines ⋈ remaining stable) between 1982 and 1985, thanks to a restructuring of the sector into specialized groups, allowing a rationalization of the product ranges and scale effects, which in turn would stimulate a domestic industry of components, motors, numerical controls, etc. To achieve this restructuring, the public authorities committed themselves through 'contrats de plan', signed by the Ministry of Industry and the various companies. They poured 2.3 billion francs as direct subsidies into the producers, plus 1.7 billion in long term subordinated loans, and approximatively 200 million for R&D.

Three years after its launching, the results registered by this policy appear very disappointing. First, on the market side, the forecast growth turned out to be a severe decline : 40 per cent between 1981 and 1983 in value for the world market. On the domestic market, the flow of subsidies allocated for the purchase of machine tools did not stop the decline of the market. More generally, the lack of accuracy of market forecasts seriously jeopardized the policy followed on the supply side : the optimistic figures prevented the drastic restructuring required.

On the supply side, the Plan suffered from a number of other shortcomings which have led to major failures : it was too ambitious and new to restructure a sector as fragmented as the machine tool industry. The State authorities, accustomed to industrial policies in oligopolistic sectors, had no experience in reshaping small or medium-sized companies (which could only marginally benefit from public purchases), nor in managing their financial support to a large group of companies. This ability would have required a very sound understanding of the industrial specificities of this sector. In fact, the restructuring did not adjust to the objective requisites of the various machine-tool segments, but rather followed the logic of financial and political concerns.

The restructuring should have distinguished between standard machines, which can be incorporated in manufacturing, and heavy machines, which are dedicated to specific purposes.

1. Standard machines. For the standard machine tools, scale effects require at least a European-wide presence, to compete with the Japanese. But not a single French producer ⊦ small or large ⋈ had that asset. Restructuring therefore had to be

transnational, either with European or Japanese partners. The 1981 Plan considered restructuring around large competitive poles as a purely national ambition, and thus did not take into account the need for international alliances. However since 1981 the necessity for such alliance has become too great to be ignored. Thus, some producers have signed alliances, like Intelautomatisme and the Japanese Hamaï. Others have ended up being acquired by foreign companies : Sagitta & Colly have been bought by Beyeler (Switzerland), Promecam by Strippit (USA), and Ernault ٦ once the French leader ٦merged with Toyoda.

Furthermore, by lack of realism or political courage, the Plan supported almost every French company, without sacrificing from the start the weakest, despite the fact that so many of them had no chance to attain the critical scale required in their segment. In parallel, a financial logic has too often preceded industrial consistency. There has been a tendency to group healthy (or supposedly healthy) companies with those which were in bad shape (as in the case of Intelautomatisme).

Finally, the public authorities made financial commitments before the companies had agreed to regroup. These regroupings never occured. This was the case of the two 'marriages' : Cazeneuve٦Sim٦Ramo and Ernault٦Somua٦ Huré٦Graffenstaden. In the first case, Sim obtained for itself in 1981 above 10 million francs in subordinated loans, plus purchases from the Ministry of National Education, plus the consolidation of 2 million francs in medium٦term loans before its 1983 bankruptcy. Ramo also disappeared. Cazeneuve, the largest of all, was eventually rescued by private shareholders, with a realistic industrial redefinition of its range of products. In particular, Cazeneuve will abandon the NC lathes for which its Japanese competitors benefitted from much higher productivity, and will focus on the lower end segment where there are no Japanese. In parallel, large investments have been made to renew the industrial sites. Interestingly enough, this rescue has been carried out without public funding, and with managers of the new company holding 10 per cent of the capital. Huré and Graffenstaden did join, but their shareholders were not very willing    integrate Ernault٦ Somua, with its repeated losses. Since the end of 1981, the

259

State financed the survival of that firm, on the hypothesis of the future grouping (450 million francs in 1982). But in 1984, the 240 million francs losses on 250 million francs sales eventually led to its bankruptcy too. In addition, Intelautomatisme - the new name of Huré and Graffenstaden -received from the State between 600÷ 800 million francs, for its 300 million francs yearly sales. For the most part, the restructuring of the standardized machine tool industry has been a failure, or exceedingly costly.

2. Heavy machine tools. The so-called 'heavy machine tool' sector has been restructured around a single pole, "MFL". This has also been very costly - more than 1 billion francs, for 1,400 jobs and 600 million francs sales, but it seems industrially much sounder : there are few world-scale competitors (and in particular the Japanese are not very strong because components advantage is minor, a small share of total cost), the scale effects are limited (the series are not long), and the industrial know-how and related investments are quite specific. Therefore, this French pole, which also widened its international presence through a commercial network, has quite a good chance of survival.

Apart from these difficult restructurings, the Plan strengthened a number of small companies (fewer than 100 million francs sales) but their insufficient scale, faced with world competition, jeopardises their future. This is the case for example of Vernier-GSP, Alcera-Gambin, etc. The Plan also supported the component supply side for numerical controls, ball-screws, etc. But chances for long-term survival remain slim. For instance, the company for the NC components, NUM, produces 800 NC per year, whereas the leader FANUC produces 20,000, and technical evolution is very fast.

Conclusion. From the beginning, the machine tool plan had unrealistic aims - it was impossible to help so many actors to become competitive - and the public authorities had no experience of guiding the adjustment of such a fragmented sector. The results are therefore limited, when compared to the costs. The trade deficit has been reduced - cut by half between 1982 and 1983 - but the world economic situation explains part of this. As the Ministry of Industry stated in January 1985 : 'Il faut prolonger l'effort', i.e. government efforts to restructure the industry are not yet over.

(c) The numerous steel restructuring plans (1965-85)
The continuing crisis of the French steel industry over the last decade illustrates dramatically how public policies may fail to assist severe sectoral adjustments, despite large financial commitments, and how this type of interaction between the State and the corporations can run out of control.

The pattern reveals a typically French bias, and it explains in part why the needed restructuring in the 1970s and 1980s has been so painful.

The interaction pattern between the State and steel companies. From the end of World War II to the early 1970s, the steel industry benefited from a national consensus which gave an exceptional legitimacy to the public support it received.

First, up to the late 1960s, the context was one of growth, the major Steel Agreement signed in 1966 belonging still to an expansionist vision. This context fitted in especially well with the more or less subjective image of steel : steel is a strategic product, its production level measures the extent of the nation's independence and of its potential external influence. As a consequence, the industry must be national. No alliances were sought, the chosen sites were exclusively French - Lorraine, Dunkirk, Fos - and even the Ministry of Finance first opposed a German stake (Thyssen's) in Solmer (Fos). Later, in 1976, France was not included in the association which grouped producers from Germany, Netherlands, Luxembourg, and Belgium. In fact, one could paraphrase the motto 'what is good for GM is good for the USA' for the steel industry in France. There was a remarkable subjective overlap between the perceived interests of the nation and of the sector.

The choice of Fos close to Marseille, for example, as a new modern site 'on the water front', was partially dictated by non-industrial concerns, originating more from long term regional planning (in particular, that of the DATAR, the regional planning agency) than from basic industrial requirements. The integration of steel policy into such broader objectives, a typically French pattern, contributed to the fact that, when overcapacity began to be a risk in the late sixties, the signs were neglected. As Pompidou formulated it : 'Fos, la grande affaire de la nation'. Uncertainty calls for tenacity in action ; risks call for State intervention, not for re*examination of the project.

A French bias is also involved in this pattern : pre*eminence is given to production, and profitability is a secondary criterion. The director of Saint Gobain at that time, who succeeded in disengaging the company from steel, explained how difficult it had been to move away from the prestige of steel and was one of the few to argue that 'La seule noblesse est d'avoir un cash flow convenable'.

The exceptional importance of steel in France *, and its impact on the bargaining power of that industry over the State *, certainly contributed to its lack of diversification, its exclusively horizontal concentration and its share of the State's benevolence.

This framework has made even more difficult the rationalisation required by the changing environment of the 1970s and 1980s.

The changing environment. The major disruption in steel production's competitive environment came from the spectacular advance of the Japanese in the mid 1970s, whose productivity was approximately double that of France (and a third more than Italy's, the highest in Europe).

Structurally, France *, and Europe in general *, had a steel overcapacity, so that they could extensively serve export markets. What happened in the mid 1970s was the devastating success of Japanese steel on the markets once served by Europe (the EC protected intensely its own internal market), fed by a very fast increase of capacity : Japan more than tripled its crude steel capacity between 1965 and 1975, while Europe increased its own by 40 per cent in the same period. The US capacity, however, remained stable.

262

In addition, in the last decade, the production share of third world countries increased, especially that of the newly industrialized countries : from 20 per cent to 33 per cent between 1970 and the early 1980s, meaning a relative decrease of Europe's export markets.

Inside Europe, and especially when the export markets shrank, competition increased very much. France faced the new Italian competition ʻ that of the Bresciani ʻ (Italy and Spain were the only European countries which expanded their crude steel production between 1973 and 1982), but also an increased pressure from German and Belgian and Luxembourg producers, who accounted for 85 per cent of French imports. French producers ʻ and public authorities (who had no data other than those from the steel trade association) ʻ were slow to understand the growing penetration of the Belgians, due in particular to an efficient dumping of long products on the French market. The lack of good statistical data, plus the understaffing of the major producers for market analysis, helped to hide this fact. The French were sensitive to the price levels and met with the Belgians to fix them (with a cartel), but not quantities. To maintain production levels, the French tolerated extremely low prices in distant export markets, which created enormous losses, and tried to compensate with high prices on the domestic market, which accelerated foreign penetration. In 1982, France was the largest customer of European steel producers, and their third supplier.

Furthermore, the world market which had expanded more or less with the installed capacities in the 1960s, and early 1970s, shrank with the 1975 recession. Unfortunately, the massive capacity investments of the Dunkirk and Fos plants, decided in France during the prosperous sixties, became operational at that time. The domestic market was itself small, and then decreased still more, given the difficulties of the automotive, mechanical, and shipyard industries.

This particularly bad timing, compounded with a lack of radical action, has progressively transformed the steel industry into a gigantic cash drain for the nation.

<u>The adjustment policies.</u> The French steel industry did not
seem to recognize the first world crisis when it occurred :
whereas the US industry shed 60,000 jobs between 1974 and
1977, and Japan shut down 18 of its 58 blast furnaces, the
French industry's workforce was almost the same in 1977 as
it was a decade before. Inevitably, the French industry called
out for public rescue.

The first Plan was developed in 1977, followed by
another one in 1978 (the first having failed), and today still,
the industry has massive financial transfers from the nation :
10 billion francs is the forecast figure of the injection needed
in 1985 alone.

Rather than detailing the various forms of financial
support and the related accepted restructuring (sites closed,
investments, etc.), we will try to summarise the assumptions
which guided public policies and explain their failures.

The restructuring and modernization have been based,
until very recently, on a double assumption :

- The Lorraine region ﹐ with Sacilor - had to remain a
  steel centre, based on its iron ore production. The
  new sites on the waterfront - Dunkirk and
  Fos -would compensate for Lorraine's mediocre
  productivity, but would not be substitutes. The three
  sites had to remain alive.
- The concentration process undertaken should respect
  the presence of two different autonomous French
  groups - Usinor et Sacilor - despite their progressive
  commonality of shareholder (the State, tacitly since
  1978) and their overlapping product ranges.

These choices clearly belong to larger political
commitments, rather than to purely industrial considerations.
As a matter of fact, they maintained a sub-optimization which
has been attacked only recently, thanks to European
Community pressures.

The 'fidelity' to the Lorraine site and to Lorraine's iron
for steel production has for years been a severe handicap. At
a time when the German or the Japanese could benefit from
much cheaper raw materials, that choice was industrially not
viable. Furthermore, it led to the technical process of blast
furnaces which could not compete with the Bresciani electric
furnaces. A huge rolling mill was built in Lorraine in the

mid-1970s for long products but (note the second assumption) it could not be filled solely with Sacilor's production. It would have required the combination of Usinor's and Sacilor's production. More generally, it seems absurd that intercorporate and interregional rivalries prevented replacing the older, smaller mills by the new plants of Dunkirk and Fos, once the decision to build these new capacities was taken. Rather than a substitution, the new plants were seen as a "compensation" for the poorer productivity of the old ones.

In fact, the concentration process never established a clear specialization of the two remaining poles, but rather maintained a theoretical competition, based on the difference of regional assets : Lorraine's iron for Sacilor, sea access for Usinor. The two groups both produce long products and flat products and even specialties (although special steels companies, when restructured, were allocated more to Sacilor than Usinor). Besides, poor world market conditions caused a decrease in the forecast cold rolling investment in Fos, for flat products, so that Fos produced only the coil, the final stage having to be done in Lorraine before being delivered to the clients.

This situation is especially absurd since the State has been controlling de facto both groups since 1978. As a matter of fact, the collusion between the steel industrialists and the State resulted (well before the 1981 nationalization) in total public control, under the Giscard d'Estaing/Barre government. The successive losses of the two groups had led them to convert most of their debt into participating loans which were non-interest bearing and to be repaid after recovery; a small part of the debt was converted into capital in new holding companies controlling the steel groups. These arrangements plus various others ended up by putting into the hands of the State about two-thirds of the industry's equity, giving therefore total public control over the industry. This allowed a few mergers - Usinor taking Chatillon-Neuves-Maisons, Sacilor Pompey - but left untouched the basic autonomy of Usinor and Sacilor.

Paradoxically, this did not favour their medium term autonomy, since the lack of radical adjustments led the French State eventually to convert the loans into equity, and

265

nationalize the two companies. The ideological bias for the nationalization of steel ¤ held by the Left since after the war ¤ did not much need to be drawn upon : no private shareholders wanted to meet the required financial injections. But, even now, the integration of the two groups has not been completed. The French need the 'friendly pressures' of the EEC to make painful decisions like the progressive abandonment of Lorraine for long products and of Fos. A coordination is slowly being imposed, focussing Sacilor in specialties and Usinor on ordinary steel. However, many borderline problems remain at a time when US protectionism is increasing. The French steel industry received about 12 billion francs in 1984 ¤ in equity and special loans ¤and will need some 10 billion more in 1985, excluding the social provisions cost of the various plans : a huge cash drain which does not even guarantee the future of what remains of the nation's cherished steel industry.

(d) <u>A case for success in free markets : French offshore oil policy (1963-78)</u>

The French Government first became concerned about the country's energy independence in the 1920s. In 1928, it took a first step in this direction by creating a national oil company, the Compagnie Française des Pétroles, partially owned by the State. Public commitment to the oil industry remained high during the 1930s, encouraging the development of engineering and manufacturing businesses around the oil companies (for example, CGG in the geophysical surveying field).

This policy of public involvement was further pursued after World War II. The increasing sophistication of the oil industry's engineering tasks and equipment requirements created a need for training and R&D. To carry out this function, the government established the French Petroleum Institute (IFP) in 1945. Its charter was to carry out long¤term R&D projects that companies could not sustain, and to create an engineering school to train a new generation of oil engineers. Soon afterwards, the government recognized the need for stronger financial resources to back policy actions. Consequently, the Hydrocarbons Fund (FSH) was created in 1954. This fund is maintained by a parafiscal levy on gasoline which provides a regular flow of money, independent of year-to-year political budgetary decisions. The parafiscal levy was not a new concept in France : it is commonly used to finance specialized research centers.

The decision to create a large research institute around a specific industry like the IFP is also not unusual. Such large institutes do exist in other fields such as aircraft, telecommunications and agriculture.

By 1960, France and its colonies were on their way to supplying their own energy needs. In addition, the 'home market' created by the activities of two public oil companies with the support of the IFP had spawned a well-developed oil equipment industry.

In the early 1960s, however, two events had a major influence on French policy. First Algeria, where most of the French oil industry had developed, became independent : France lost its oil-rich territories and the problem of energy independence became more acute than ever. This also meant that the French equipment industry needed to find new markets in order to survive. Secondly, Elf, one of the two state-owned oil operators, discovered hydrocarbons offshore in Gabon. Elf had to use American technology to develop the field, although it tried to initiate inexperienced French contractors in the problems of offshore oil.

The offshore oil industry was of interest to France for two reasons : it could provide a means of achieving complete energy independence and it provided an opportunity to develop technical capability in an emerging industry. The first reason was the most important at the time the offshore policy was formulated in the early sixties. During the following decade, however, the second motivation gained in importance  because no oil was found in French waters, and also because the political independence gained by the oil-rich countries meant that resources discovered by foreign oil operators no longer represented a secure source of supply for their countries of origin. The following section reviews the actions taken by the government in the 1960s and 1970s in the off-shore area and discusses this evolution of perspective.

By 1960, three decades of consistent government policy in the oil business had created some of the major elements

needed to reorient the oil industry :
- France had two partly or wholly state-owned oil operators which had gained experience in on-shore exploration and were moving off-shore ;
- a successful French oil equipment industry had developed since the war ;
- the oil industry felt supported by thirty years of consistent government policy ;
- thanks to the IFP, the French were among the leaders in oil technology and had a major R&D capability.

Building on the existing base, a geographical and technical reorientation of French efforts had to be achieved. The industry had to learn to operate in and serve the off-shore market as well as it had the on-shore fields. In addition, the equipment industry had to be weaned off its dependence on French customers.

The main institutions responsible for policy formulation and implementation are : the Ministry of Industry, the oil companies, the IFP and the CEPM.

The Ministry of Industry. The General Direction for Energy at the Ministry of Industry is the 'home' for the major participants in the off-shore area - IFP, CEPM, Elf and CFP (the oil companies), and the FSH (Hydrocarbons Fund). The fact that the off-shore industry is linked with energy rather than industry at ministerial level reflects the government's approach : off-shore policy is based upon the national policy of energy independence rather than on purely industrial considerations.

In high technology industries, the influence of the Ministry of Industry is generally superseded by other Ministries (Defence, Post and Telephone, Transportation), or very restricted by the autonomy that public corporations or research centres have gained (in nuclear, space, electricity). In the off-shore equipment industry, the Ministry's strong position is derived from the very clear charter that it was given in the area of oil policy and from the resources drawn from the independent Hydrocarbons Fund it has at its disposal.

Between 1963 and 1978, the FSH provided 1,790 million francs of subsidies (in 1978 FF) of which 730 million went to off-shore oil R&D projects carried out by engineering companies, the IFP or the oil operators themselves. The remainder of these expenditures was allocated to on-shore oil R&D, exploration and production. The pattern of FSH subsidies has dramatically shifted towards offshore R&D, which went from an average of 30 million francs to 80 million francs a year during the 1970s. Over the whole period, government spending represented 38 per cent of total R&D expenditure within France.

The authority of the Ministry of Industry has been further reinforced by strong leadership and a network of personal relationships between government officials and executives of both private and public firms. The former Minister of Industry, M. André Giraud, had been head of the Hydrocarbons Division and his successor, M. Leblond, created the CEPM and is now managing an off-shore company as well as being chairman of an industry association.

The oil companies. Elf is the result of a succession of mergers of public and private oil firms. It first undertook off-shore exploration in the early 1960s, in Gabon. CFP, created by the Government in 1928, became involved in off-shore oil only in the late 1960s. Both firms developed an early interest in off-shore technology and created in 1963 a joint marine studies department. They played a pioneering role in the development of the North Sea, although their total share of blocks did not exceed 5 per cent. The two oil companies have played a central role in policy formulation and implementation :

- they directed the R&D effort of the country towards market needs and participated in the definition of national priorities along with the IFP and engineering companies ;
- as oil operators, they gave long-term contracts to service companies or paid for full scale tests of new technologies (Bay of Biscay, Gabon) ;

* they acquired shareholdings in equipment manufacturing and operating firms (e.g. COMEX) or purchased expensive equipment to lease back to operators ;
* given their financial resources, they were able to undertake large scale and long-term R&D (e.g. the Deep Sea Programme).

The IFP. The French Petroleum Institute (IFP) carries out long-term R&D in all the stages of the oil industry : from geophysical surveying to petrochemicals. It also controls the National School of Petroleum and Motors (ENSPM). The IFP has been involved in several other ways in French off-shore industry development :
* it has carried out R&D mostly in cooperation with oil operators or manufacturing firms (e.g. the Pentagone platform developed jointly with Neptune) ;
* it has created subsidiaries for the commercialization of some of its findings ;
* it has taken equity positions in newly created firms.
A central element in the successful role played by the IFP has been its close links with the industry, which favoured transfer of technology and mutual understanding. Engineers from industry often team up with IFP people for joint projects, and it is not unusual for IFP employees to join the industry.

The CEPM. To implement the off-shore policy, attention was given to the interface between market needs (oil operators), technical capabilities (IFP) and business competences (engineering companies). A special body was created for this purpose, the Marine Petroleum Committee (CEPM), whose role as coordinator of all the actors has been critical. In addition to being a forum for industry members, the CEPM has a crucial role in channelling funds towards companies for financing high risk ventures.
The CEPM was created in 1963 by the head of the Hydrocarbons Division of the Ministry of Industry to assist the French oil industry diversify into the off-shore area. By 1980, it was managed by an eight member committee,

including senior executives from the oil firms (Elf & CFP), the IFP, the CNEXO and the equipment industry. Two technical committees, also with a broadly-based membership, have responsibility for exploration and production problems. CEPM had a permanent staff of only four people. Its role as a meeting place for the French off-shore community expanded over time : Elf and the IFP were the only committee members in 1963, CFP joined by 1968 and oil equipment firms were admitted in 1971.

CEPM's tasks include reviewing projects submitted by equipment companies with regard to the needs of the oil operators ; it then makes recommendations to the MOI. The Ministry's Hydrocarbons Division then examines the project on financial grounds before a final decision is taken.

The CEPM has proved very successful in fulfilling its coordinating role and creating a dynamic towards the development of the off-shore industry. Its existence favoured :

- a division of labour between the IFP (long-term R&D), the equipment firms (applied R&D) and the oil companies (information on market needs and major resources to fund prototypes) ;
- healthy competition in terms of R&D ideas between industry members ;
- concentration of resources at the development stage : a single project is funded in each area.

Growth of the French off-shore equipment industry. In the mid-1960s American technology had an important lead over competitors in the off-shore field. To catch up, French companies with the help of the government launched very ambitious projects representing technological breakthroughs such as the articulated column (Elf, EMH), the floating platform (IFP, Neptune), or the dynamically positioned drillship (CFP, Foramer). Some of the projects took nearly 10 years to become commercially viable, others were never successfully completed (e.g. the transmediterranean pipeline). On the whole, this initial effort in the off-shore area enabled French firms to gain a technological edge in various areas. Some of the advantages gained were transformed into commercial successes (e.g. the Pentagone floating platform) ; some others failed to develop strong business positions (e.g. Cit-Alcatel in dynamic positioning equipment).

Around 1970, a second phase in the industry's development took place ; the exploitation of the North Sea fields provided a unique opportunity for French firms to commercialize their know-how. Within a few years, the French off-shore industry grew into a multi-billion franc business, second only to that of the US.

By the late 1970s new problems arose for French industry : protectionism grew rapidly in Norway and the UK, creating barriers to French penetration. At the same time, no oil was struck in French territorial waters, despite all the exploration efforts. Some companies, however, have been very imaginative in their efforts to overcome these barriers through joint ventures with local partners (e.g. Doris in UK and Norway) or acquisitions (e.g. UIE in Scotland).

In order to hold their market position in the equipment sector, the French decided to engage in a new and costly round of R&D. The projects chosen are for the needs of the late 1980s in the area of oil exploration and exploitation in deep waters. They involve, for example, floating production platforms, underwater wellheads and J-curve pipelaying, requiring new technological developments in various fields such as robotics, remotely controlled machinery or welding.

During the whole period, the dynamism of the entrepreneurs involved has been an important factor in the development of the off-shore equipment industry. Since the early 1960s, around 20 companies specializing in off-shore or diversifying from on-shore technologies have been created, often with some help from the IFP or the oil companies.

Oil equipment manufacturers have their industry association, the GEP, which participates in trade fairs and carries out market studies. Another industry association, ASTEO, represents firms involved in every aspect of ocean exploitation. In addition to a marketing role, ASTEO provides advice to the government on specific topics.

Conclusions. The French off-shore oil policy was initiated as a new chapter in the long history of governmental search for energy independence. However, the growing independence of oil rich countries, added to more acute concerns for the level of industrial activity in France, shifted the focus of the programme towards the promotion of a growing high technology sector.

The success of the policy is the result of the commitment of all the actors involved, together with a remarkable degree of co-ordination :

- policy formulation has always been grounded in good economic analysis due to the numerous opportunities for exchange of views and interchange of staff ;
- the government acted very early and consistently throughout the period : public funds have been uninterrupted and steadily growing and the same people have been in charge of policy implementation over long periods of time ;
- the oil companies have provided the essential inputs from the market and have continuously favoured the development of new technology within French firms ;
- the IFP carried out a major part of long-term R&D and has been very efficient in transferring its knowledge to business firms ;
- the equipment manufacturers have shown an entrepreneurial spirit and a management expertise that contributed greatly to the success of the industry ;
- apart from its advisory role for the R&D projects, the CEPM has been a forum for industry members ; the links it helped develop between members of the off-shore community contributed greatly to the momentum created in France to develop off-shore oil businesses.

# 6. CONCLUSION : INDUSTRIAL POLICY WITHOUT STRATEGY ?

Since Louis XI and Colbert, France has had at its disposal an impressive arsenal of means of intervention in business, but it has lacked a strategic vision of its industrial development. And unlike some other countries, France has openly pursued the objective of a national "industrial policy". The institutions of the Fifth Republic were to give new lustre to this royalist and centralist tradition, and above all to facilitate the continuity of State intervention which is by its nature difficult in a democracy. The great faith expressed in the successive sector-based priorities of the fifth, sixth and seventh Plans, Pompidou's 'industrial imperative' programme, the great technological equipment plans (in defence, nuclear power, the telephone and the TGV), and the many games of Monopoly played between the State and interest groups have been the most spectacular (and still current) manifestations of this ambition. However, these incessant interventions are not sufficient to create a real strategy for industrial development –that is, to increase the value added of a country with a competitive traded sector. France loves to talk of its industrial policy, but lacks a strategy to match ambition.

## A harsh assessment

Although it is hard to draw the line between responsibilities of State and business, a global assessment of French industrial policies is probably less positive than either the Right or the Left would like to admit. In infrastructure, for example, France is now generally well-equipped technologically, but this has often been achieved at a higher cost to French users and taxpayers than to their American, German or Japanese counterparts. Telecommunications rates for business uses, railroad and road freight prices, airlines rates are significantly higher than in the US, and sometimes higher than in more open, free competitive economies like Germany or the UK.

What is even more serious is that France's gigantic catching up in infrastructure, unique in Europe, never really allowed for the creation of world competitive businesses, with the exception of defence. French industry exports very few nuclear power stations, not yet the TGV (will it ever ?) and export of telephone exchanges is clearly below initial objectives. Of the three industrial sector priorities set up by the fifth Plan 18 years ago, chemicals and mechanical engineering are encumbered by lifeless, subscale businesses continually in the process of restructuring themselves, and electronics remain a priority, while not one of its companies has become globally truly profitable. The successive plans for electronic components have certainly facilitated investments in research and modern production facilities, but the target is a moving one. Few computer companies are able to finance themselves with the exception of certain service companies. Aeronautics and military electronics are brilliant exceptions, but in this domain the rules of competitiveness are far from being strictly economic.

As for the many boundary modifications, mergers, and regroupings encouraged by the State, few have been fruitful. Some have ended up as incoherent and ungovernable conglomerates (Thomson Brandt CSF, Pechiney Ugine Kuhlman) which, paradoxically, had to wait to be nationalized before they could refocus on their original business strengths. Others were delayed too long and now absorb the greater part of the State's resources : steel, shipbuilding, heavy mechanical engineering, paper, petrochemicals, heavy organic chemicals, and fertilizers have been awaiting serious rationalization for 10 to 20 years, and losses will continue to amount to billions. There is no end in sight to rescue plans, with no sign of these industries becoming financially autonomous. The automobile industry, formerly France's jewel and still its principal source of foreign earnings and of technical pride, has been sinking for several years into the vicious circle of non competitiveness : loss of market share, job redundancies, heavy losses, demoralization, etc.

In the more fragmented sectors where the State cannot play a leading role with public procurement or strong industrial players, successive Ministers of Industry have announced many sectoral 'plans' in textiles, toys, mechanical

275

engineering and of course machine-tools. The common denominator of all these plans (apart from that for machine tools) is that they have lacked a serious diagnosis, and have rallied too few funds to solve any problems. The machine tool plan failed to be implemented rigorously, and was too limited to national boundaries to give birth to more competitive companies.

This rapid assessment can only repeat already wellknown critiques of the entire interwoven array of public aids, and more broadly of the more specific privileges built into the credit distribution system in France, of which a good half is driven not by market mechanisms, but by bureaucratic intervention.

At the risk of seeming provocative, one might say that the all too rare new industrial successes of the last twenty years have been caused by corporations which are largely autonomous and even sheltered from State policy : public works (Bouygues, Dumez, SAE), food (BSN, Moët, Pernod-Ricard, Bongrain), cosmetics (L'Oréal), distribution (Carrefour, Auchan, Euromarché), the hotel industry, Club Méditerranée, Air Liquide or Lafarge, to cite only some of the most important. All of them, however, are protected against international competition and export little domestic value added even if they have internationalized. As for the true success stories of industrial policy conducted during 'thirthy glorious years' , such as in aeronautics, oil, and railways, their roots reach back to the prewar era ; ironically and sadly, the sole postwar success among new companies has been in the military industry.

A general strategy for industrial development, which would be based on a thorough understanding of structural evolutions imposed by competitive and market forces, has been lacking in France. A comparative assessment of French industrial policies with those of its most successful rivals suggests some useful lessons for managing industrial decline, promoting growth, and organizing economic development within advanced industrial societies.

## Managing industrial decline

Societies have varied significantly in their ability to address the problems of "crisis industries". Some, such as in Britain, Sweden, Belgium and, more recently, France have spent billions to keep bankrupt companies above water, deluding themselves for years about the chances for revival. Others, such as Germany and Japan, have been more successful in holding down the absolute level of expenditures and gaining greater results from funds utilized.

A number of principles can be distilled from these examples. First, it is crucial to act in **anticipation** of events whenever possible. Structural declines of industries or companies can often be seen a number of years in advance ; at least one or two troughs of the business cycle are evident before serious bankruptcies develop. Thus, the need for rationalization of the German steel and coal industries was seen and acted upon in the late 1960s when the government began a major programme for industrial reconversion in the Ruhr region. Over one billion dollars was spent between 1969-76 to build new industry in the area and to rationalize existing coal and steel operations. Similarly, the Japanese MITI began in 1975 urging limitations on investment in steel and shipbuilding in Japan, despite the fact that these industries were then world leaders and still in expansion phases. Many of the companies did not share MITI's view and had optimistically planned for the future. Nevertheless, a dialogue began which has assisted reconversion developments in the late 1970s. When the steel crisis came in the late 1970s, the dislocations were far less severe in Germany and Japan than they were in France, which had been adding steel capacity at Fos and Dunkirk during the same period and not retiring old mills in Lorraine.

A corollary to this principle is that government must be capable of distinguishing between major structural declines and temporary problems that can be overcome with adequate funding. The tragedy of much government intervention, particularly in steel, shipbuilding, coal and iron ore in Europe, is that the government often provides huge subsidies from the public treasury, after which more funds must be added, and more funds a few years after that. This has been the case for the French steel industry : the government has been forced to finance five successive rescue plans (1967, 1975, 1978, 1981 and 1984) while claiming each time that it would be the last one. Meanwhile, workers are still laid off, and communities and regions suffer the consequences of gradual economic decline due to obsolete plans and uncompetitive organizations. By contrast, in successful cases, the government and the banks that would suffer from any bankruptcies have helped industry to devise a rationalization plan accompanied by labour market and regional policies designed to ease the adjustment. This ensures that government funds will be spent in a way that salvages potentially competitive parts of the industry and minimizes the hardships to workers and communities.

A third lesson involves decision making mechanisms for industrial policy. A number of countries have established various forms of tripartite bodies (representing management, labour, and the public authorities) for considering the problems involved in an industry. When these have been formed after an industry is already experiencing competitive problems, and exist primarily at a centralized level, they have tended to be unsuccessful. As in France or Britain, they have often become mechanisms for government and management to convince unions to accept lays-offs and wage declines, or for management and unions to demand more government assistance. Consultation of this type is most successful when it is part of an ongoing process within subsections of industry, and when it is open to participation by broad cross-sections of affected communities. Under these circumstances, such bodies can be forums in which rationalization plans are created, and creative solutions are found.

A final lesson, which Japanese and German policymakers have long understood, and the French have embraced only recently, is that the only long-term solution to competitively declining industries is the creation of new industries to replace them. In Japan, the primary responsibility for identifying new competitive opportunities rests with the companies themselves, which often encompass a mixture of businesses, some of which are growing, while others are in decline. The major consumer electronic companies for example have been able to drastically reduce

278

their employment in colour TV production following automation of circuit board assembly, while at the same time creating new jobs in videocassette recorders or integrated circuits. When whole companies fail, other companies in the region often provide assistance. The Japanese government provides funds to assist these new growth opportunities. The German government likewise provides incentives to expanding firms for new plants in regions where declines in traditional industry are expected. In both cases, funds are distributed to growing companies within an industry suffering overall decline, or to growing industries, rather than to declining companies and industries.

The worst of both worlds is either to prevent any structural adjustment by artificially maintaining employment, or to allow companies to fail, but to make insufficient effort to encourage companies with growth opportunities to fill the gap. The first error has been that of the successive French governments from 1975 to 1983. The second one has been the British policy for the last few years, and thus far has had dire consequences. As a political reaction against seemingly limitless subsidies of uncompetitive companies, this policy initially gained short-term popularity. In the long run, however, it is proving to be painfully unproductive.

In summary, industrial decline is necessary and inevitable in a vital economy. Successful industrial policies minimize the hardships associated with this process by accelerating the generation of new companies and industries to replace the old. In this way, successful industrial policies promote market changes rather than resist them. They employ the following measures :
- mechanisms to anticipate problem areas well in advance ;
- realistic rationalization plans to accompany aids given to declining companies ; funding to lead to a solution rather than just to maintain the status quo ;
- long-standing consultative mechanisms through which affected parties can together develop solutions to a crisis from a basis of mutual cooperation and trust ;

* long-standing and effective labour market and regional programmes to ease dislocation, attract new industry, and retrain people.

## Promoting growth

Programmes designed to stimulate industrial research and development have existed since the early 1950s in France as in other advanced economies. In the early years, they focused on universities and research institutes undertaking basic research. Since 1970, both the level and mode of operation of many of these programmes has changed. Governments have significantly increased their R&D funding, and more funds have been directly allocated to industry for applied research. This change derives from the realization that development and commercialization of new technology is often more expensive and risky than basic research, and that better coordination between industry and universities provides a quicker diffusion of new innovation.

Increasingly in technology - driven economies like the US, Japan, and to a lesser extent Germany, projects are funded at the initiative of companies that put up a share of the total budget. Consideration is given to the international competitive environment for the products that might be generated from research efforts. Moreover, funds are often divided among companies in such a way that each pursues a different technological solution to a common problem and then shares the information with the others. Commercialization of the innovation, however, is competitive.

In contrast, the French government has supported large-scale, government-pushed, industry-wide programmes designed expressly for national independence. Some of these programmes - Concorde, Plan Calcul, Secam TV, Graphite Gaz - have been failures. Others, such as in off-shore industries, Airbus, power generation, airplanes and helicopters, have reached commercial success although profitability is still a subject of much debate.

Increasingly, it is recognized that large-scale industry-wide programmes are too broad, and that the key to success lies in specialization and dominance of specific businesses. In most countries, industry-wide programmes are giving way to more specific business-based projects, in which governments provide targeted assistance for marketing, foreign investment, or consumer financing. Mechanisms for promoting new industry in Germany are beginning to resemble those that have been used in Japan - featuring a combination of incentives administered according to the competitive economics of particular businesses. France has yet to integrate fully the dynamics of a market economy in its industrial policy thinking. Government agencies do not interact with companies, or respond to their requests but rather dictate too often new areas of investment. Government officials in France have not yet fully recognized the importance of investment in marketing and distribution overseas and merely subsidize exports rather than placing greater emphasis on measures to assist the growth of competitive productivity.

**Structure and organization**
The most effective organizations for industrial policy appear to be those in which policy explicitly emanates from only one or two places in the government and where jurisdisdictions are clearly defined. In Japan, MITI has clear authority over industrial affairs. Although its budget must be approved by the Ministry of Finance, and it works through certain other institutions to implement policy such as the Japan Development Bank, it is clearly in charge. In Germany, the Ministry of Economy and the Ministry for Technology have clearly-defined spheres of responsibility, as do the agencies responsible for export and overseas investment assistance. On the other hand, the French structure is a fragmented and unstable collection of agencies, ministries, boards and ad hoc groups. As a result, policymaking is often diffused among groups and is subject to political infighting. This has been a source of weakness for French industrial policy.

A second principle for effective organization of industrial policy is that a competent group of civil servants must be responsible for designing and implementing it. Business leaders in all countries naturally resist government intervention. Nevertheless, this resistance has been overcome in countries like Japan and France, where the calibre of government officials responsible for industrial policy is extremely high. The traditional prestige attached to careers in the French government and the severe elite selection through ENA have been, however, a source of misused power.

A third principle is that individual policy must be transparent. Public knowledge of government programmes helps to ensure public confidence in industrial policy. In Germany and the US, for example, the amount, type, and destination of government aid by company is made public. In Japan, such information also is available to the public, although one requires great persistence to uncover details. This is far from being the case in France where all attempts at publicizing reports on government aids to industry have been covered up in the past by the highest political echelons.

A fourth principle, related to transparency, is that the public must support the broad goals of industrial policy. At its most basic level, effective industrial policy rests upon social consensus - a collective commitment to productivity on the part of the public·at-large. In countries such as Britain and France, in which different groups of workers and producers fundamentally disagree about how the economy should be organized and how the fruits of new produtivity should be distributed, industrial policy falls prey to divisiveness. Social consensus cannot be contrived, of course, but it can be facilitated through decision-making processes in which many segments of the public are consulted and informed.

Finally, industrial policy should not depend upon a large bureaucracy. A large bureaucracy only complicates effective administration, rendering internal transactions less efficient and confronting business leaders with bewildering red tape.

The lessons to learn from France's past experience with industrial policy relate more to the discipline and conduct of analysis and to the process by which industrial policy is undertaken than to the content of specific programmes. Below are some general principles that are emerging within the most successful advanced industrial countries :

- economic restructuring and improvement of competitive productivity are becoming the key goals of industrial policy. The common aim is the maximization of wealth creation in sustainable financial conditions ;

- well-established labour market and regional policies administered with long-standing and well-defined participation from management, labour, financial institutions, and government are necessary. The presence of these structures in Germany and Japan and their absence in France and the UK have made the difference between success and failure for many projects ;
- industrial policy instruments must be matched to the needs of a given competitive situation. No general policy will succeed in all competitive situations. Mechanisms such as across-the-board export subsidies or employment subsidies which do not foster industrial restructuring are being discouraged. Such policies in France and the UK in particular have generally been unsuccessful and wasteful of national resources. Matching specific actions to the key competitive levers in a business ensures success and cost efficiency. This has been a major factor in the success of Japanse industrial policy and has been learned by some governments in the world who now are becoming more sophisticated in their use of policy tools as illustrated by South Korea, or Singapore ;
- investment decisions should not be dictated by government but should be initiated by businesses which are close to the market place. The role of government has been most effective when it has involved intelligent response and dialogue with businesses rather than heavy-handed direction.

The political changes in France of the last decade have caused turmoil and rigidities in industrial policies. The Chirac government from 1975 to 1978 did little to adapt France to its new competitive environment and initiated a series of counter-cyclical measures which still account for part of French industry's cost penalties. The Barre government from 1978 to 1981 did a lot to restore corporate and State financial health, and at the same time invested in new technologies. It failed, however, to convince public opinion and the unions of the fairness of the structural adjustments and could not reverse the trend of declining investment, R&D and

283

market shares. The first socialist Mauroy governments (1981-83) focused the debate on ideological changes (nationalizations) and adopted countercyclical measures which proved to be short-lived and costly for the nation. With the help of the Delors 'plan of rigour' and more recently the new Fabius government, France has at last realized, many years after its neighbours, that the restructuring of industry would be long and painful. It still has to realize that it is in fact endless, as competitive positions evolve and markets mature.

From the official declarations and the policy decisions of the last two years, it is possible to summarize the objectives of French industrial policy in six priorities. Indeed, these objectives will undoubtedly be those of any government which will be in power after the 1986 elections, however different the rhetoric or the style.

**The present directions of French industrial policy**
The French government's priorities for the future appear to be the following :

- to restructure basic industries and those of intermediate goods (and, in the future, the auto industry) which constitute the foundation of the public sector, through continued budgetary support in order to permit investments in productivity which companies cannot finance through their internal cash flows ;
- to modernize the rest of industry by furnishing businesses which can invest productively with subsidized loans through new saving channels (Codevi, Industrial Modernization Fund) ;
- to convince the entire array of social forces of the cruel necessity of reducing jobs, when market growth is inferior to productivity growth ;
- to make up for France's technological lag with budgetary support of industrial R&D, and especially with large 'mobilising programmes' linking public and private centres, with priority given to computer technology, aerospace and, to a lesser extent, biotechnology ;

* to steer the present generation into new disciplines corresponding to the new requirements of international competitition : training in electronics and biology, international trade schools ;
* to anchor France's position in Europe by weaving new cooperative threads with EC countries (in technology, infrastructure and industry).

This industrial policy is geared towards providing business with the financial and human resources they need. The implicit wager is that they will transform these resources into equipment and research which will raise them up to an internationally competitive level. Is this quite liberal vision adequate for French industry's competitiveness ? In other words, do such investments necessarily lead to an increase in competitiveness ?

## What is competitiveness ?

In a competitive world, the most successful company is the one with the lowest cost for a given service, or the best service (and therefore a higher price) for equivalent cost – that is, the one which knows how to use resources most efficiently.

In any industrial activity there is always a leader, generating a higher profit than its rivals and thus growing more rapidly ; its followers, who live more or less comfortably ; and those companies whose costs are above the price level imposed by their more efficient rivals, and are thus condemned to extinction.

Improving competitiveness means among other things reaching cost advantages through scale : instant scale effects and the benefits of cumulative experience. In an open economy, such a scale objective is a moving target which evolves with market growth and the globalization of trade. In consequence, research and investments attempted by underscaled businesses are a squandering of resources and an inflation factor when they neither achieve nor lead towards competitive scale. France has invested as much as its neighbours, but large investments have been accomplished by loss-making businesses which could not or did not know how to change their scale. It is not a question of calling for gigantic proportions : Salomon (2,000 employees) is of competitive scale while Usinor (20,000 employees) is not. The list of underscale capacities, refusals to specialize and the scattering of efforts of the last 20 years is overwhelming : petro- chemicals, thermoplastics, fertilizers, steel, shipbuilding, telephone, computers, automobile parts, industrial vehicles, electronic components, machine tools, farm equipment, paper, textiles, to mention only those principal French industries which have clearly not achieved world or even European competitive scale. The gravity of their situation is not caused by under-investment, as the materialist vision of industrial development would have us believe : CDF-Chimie, Usinor, Renault and Bull, for example, have probably invested too much, ill-advisedly. It is caused, rather, by bad strategies, and sub-optimal run lengths, industrial sites, and distribution networks. France does not lack material investments but rather immaterial ones - product modifications for foreign markets, factories adapted to long runs, world marketing, and team organization.

With such a list of failures concerning sectors where the State has intervened as well as others where it has abstained, the prime objective of industrial policy becomes : how can French industry achieve the required scale and technology lead, within each business, while increased competition does not leave time for rest ?

**Competitive scale and access to technology through cooperation**
Everyone agrees that if all businesses performed and organised themselves like L'Oreal, Bic or Dumez in the search for the advantages of world scale, French industry would not need an industrial policy. France has few Stars of this kind and not a single one in growing technology-based businesses except oil. If French business cannot achieve world scale on its own, it must conduct its search through a policy of alliances and judicious associations. The overlapping of technologies which had been separate (electronics and mechanical engineering, for example), and the integration of world markets, force the strongest to break out of their isolation. IBM is diverging considerably from its usual behaviour in proceeding towards external acquisitions in telecommunications (Rolm) and in components. Firms as

powerful as Control Data, Honeywell or Sperry have decided to create a common research laboratory. Philips and ATT are sharing with each other their access to markets and their technological resources, respectively. France remains in splendid isolation.

Intercorporate cooperation does not just happen spontaneously ; it requires great experience often acquired first on the national level. Swedish, German, Swiss and Japanese industries have generally speaking known how to combine the competitive and the cooperative spirit. In France, family or professional rivalries, misapprehensions of real competitors, or simply atavistic individualism and/or arrogance have prevented the formation of necessary alliances. They have often ruined agreements for cross-specialization (as in German chemicals), cartels for consolidation (as in German and Japanese steel), and research associations (as in Japanese electronics). The weakness of France's sub-contractors and component manufacturers - a sign of the unreasonable diversification of large groups - has prevented the constitution of scale economies shared by French users. Contrary to ZF which in West Germany wholly supplies truck manufacturers with transmissions, Berliet, Saviem and Unic in France have always maintained integrated manufacturing of short runs, based on incompatible standards. This uncompetitive structure is unfortunately repeated in the machine tool industry for key components (ball screws), in farm equipment (motors), in cars (electrical equipment) and many segments of the textile industry.

Thus it seems that, faced with rivals which are better organized or which gain additional strength through successful mergers, French businesses can no longer retaliate in isolation. Most often, exclusively French alliances do not suffice. The CGE-Thomson agreement must be a prelude to cross-specializations and to the corollary : opening of public markets with West Germany. The only solution to the machine tool crisis is a European one. To summarize these often complex situations, interdependence of business strategies is provoked by one or many of the following factors :

∗ the fragmentation of component manufacturing is no longer viable when faced with foreign competitors centred around a dominant world supplier (Fanuc in Japanese numerical controls) ;

∗ access to world markets requires a common approach to distribution, after-sales service, and engineering of a range of complementary products (Japanese trading companies in machines or in textiles, Danish or Dutch food distribution companies) ;

∗ optimization of run lengths, of overhead costs, and of business cycles requires integrated management of a "chain" of businesses situated at different levels of the manufacturing process (the woollen industry of Prato in Italy).

In these situations, how can French industry regain its competitivity without a profound modification of its structures ∗ that is, of the companies' respective specializations, of links between supplier and client, and of product range ? The major drawbacks of policies like the textile 'plan' of 1982-83 are in giving respite to the weakest at the expense of the strongest and in putting off the painful sacrifies necessary to structural redefinitions. Likewise, simple juridico-financial reorganizations like the steel 'plans' of 1978 and 1985 artificially maintain the survival of underscaled groups. General financial support or a backing of hozizontal research, like those currently envisaged by the government, take the risk of maintaining ∗ even of reinforcing ∗ a company's lack of scale.

### Who must take the initiative ?
The cure is more difficult than the diagnosis. If everyone (or almost everyone) agreed that it were better to wait for businesses to take the initiative, the State could not remain indifferent to the structural flaws in France's industrial fabric. The textile plan is not a response, but rather a short-term economic measure (both costly and harmful, we might add). The Modernization Fund's loans (like the subsidized loans introduced in 1978) and the praiseworthy support of research, both of which have grown since 1981, are at risk of becoming dressings on a limb that should be amputated to save the body. Moreover, the State's responsibility is directly

engaged wherever its implicit behaviour is determinant : activities dependent on public procurement,and those dependent on the State as tutor, regulator or as shareholder, constitute more than half of French industry.

When business leaders (private or nationalized) themselves take the initiative in specialization, cooperation, and the search for competitive scale, the State must at the least not hinder them, and should diligently help them, as in the Thomson-CGE agreement, and Pechiney's. It is rather paradoxical that it was only after the nationalizations ≉ which everyone expected would mean additional inflexibility ≉ that one saw the huge monsters born in the euphoria of the 1960s return to their original vocations. It seems that finally - under pressure from competition and deficits ≉ the large French groups have become conscious of the lack of scale which was the corollary of the disorderly diversification of their business portfolios. The French chemical companies neither regrouped among themselves nor with foreign alliances, but through heterogeneous financial constructions like Pechiney≉Ugine≉Kulhman. The same went for heavy mechanical engineering and electronics (apart from consumer electronics). When business leaders cannot or do not know how to take the initiative in the search for scale, the State must either allow natural selection to take place or must itself establish a strategic diagnosis and spur them on towards specialization and scale effects. A laissez≉faire approach accompanied by the opening of financial floodgates (loans, capital endowments to public enterprises, research credits) is the worst possible reaction to a deficiency in business initiative. Thus to leave Usinor and Sacilor to develop their own commercial strategies and independent investments (from behind the mask of 'public enterprise's managerial autonomy') reveals a blindness towards the new conditions of competitivity. But how can State intervention work without creating a cure which is worse than the disease ?

The French State is poorly equipped for the task of changing its role as tutor or as benefactor into one as a catalyst of intercorporate or international cooperation.

State intervention in business structures has been much rarer than is usually thought : as we have shown, sector≉ based 'plans' are typically rather timid about promoting changes in specialization and scale. This has been the case with plans for heavy organic chemicals and fertilizers (especially in the public sector), steel, shipbuilding, and innumerable machine-tool and heavy mechanical engineering plans.

Conversely, the French State's initiatives have only rarely resulted in, or even aimed at, world scale competitiveness. Thus the Plan Calcul was initially designed outside, and even in opposition to, the single French business with a European network (Bull). Subsequent agreements with Honeywell were reached at the expense of a European solution and involved giving up access to two important markets : Britain and Italy. One could likewise cite errors of judgment and failures in the telephone industry, in which France claimed to be the only European country to favour four underscaled suppliers (of which two were national with no international ties). The failures have certainly been more numerous than the successes, but might we not draw a moral from the sucess stories of those who have been in charge of Airbus, of the military cooperations, of Ariane, and of the development of an oil and oil-related industry on the international level ?

The time has come seriously to draw lessons from the successes and the deficiencies of French industrial development, and from the respective roles played by the State and business.

### The role of the State

Methods of intervention require improvements in four domains : diagnosis, animation, negotiation and decision making.

**The capacity for diagnostic strategy** is the starting point of any industrial policy and is the greatest defect of the French administration, not from any lack of brainpower, but from defects of methods and from France's withdrawal into itself. Industrial diagnosis - if it wishes to be effective and thus established on a detailed level - requires great experience in world-scale information retrieval, processing and especially analysis.

When it comes to economic data, France is cruelly lagging behind Japan, the US, and West Germany. The foreign public networks (DREE) are time-worn and poorly linked with interior networks. The Chambers of Commerce and the Professional Federations are completely underequipped in relation to their German counterparts. The statistical services INSEE and STISI are incapable of keeping up, in a reasonable time span, with many essential variables of industrial enterprises (such as profits, R & D, or foreign investment). The data available on French businesses is mediocre, non-current, and discontinuous. In the US, all businesses listed on the Stock Exchange are required to reveal their profits and investments by divison and by geographical zone. In France, corporate accounts are still misleading. Industry has everything to gain from an ethic of transparency and truthfulness.

**The capacity for animation, encouragement and education** is not a tradition of the French administration, either. The French State knows how to constrain. It is crippled in a changing and uncertain world like that of international industry.

French people often have a false view of Japanese industrial policy. MITI has no coercive power (except in the domain of foreign exchange), nor does it distribute any financial manna. It is quite contrary to our top civil servants' old fantasies. Its prestige - and it is a great one - arises above all from its analytic capacity, its contribution of data on foreign markets and competitors, and its capacity to animate dialogue. MITI continuously and in great detail encourages **hundreds** of diagnostic and strategic groups, bringing together large and small businesses, customers and suppliers, researchers and industrialists encompassing the most diverse activities : from aluminium electrolysis, to synthetic silks, to fifth-generation computers.

France should draw on its own history - the lessons from successful strategic dialogues which have more often than not occurred without great publicity. The Comité d'Etudes Pétrolières Marines (CEPM), for example, has for 20 years been the privileged meeting-place of oil companies, equipment firms, engineering specialists and research centres, where the great technological and commercial successes of the French offshore oil industry have been decided and developed. This kind of structure which is informal, low-key, competent, and stable, lends itself to the creation of cooperation agreements, cross-specializations, and the search for world scale in each business segment. This step should, in general, be taken in the European arena, and on the intercorporate level. It has already been fruitful in computer technology : the ESPRIT programme of European research was prepared over a period of 18 months by 16 companies.

Such a step is the inverse of sector-based plans. It sets no short-term objectives such as employment or balance of payments ; it focuses more on structural effects and strategic spin-offs than on spectacular financial or legal measures. It is progressive, flexible, pragmatic. No sector-based plan could rapidly improve the machine tool, the computer, or the paper industry's competitiveness. Only a long-term, realistic, detailed and continuous process of intercorporate dialogue can face these challenges. The Directors of the Ministry of Industry must initiate no further 'plans'. They must submit to a cultural renaissance and transform themselves into diffusers of information, into advocates of diagnostics, and into leaders of dialogue. Such a transformation calls for great modesty but also great professionalism.

**The capacity for State negotiation** is presently corrupted by its tentacular power. If the Administration is to abandon its pernicious role as tutor or as benefactor of uncompetitive businesses, it must regain its capactiy for negotiation. In order to do this, the identification of choices must be more rigorous : every industrial problem has a strategic dimension ~ products, market shares, investments ; an organizational dimension ~ management, time limits ; a social and a financial dimension. The first two are too often neglected in favour of the last two. Negotiations are led by the Director of the Treasury and political staff within Ministers' 'Cabinets'.  It is as if the State had to arbitrate between its concern about budgetary rigour and its concern about saving or creating jobs.

A good industrial negotiation between the State and business requires a working out of all the dimensions, a coordination of all the Administration's various services, and a leader recognized for his knowledge of the field and for his strategic sense.

**The State's capacity for decision making** must be aimed towards gaining the essential qualities one expects of industrialists : rapidity, firmness, commitment to agreements. The French State has discredited itself for twenty years in the eyes of German and Dutch industrialists, when it made an about-face in the Unidata affair shortly after signing an agreement. An industrial decision is not really made until the file is closed ; otherwise, competitors take advantage of the transition and employees become discouraged.

When one takes the magnitude of the nationalized sector into account, one of the major challenges in the years to come will be to arbitrate in the same way - that is, in taking note of the strict merits of business - for both private and public businesses. Public businesses must have the same constraints, the same duties and the same autonomy as private business, when questions of scale and of cooperation are at stake.

Such a reversal of the Administration's methods of intervention cannot take place in one year, nor even in one term. This makes it all the more urgent to start working at it right now. Just as a new business strategy requires new structures, so must the Ministry of Industry be profoundly reorganized. The new capacities for diagnosis and for animation must be decentralized and entrusted to professionals, while the new capacities for negotiation and decision making require new work methods in the Administration.

As for diagnosis and policy implementation, new skills and new methods can be progressively injected into the current Direction Générale de l'Industrie and into industrial leadership. But besides the fact that it is hard to construct something new out of old materials, the present range of the Ministry of Industry's responsibilities is too limited : fortunately, it includes telecommunications (budgetarily, at least), but it excludes the food industries, construction, shipbuilding, aeronautics, and military electronics industries, notably. Moreover, despite the recent Modernization Fund's protection, most financial inducements and horizontal policies ⊣ export financing, regional development, fiscal agreements ⊣ elude industry's participation. France lacks the advice and the implicit consensus of high ranking public officials and of industrial leaders well known for their business success and their concern for the general interest.

The existing capacities for diagnosis and for implementation are scattered and poorly utilized, such as the IDI which treats the problems of small companies, the technical Ministries, and the large national monopolies (EDF, SNCF, PTT). The State also needs new and fresh engineers and professionals from the "traded" industries, French people with experience in other great industrial nations, and consultants trained in international forums.

The capacities for negotiation and decision-making must, of course, remain closely tied to the Administration. The structure which was proposed for the defunct CODIS was quite pertinent : to coordinate services, to determine priorities,to decide quickly and directly. The CODIS succumbed to power struggles carried on by its top officials, and more fundamentally, to several errors in objectives. The CODIS ⊣ in the great tradition of the French State ⊣ confused its financial responsibilities with those of a strategy catalyst. It was no longer the objective and demanding instigator it had been, as soon as it became also a distributor of aid, the ultimate symbol of a top industrial manager's power.

There is a great danger that the French Administration will not break out of its old shortcomings ⊣ a narrow minded esprit de corps, inflexibility, lack of realistic objectives, feelings of superiority, etc. The best way to force it into modesty and professionalism is to allow it only to take initiatives in a progressive way, and to continuously confront it with reality. France has no shortage of either brainpower, energy, ambition or even of money. What it cruelly lacks is the realization that it has never caught up with the great industrial powers of the early 20th century (USA, West Germany), and has already been outrun by that of the late 20th century (Japan). What France needs now is to get back to work, to 'modernize' without cease, and, in order to do this, to better understand the forces of competition and of world markets. Such must be the virtues of a new industrial policy, with a strategy.

# POSTSCRIPT : THE NEXT FRENCH MIRACLE ?

## An irreversible choice for international competition

In its long history, France has never been a leading nation in trade and industry, but it has often been one of the wealthiest or at least one of the most attractive places to live. The French have lagged behind the Italian or Dutch merchants and navigators, behind the British and German industrial capitalists, and are now lagging behind the American and Japanese multinational corporations. They have however been well endowed with a rich and diversified farmland, a temperate climate, a long coast line and a convenient geographical location. The French have therefore been sufficiently satisfied with their relative situation to emigrate much less than their European neighbours. They have always felt that they could improve their standard of living by tapping domestic resources (and colonies). As a result they have not developed the same sense of international competition, which is at the root of modern capitalism.

After the costly victory of 1918, France entered twenty years of economic lethargy and social division which led to the most humiliating defeat of its history. Five years of coma followed, while most of the other major nations had their industries boosted and their people united by the war effort. The 'thirty glorious years' of 1945-75 were therefore remarkable not only because the country experienced the highest growth rate in Europe, second in the world after Japan, but also because it embarked on a fundamental structural evolution from a protected agricultural society to an industrial economy open to trade and foreign competition. The country had to fall far in its standard of living, and its international presence, before it could rebound. The postwar period was thus the time for France to catch up with its predecessors in the industrial revolution and to transform its economic structures.

Free trade, international competition and industrial growth have brought enough benefits in terms of jobs and standard of living to make these strategic choices irreversible for the French people and its leaders. When the Left came to power in 1981, it was tempted to 'break away from capitalism' as its programme explicitly stated (e.g. nationalizations, trade protection, credit planning, etc.) but it quickly returned to the model of a mixed economy. When hard choices had to be made in 1983, the French government decided to stay in the European Monetary System, and restore its fundamental macroeconomic equilibrium (trade balance, budget and social deficits, corporate cash flows). Since then, the actions taken and even the rethoric used by the French Left have more and more resembled those of Nordic and German social democrats, embracing the virtues of the market system and free trade.

All the polls show that a majority of the French people is now convinced of the long term benefits of open competition and open borders, even if they are also attached to their system of social security, unemployment benefits and to some extent to an influential role of the State in the economy. The conversion of nine tenths of the French to a free economy close to the German or the Scandinavian models is not a small event, at a time of record unemployment, public sector restrictions and trade deficits. After all, if the traditional attitudes and beliefs still held in France today, people in disarray would turn to the almighty State for assistance, and the creation of new companies would not be at a record level.

If France has definitely chosen to be a market economy open to foreign competition, it has yet to learn how to succeed in bad times, as well as in good times. The postwar miracle was one of reconstruction, physical transformation and fast growing trade. The performance criteria were those of quantitative growth, and productivity. As we saw in part II and part III, a new wave of entrepreneurs and State ventures could thrive in what was a fairly stable and supportive environment where every European country was becoming wealthier. If France wants to stay a leading industrial nation by the year 2000, it needs a miracle of another kind : one which will be characterized by mental and organisational transformation. Performance criteria are those of qualitative development and adaptability. Innovation and investments alone will not create wealth automatically, they have to result in greater value for customers and greater advantage against competitors. Not every nation will become wealthier in trading with others ;

297

some will slowly become obsolete and live off their reserves, while others will adapt and continue to progress. The time has come for the selection of the fittest.

In an environment characterized by constantly emerging new technologies, new businesses, new customer groups, and a more and more integrated trading system, there are ample opportunities for new competitors to enter and old ones to disappear, for new industrial countries to grow and old ones to decline. More than ever, and for an increasing number of industries, success is not based on technical excellence or physical investments, but on better global performance. Ariane is not a success because it puts into geostationary orbit payloads of several tons for the first time in Europe, but because it satisfies the needs of many new customers at a lower cost and with more reliable deadlines than the US Space Shuttle, its only commercial competitor. Super Phenix, on the other hand, might be the best fast breeder reactor in the world on technical grounds, but it does not have a market because it produces more expensive electricity than alternative sources of energy.

More than ever before in man's history, and excluding the unthinkable scenario of a nuclear holocaust, the fate of a nation will depend on its ability to sustain international competition in a number of businesses proportional to its population. What then are the chances of France remaining among the leaders by the year 2000 ?.

## France's handicaps and assets for the year 2000
In the worldwide redistribution of power and wealth between Europe, the USA, Japan and the newly industrialised countries, France suffers from many of the same handicaps which other European economies face. It has in addition some handicaps of its own and fortunately some assets which can shape its destiny.

### The handicaps of a European nation
Like its European neighbours, including the most prosperous, France is marked by many signs of obsolescence and decay. The proportion of active to inactive people is decreasing dramatically as the population is ageing and the birth rate has now declined below the point of generation renewal. This

is compounded by earlier retirement and pre-pension schemes in industries with redundant workers. Rising unemployment and health costs cannot be matched by similar increases in the nation's production base. This means a loss of competitiveness against younger or more dynamic nations.

But more fundamentally, European economies are caught in a constantly evolving competition to which they have more and more difficulty to adapt. They do not have the resources and scale of the American economy and are less adaptable and combative than the Asian nations, including Japan. Having reached a remarkable degree of prosperity after pioneering many new industries, they find themselves trapped into old structures, obsolete investments and archaic attitudes. France is a newly industrialised country compared with the UK, Belgium or Germany, but suffers from the same syndromes : its workers do not emigrate away from declining regions where their roots have always been, its managers lack faith and conviction, its young people are not offered an exciting future, its education system tends to reproduce the values and knowledge of the establishment rather than prepare the new generations to cope with a different world.

It is therefore difficult for political and business leaders to convince the society to adjust from one employment level to a lower one, from one industry to another, from one region to another. In an environment where fluidity, rapidity and pace of adaptation form the basis for success, European economies are all plagued with rigidities, slowness and fragmentation. European markets are all different, societies are still confronted with class conflicts, large companies are less adaptable than their US or Japanese rivals, political parties are boxed in ideologies.

In this context, French handicaps are those of a continent and of a civilisation. If Europe continues to decline, France will follow. If there is a future for Europe, France could hold its position as its second most powerful engine. In both cases however, the country has to face specific obstacles and can capitalise on specific assets.

#### France's handicaps in open competition

France has the handicaps of a centralised and protected society which has only recently come to grapple with a decentralised market economy facing intense competition. These handicaps are of five general kinds and constitute the fundamental obstacles to the modernisation of French enterprise and French society.

(a) Poor traditions of industrial organisation and labour relations. The French genius is better at exploring new paths and breaking new ground, than at reproducing constant quality and performance. The education system, the social values, the forms of organization, the role models are all geared towards uniqueness, heroïsm and individual prowess, rather than long series, hard work and collective results. This cultural environment is more favourable to the creative explosion of artistic talents, technical inventions, and original designs, than to the harmonious development of industrial activities. At all levels of society, the French mind resists and sometimes rejects the disciplines and routines which make industries efficient and competitive.

The management of production is an obvious illustration. Process engineers look more for breaking records in cycle times and machine speed than for maximizing capacity utilization and reducing maintenance costs. Product engineers and R & D departments rarely understand the requirements of mass production : transfers of people between the shopfloor and the labs, which are customary in Japan, Scandinavia or Germany, rarely occur in France. Nordic and Germanic corporations are far ahead in terms of organisational development and the management of human resources. French management and French unions are both at fault. Decisions are taken subjectively and without preparation. Information systems are obscure and partial. Conflicts are resolved by brute force or ruse, not by negotiation and learning. People are considered as a constraint or a source of headache, not as the most precious asset. The immediate postwar period was fertile in social reforms in most European industrialized countries. France went half way with the introduction of the Comités d'entreprise. It has taken forty more years (with the lois

Auroux) for many French companies to discuss corporate decisions with the unions, in a manner which German and Scandinavian companies have experienced ever since the Second World War.

French leadership has been trained to optimize resources along a single dimension, not to make trade-offs in condition of uncertainty. French leaders are still more comfortable at managing 'vertical' and bureaucratic organisations driven by a single performance measure like technical achievement (e.g. research agencies, utilities) than decentralised 'matrix' organisations driven by a complex set of measures. It seeks to achieve the best result whatever the costs are rather than the best return on inputs employed.

Larger corporations suffer most from the French cultural archetypes. The French people still treat industry as a personal venture. This favours the emergence of strong personalities able to start up new companies and develop them up to a certain size, but not managers of large complex organizations. It turns out successful capitalists like Marcel Dassault, Baron Bich, Sylvain Floirat (Matra) or Fournier and Defforey of Carrefour, or bright administrators for public utilities, but not enough of the thousands of pragmatic, consistent, reliable and stable executives who make large multinational companies successful. The popular role model in France is Bernard Tapie, not the chief executive officer of Schlumberger or Elf Aquitaine. France has always been a fertile ground of creators who can hold an organisation on their own. It is however dramatically poor in talents such as Cesare Romiti, Lee Iacocca, or Per Gyllenhammar who have turned large and complex structures in bad situations such as Fiat, Chrysler or Volvo into profitable striving companies.

Executive teams who were considered as role models by their peers in the 1970s, in companies such as Renault, Peugeot, Michelin or Thomson, found themselves overwhelmed in times of crisis. Management became divided, decisions got postponed, the workforce was left in disarray. Charismatic leaders, founders or long established grass root managers of somewhat smaller corporations like A. Riboud (BSN), F. Dalle (L'Oreal) or F. Bouygues, were much more successful at sailing their ships through rough waters and making quick decisons while maintaining the integrity of their firm. These talents are dramatically lacking in larger corporations.

(b) Nationalistic attitudes. France is the last nation-state in Europe, together with England, with a sense of superiority or at least self-sufficiency. Everyone in Brussels will agree that the best European citizens are the Italians and the smaller nations. The Germans are still eager to prove their goodwill and contribute to a peaceful and prosperous continent. The French have missed their historical chance in 1958 to become the soul of a new Europe through ignorance, arrogance and some degree of fear of being overcome by more efficient nations. French corporate leadership has failed to build truly transnational enterprises – there are only a handful of them in Europe –and has left the field wide open for more dynamic and farsighted German, US, Dutch, Swiss or Swedish rivals. There are too few Frenchmen abroad, and too few executives speak foreign languages. French companies export as much as their rivals but they are not as truly international : they have not established their presence in distant markets as solidly, and rarely take their decisions with a world vision. The true multinationals – Air Liquide, Schlumberger or Michelin – are rare exceptions among large corporations and these are not very large corporations by world standards. Most are mere exporters of French products designed for the French market, or investors in unrelated businesses abroad.

Only half of the union membership belong to the European confederation and few of their leaders have any concern about the fate of Europe. Out of the four main political parties, two form a purely nationalistic separate group in Strasbourg (the Gaullists and the Communists). It is now 'chic' among political leaders to laugh and joke about the EC inefficiencies whereas most of them are due to national attitudes, the first one being the disastrous adjustment to the treaty of Rome imposed by de Gaulle in 1967 and known as the "Luxembourg compromise" which introduced unanimity instead of majority rule.

Many political leaders think that the French franc is still a major reserve currency which allows them to conduct economic policies independently from world business cycles.

Many leaders and media reject imports and applaud French quotas on Japanese cars and colour TVs, or road blocks against Italian wine. In summary the French people are too satisfied with their life style and too sceptical about the benefits of a new style of leadership, to be positively influenced by their foreign neighbours, or eager to succeed on foreign soil.

(c) <u>Anachronistic education and research institutions</u>. The French education system is at least one century old and many of its most prestigious schools were set up almost two centuries ago : Ecole des Ponts et Chaussées and Ecole des Mines, in the eighteenth century, Arts et Métiers during the Revolution, Polytechnique under Napoléon. The French primary school is considered one of the best in the world and combines quality, creativity and free access for the largest number. The secondary school however is still built on nineteenth century intellectual models and does not prepare youth for the diversity and uncertainties of modern life. Only 37 per cent of the youth gets its baccalauréat, while the others are more or less rejected from a recognised career path. No society can function properly with such a failure rate.

The higher education system is geared to selecting the best minds, for the top, not at developing a wide range of skills and motivations for a wide range of professions. The best engineering schools (Polytechnique, Mines) teach mathematics and physics not engineering. The top graduates will never be engineers in their life but will belong to a special caste of super citizens who will manage anything from a ministry to a bank or a nationalised company. The top government school (ENA) is not a learning instiution for civil servants and public administrators but a selection mechanism with similar objectives. French education teaches too much analysis, and not enough integration : it gives a sense of intellectual superiority (or inferiority) but does not help to cope with uncertainty, changes or differences. It is still too much written and systematic, not verbal and experimental like anglosaxon or nordic education. The reward system is based

303

on the elegance and the brio of the solution not on its usefulness. This has moulded a style of leadership unfit for managing large companies undergoing change (see above).

The research institutions are modelled and managed to satisfy the researchers, not the society. Fundamental science is of an excellent level in France, particularly in mathematics and physics. Applied sciences, however, are lagging.

The emergence of computer technology and biotechnology is posing a great challenge to existing insitutions, not only because, as new fields, they require the channelling of resources, but also because they present specific requirements in ways of conducting research and education. Computer science involves at the basic level (among others), mathematicians, solid-state physicists, psychologists ; biotechnology involves biologists, chemists, medical doctors, etc. Both also require an innovative mix of research teams, new student curricula, new labs and equipment. Thus, they cannot be **part of** existing units or programmes. Both fields also need a very good interface between basic science and engineering : theoretical research on computer architecture can hardly be divorced from the design and fabrication of hardware which in turn require competences in electrical and mechanical engineering.

Overall, France (as well as Europe in general) has proven ill-equiped to deal with this challenge both in terms of research activity and in terms of trained researchers. Although it can still compare favourably with any other system in some areas of basic research and in the quality of its preparatory schooling (undergraduate level), France has not structurally been able to come up with adequate research-led education and with the necessary blend of disciplines and of basic science and engineering.

The reasons are numerous. First, most of the research work in France is performed in very large government labs (CNRS, CEA, CNET), which have no institutional link with universities (they often report to different ministries) and have no educational role. Second, universities have been short of money to conduct experimental research ; most of the equipment money has gone to government labs whilst university money has been used to deal with the increasing number of students. Third, the institutional split between universities (mainly basic disciplines) and engineering schools (applied research) has made the integration of both aspects very difficult. Finally, the ability of the French scientific education system to evolve towards new fields has proved very limited. Reallocation of resources is almost impossible in a public service mode ( most of the scientific staff and faculty is fully tenured). New programmes can only be developed with additional resources and those have been scarce. The pressures put on French institutions to evolve have been very small : research budgets are repeated from year to year (with no real evaluation of topics nor of quality) and the weak links between industry and university have prevented a fast response to new missions.

(d) <u>Underdeveloped market mechanisms for resource allocation</u>. France has too recently converted to open competition, to have replaced all bureaucratic mechanisms by market mechanisms. This is a cause of grief and inefficiencies which will take long to disappear despite all the promises of the opposition parties, and the recent changes of the Socialists.

Despite recent reforms (see part III, chapter 3) France is far from having a market based financial system. Banks tend to prolong unduly the life of inefficient companies as long as they are large and pre-eminent, rather than facilitate structural evolutions. The reorganisations of Boussac or Creusot-Loire have been instigated by the State or individual capitalists, not by the banks as in Germany (with AEG-Telefunken), Japan or the US. The stock market is still very small and the bond market can be crowded out by the public sector at times when the real estate market is also attractive. There is no real competition for money. Corporate ownership is either family based or institutional (State and insurance companies) and there is little fluidity : unfriendly take-over bids are rare and very few companies go public.

The various sectors of the economy are not competing for the same funds : each sector has its own sources of credit, its own structure of interest rates, and its own subsidies. More than half of the fund flows are channelled by bureaucratic decision not by market criteria. This was necessary at a time of reconstruction, sectoral priority and limited foreign competition. It creates frustrations and inefficiencies in a complex economy open to ever-changing trade and investment patterns, where the best decision makers are the customers and the business managers. Everyone agrees that the nation should continue to set aside public funds to invest in risky ventures like Ariane or Airbus, but why subsidize the small machine tool industry and not the automotive components sectors ? Why does a textile firm in the Vosges benefit from at least two different incentive schemes (a sectoral social security reduction and a regional investment subsidy) while a computer software firm based in Lyon gets nothing ? The ambition of mastering the market forces by State planning is so ingrained in French attitudes that it transcends political parties. An assistant to the last Minister of Industry in the Barre Government even tried to establish sectoral priorities based on a complex series of 'multicriteria' analyses including the relative weights of exports, technology, employment and capital intensity[1]. This served as the intellectual basis for the now defunct CODIS (see part III, chapter 2) which was one of the most sophisticated attempts at planning industrial policies in modern France.

Even in opposition when the conservative parties have had the freedom to embrace a lot of 'Reaganomics', the belief in a strongly State-planned industrial strategy still prevails. In a recent press conference, the Gaullist Michel Noir, responsible for industrial affairs in his party, declared about high-technology investments : 'our former PTT Director had to <u>force</u> the chief executives of our telecommunications companies so that they could achieve the successes which they experienced. The Gaullist idea to give France a computer industry was born with the nuclear defence effort. Today the conquest of <u>independence</u> goes through the same process in integrated circuits'. Obviously all notions of market success, competitive position and financial return are replaced by those of independence, prestige and political will.

1

Christian Stoffaes, <u>La Grande Menace Industrielle</u>, Calmann-Lévy, Paris, 1978.

Market mechanisms are underdevelopped or even non-existent in many other parts of French society. They play no role in publicly owned research institutions which carry almost half of the country's R & D effort, in the education system, in health care, or in transport. France is unique in the respect in the western world. Holland and Germany have very active private pension funds, competitive banks and autonomous regional universities ; the UK has a well developed stock market and prestigious private education institutions ; the US and Japan have company owned education, pensions and health insurance schemes and very dynamic capital markets.

The atrophy of capital markets and the degree of State control over resource allocation mechanisms have altered the way corporate managers make investment decisions. Too few French executives are convinced that return on capital employed is the only valid measure of their performance. Managers who grow faster than inflation, and balance their books without too much social conflict are heroes. The French model is a market economy without capital. This has worked at a time of high savings and negative real interest rates, but is now turning into a disaster when cheap money is running out.

(e) Demagogic and protective macro economic policies

Despite 23 years of political stability and the strong authority of the President under the institutions of the Fifth Republic, France has had very few years of consistent and productive macroeconomic policies. They have in general been demagogic, chauvinistic and in conflict with the requirements of an economy open to foreign competition.

Except for short periods when a strong medicine had to be imposed to confront crisis (in 1958, 1979/80 and 1984-85) political leaders from all ideologies have primed the pump or cooled the engine with little concern for structural consequences. Reflation policies have resulted in higher inflation and trade deficits (like in 1975/76 or 1981-82) while deflation policies have allowed companies with smaller cash flows and less opportunities to invest (as in 1967 or 1980). Furthermore this too easy stop-go has only aggravated the traditional bad habits of the French economic system which now appear as clearly incompatible with the constraints of a market economy :

- public deficits which until two years ago were lower than in any other major OECD country have been more damaging because a larger proportion were financed by monetary creation rather than by savings ;
- the cost of health care, pensions and unemployment benefits has resulted in higher labour costs rather than higher taxes, therefore contributing to a cost-push inflation and little incentive for job creation ;
- price controls, subsidies and monopolies have generated price fixing practices and unequal treatment throughout the economy, thereby fuelling inflation in protected sectors ;
- negative interest rates through subsidies or monopoly banking pratices have artificially compensated for low returns on capital, and encouraged inflationary expansion policies, and investment decisions.

Owing to these structural biases, France has found it more difficult than most other OECD nations to break the vicious combination of high inflation, low investment and soaring unemployment pervasive since the first oil shock. It has taken France ten more years than Japan and five more years than the UK, Scandinavia or Germany to understand the three principles of an open market economy, namely that :

- GDP growth is conditioned by the trade surplus (except when the domestic market is large enough like in the US),
- wage increases should be pegged to productivity increases not to the price index,
- increases in corporate investments require higher cash flows if debt is going to be paid off.

After the second oil shock, the Barre government started to lead France in this direction. Since then, the country has gone full circle, experimenting with another disastrous counter-cyclical expansion programme in 1981-82 before having to deflate brutally. France is now on the same trend line as it was in 1980 : the trade deficit is being reduced, wages are increasing less rapidly than prices, inflation is down to around 5 per cent, corporate cash flows are improving. The price paid by the contradictory stop-go is however very high : GDP growth is lower than for most OECD countries, unemployment continues to grow while it has stabilized in other OECD countries and investments are still too low. Has the medicine killed the patient ? There is unfortunately no alternative as the margin for manoeuvre is lower than ever. In fact the French have never accepted to pay the price of these policies by cutting their consumption level as in neighbouring countries. Instead they have tapped their savings (the saving ratio is lower than it was in 1958) and their leaders have borrowed abroad. This makes impossible any change in economic policy. Business cannot count on a more prosperous domestic market. It has to earn its living by increasing market share and penetrating new foreign markets. It is for business leadership to take up this challenge and utilise the best assets the country still offers.

France's assets in restoring its competitive power
    Compared with other European countries, France has a few assets which can allow its leadership, particularly in business, to strive for a new phase of economic development. France's destiny is linked to the future of Europe. If Europe as a whole can bring its act together and function as an integrated market, France still has a fighting chance to be one of the leading industrial nations of the next century. Its distinctive assets are of four kinds :

(a) A dynamic population still striving for wealth creation. The French social and demographic fabric is half-way between those of Northern Europe and the US. It has a lower birth rate and immigration flow than in the US but somewhat higher than in Germany, Scandinavia or the UK. The birth rate has recently picked up and public campaigns and tax exemptions for new babies are quite popular. The French people are still fighting for a better standard of living and their confidence has been less affected by economic depression than in Belgium, Holland, Britain or even

Scandinavia. Although average working hours have been substantially reduced, they are similar to those in the rest of Europe.

The sense of national identity and the attachment to the national soil is stronger than in divided Germany or Italy. Political leaders from all horizons have drawn on national pride as a support for their policies, at a time when their nationalistic rhetoric would seem archaïc to many Europeans. If the widespread belief in France's unique historical desting is often an obstacle to open attitudes towards foreign markets and foreign partners, it can also be turned into a cement to weather difficult times. The French have not been hit by fundamental doubts about their future like the Germans. They are not as threatened by the division of the world and are more confident of their ability to survive.

Furthermore the attitudes of the French people towards business success and financial rewards are changing in a fundamental way. The traditional catholic and agrarian resistance to salient material wealth is giving way to new values. Business leaders like Bernard Tapie or Gilbert Trigano are becoming media stars and their personal wealth does not scandalise anyone. Business creation is at record levels, venture capital is popular, and young graduates are willing to take more risks than ten years ago. Of course, French society is not prepared to sacrifice consumption levels and invest at a rate equivalent to Japan or the other Asian countries. But there is a desire to create new sources of wealth.

(b) A well developed infrastructure. France has now caught up with its most advanced neighbours in term of transport, communications and energy infrastructure, and is even ahead in some areas. Its road network is one of the densest and best maintained in the world even if some motorway links are still missing. Its railway system is efficient, comfortable and reliable, with a remarkable high-speed train link between Paris and the South-East, and a new one planned between Paris and the South-West. Its harbours have been modernized even if none of them is on a par with Antwerp or Rotterdam.

The telephone network is now one of the most digitalized in the world and in data transmission, with Transpac and now the satellite Telecom I, France is considerably in advance of the rest of Europe. In new telecommunication services, France is ahead of Europe, with its millions of free videotex terminals (Minitel) installed and plans for an aggressive cabling in optical fibers. The production of electricity is now 50 per cent nuclear - the highest proportion in the world, thus giving France a cost and capacity advantage over its neighbours. The country has become an important exporter of power.

The country has modernized many regions which used to be mostly agrarian : new universities, hospitals and airports continue to be built in many cities like Grenoble, Montpellier, Lyon, Nice, Toulon, Strasbourg, Nantes, which can rival Paris in attracting corporate investments.

(c) Stable resources from its soil and its geography. Owing to its large and diversified agricultural sector, France is likely to remain the largest European exporter of commodities (cereals, sugar, wine, butter) but the income derived from the often higher-cost commodities is totally dependent on the future of the Common Agricultural Policy. It can develop a series of other agribusinesses with more value added per acre or per worker : cheese, fruit and vegetables, flowers, dairy products, etc., where it has often let other countries take the lead.

The diversity of its geography and its long history are the best basis for its tourist industry. Foreign income earned through tourism has increased significantly in the last few years. With road and hotel infrastructure improvements and a high dollar France is the only country with a positive tourism balance among the five largest industrial nations.

(d) A national ambition for technological leadership. France can continue to use the power of the State to catch up in technologies which require massive and risky front end investments like defence, space, or marine exploration. These efforts will benefit from a broad political consensus, and will be led by a dedicated and well trained technical and bureaucratic elite. They will have in turn spin off effects on key industrial areas like semi-conductors, computers, lasers, etc. where French corporations are too weak to confront international competition on their own. France has a tradition of technical invention, and excellent education in the basic sciences.

These assets, however, can only bear fruit if the country adapts to the organisations and values of a modern industrial society. These require changes in management, in labour, in politics, and in the society at large.

## What remains to be done : the next miracle

France has missed the industrial revolutions of the nineteenth century to the benefit of other European nations like Britain and Germany. After a more rapid growth in the postwar 'thirty glorious years', and with more untapped sources of wealth creation than any other European economy, France can still become a leading economy in a revitalized Europe. The next miracle will be one of cultural transformation, which will affect all groups in French society - as with any fundamental change, it is the role of leaders to understand and explain the objectives of such a transformation, and make it happen.

(a) Corporate leadership has the primary task in any market economy

France has successful and often wealthy entrepreneurs, and business creators, but suffers a major shortage of professional managers. French corporate leaders have yet to learn how to manage complex organisations in changing market conditions. Positive changes are underway which suggest that France is at last entering the managerial revolution (see part II). Business portfolios are being restructured along more rational lines, hard decisions on plant closures and staff reductions are being made with more courage than before. Younger teams of executives are less conservative about social dialogue, and less chauvinistic in their search for scale. They are also more profit-minded and less sensitive to size or prestige than their predecessors.

Companies whose management has changed from the old establishment to younger and more professional teams - e.g. Thomson, Bull, Pechiney, Schneider, Hachette, Boussac or

DMC have moved further towards international standards in the last five years than in the two preceding decades. Another group of somewhat smaller corporations in food, oil and sheltered businesses (the Stars described in part II) had already shown that French talents could give rise to excellent companies : BSN, Moët-Hennessy, Perrier, Bongrain, Schlumberger, Geophysique, Air Liquide, L'Oreal, Lafarge. These two groups together with the spin-offs from foreign multinationals could form the training ground of a new generation of competent, internationally and profit-minded managers which French industry badly needs.

Despite recent changes in several large corporations, French management still has to learn the rigorous discipline of efficient leadership : the merits of routine procedures, fair systems and consistency over improvisation, subjective judgements and hazardous turnarounds ; the value of training and motivating people rather than managing by charisma or fear ; the courage to act decisively on hard matters, and the commitment to the firm's long term interests, rather than the uncertainties of political management. Modern corporations are complex, interactive systems, not the simple vertical organisations of the nineteenth century. French managers are too often top engineers, or top bureaucrats, not system integrators.Successful managers are those who manage interactions between the various elements composing the system : customers, employees, distributors, subsuppliers, not the ones who are seeking to break records on a single dimension.

Beyond the stage of survival in more intense international competition, France will need a new breed of managers who can develop their corporation in all dimensions : who can develop its human resources as its main asset, and continously adapt its strategy and organisation as markets and competitors evolve. In the past, growth has hidden management shortcomings. In the future, the winners will require constant care and improvement in management.

(b) Labour leadership
The French labour movement has traditionally been too ideological, too weak and too divided to influence in depth either the management of corporations or economic and

313

social policy. In its rare influential periods - 1936, 1945 and 1968 - it has resorted to violent reactions and political changes, rather than negotiation and progressive steps. Of course, corporate leadership shares the blame, but union leaders have rarely helped their organisations to adapt to modern industry.

In this domain as well, fundamental changes might follow the structural crisis in which the labour movement is sinking. Membership is half what it was during the growth period. The once feared CGT, which could decide on a national strike at will, is incapable of putting more than a few thousand workers on the Paris streets, and is retreating into its traditional strongholds publicly owned monopolies and heavy industries - with very little influence in new industries and service sectors. The once intellectually prestigeous CFDT which was the most innovative social organisation in the 1960s, is now being surpassed by the very traditional and conservative FO, in all elections. None of these unions has had the courage and vision of the UAW in the US, LO in Sweden or the Italian unions in negotiating with management new forms of organization and flexibility in wage structure and employment status.

Union leaders are more political figures than managers of complex organisations. They devote more time to public speeches and summit meetings than to dealing with the rank and file. In the last important bargaining session with the Patronat on flexibility, four out of five unions agreed to sign important reforms, to be subsequently turned down by their own membership.

In all countries, the unions, like all bureaucratic mass organisations - the Church, the Army, the Parties - have a difficult time to adapt to changing values and life styles. The division of French unions among three basic ideologies, communist, socialist, and christian-democrat, is yet another factor of weakness which make them relatively ineffective in managing changes. Multiple representation leads to competition, and demagogy makes courageous changes almost impossible.

In France more than in any other western society, the world has been seen as too dualistic : stalemate or compromise, win or lose. The recent economic history of

Asian societies shows us that everybody can win or everybody can lose depending on the way a conflict is managed. Unions and management will both have to learn that leadership is not dreaming about consensus, but being able to solve conflicts.

## (c) Political and government leadership

The changes in public management will not come automatically from political changes. Some fundamental beliefs and attitudes are shared throughout the spectrum of ideologies and parties. Political leaders often come from the same schools and have gained similar experiences in ministerial cabinets. Whether their credo is a new breed of socialism, or neo-liberalism or a mixed economy, they all resort to the State on many occasions where the market should do the job, and and too often manage State enterprises like political "colonies" whereas they should be run like corporations.

French political leaders, and the extremely competent bureaucrats whom the State has attracted for the last three decades, will have to learn the virtues and the subtleties of a market economy, without giving up the benefits of a strong and resourceful public apparatus. They will have to manage the combination of the three models described in part III, chapter 3 : the spontaneous economy, the contractual economy and the guided economy, and manage the transitions from one model to another, as business conditions evolve.

The spontaneous economy has recently been making some paradoxical advances in France under the socialist government. As we have seen in part III, the legal and fiscal measures taken by the former Minister of Finance J. Delors in 1982 and 1983 have considerably boosted the stock market - which has had its best performance ever -and created a dozen new financing instruments for corporations and individuals. The 1983 Bill on economic initiative has introduced in France pure capitalist tools like venture capital, stock options, and management buyouts. More recently, the new Minister P. Beregovoy has created more market mechanisms in the French financial system than have ever been tried before. Subsidized loans have been cut by half, banks and stock brokers have been subjected to more competition, large corporations have gained direct access to the money market, banking monopolies are being reduced in many operations.

At the same time there is a desire to let free competition, rather than State decisions, regulate resource allocation. R & D incentives are more in the form of tax exemptions than direct subsidies ; business creation is encouraged by a five year tax exemption on profits ; wage negotiations which promote flexibility are being encouraged. Political leaders of all parties – except the Communist – are committed to reducing the burden of taxes and social security levies.

However, before France can conform totally to the rules of international competition, future French governments will need to dismantle a number of other regulations and constraints which have frozen the free movement of resources for one, two and sometimes four decades ; among them are price controls (on 25 per cent of industrial goods and 75 per cent of consumer purchases) foreign exchange and foreign investment restrictions, administrative authorizations for layoffs and investments in certain congested areas (Paris), or certain sectors (distribution, banking), distribution monopolies (for drugs) and professional numerus clausus (for notaries, stock brokers, doctors, taxis, etc.), import quotas (on cars, TVs, VCRs, machine tools, etc.).

The contractual economy which should have received a new spirit with the Socialist programme for a renewed planning system has not yet found its way. The unfortunate interventions in the recently nationalized companies, the ambitious programmes launched for machine tools, or the 'filière électronique' announced by the first Minister of Industry, Jean-Pierre Chevènement, have given way to a very pragmatic, low key approach by Laurent Fabius and his successor Edith Cresson. The latter speaks more highly of privately owned Peugeot than of Renault and has received too little budget to embark on any grandiose industrial strategy. France still lacks, however, the pluralistic and catalytic tradition of the Japanese or the German administration in fostering cooperation between business interests and the national interest.

The guided economy is still as powerful as ever in State-driven sectors, such as defence, telecommunications or energy. But many subtle changes are underway which will leave more room for market forces. The PTT monopoly is allowing some competition in several new areas including the exploitation of cable TV, electronic mail, and the use of Minitel for corporate communications. In energy, the price of gasoline has been deregulated for the first time in France. The State is also introducing private ownership and management in TV (including the new satellite station TDF), after having deregulated radio.

In France, as in almost all other industrialised countries, the trend is undoubtedly towards less regulation and more competition. If the opposition parties come to power they will according to their official platforms proceed to the privatisation of the whole banking and insurance sectors, of most industrial companies (except the ones suffering heavy losses), of the TV and radio State holdings (Havas and Sofirad) ; corporate and personal income taxes would be reduced (a total of 40 billion francs according to the programme of the RPR). State controls on prices would be lifted, and exchange movements and corporate lay-offs would be partially deregulated. Monopolies in the energy, telcommunications and transport sectors would be dismantled or at least reduced. Credit would be deregulated and the Banque de France would become autonomous as in the US or Germany.If the Socialists were to stay in power or form a coalition, they would probably accelerate the deregulation of financial services, the media and maybe some telecommunications services. Public ownership is still an integral part of the Left's ideology but pragmatic leaders like Laurent Fabius, Jacques Delors or Michel Rocard would certainly find ways to allow nationalised companies to 'breathe' : by selling off part of their assets, or issuing private paper like 'titres participatifs' or 'investment certificates' as has been done recently by Rhône-Poulenc.

The mix of spontaneous, contractual and guided economies will however always be tilted in France towards the last group, given long established traditions. No political party advocates for example the total privatisation of the

PTT despite the success of British Telecom. Everyone agrees on the need to use public purchasing as a lever for new investments in risky ventures.

## (d) Intellectual leadership and public opinion

The opinion leaders in France can come from a variety of groups including universities, research institutions, parties and political forums, the media and business. Together they reflect and contribute to society's values and attitudes. They also have a key role in promoting changes towards a modern and decentralised economy open to international competition.

Never before in French history have the words liberalism, market, profit, enterprise, freedom, individual choice been more popular. Real attitudes have not changed as quickly as terminology, and political parties have changed even less than public attitudes, but it remains that the widespread confidence in an almighty State is diminishing. People tend to count more on their own initiative, as demonstrated by the creation of many new local associations, clubs and forums of all sorts. The intellectual debate has also moved from philosophical and ideological issues to more pragmatic ones : book sales on economic policy, management, social changes, money, careers are at their record level and best sellers, like François de Closet's 'Toujours plus' or Michel Albert's 'Le Pari français', break new ground against all conventional wisdom.

In a recent poll, the economic magazine l'Expansion (February 1985) gave a few illustrations of what was called the 'tidewave of liberalism' : 61 per cent of the people preferred a system of wage increases based on individual merit and company's bonuses rather than seniority (55 per cent of blue collar workers) ; 43 per cent were in favour of facilitating authorizations for lay-offs (vs 43 per cent opposed) ; 59 per cent thought that a more liberal economic policy would stimulate growth (vs 8 per cent of the opposite opinion) and 48 per cent thought that it would stimulate job creation (vs 15 per cent). Very few opinion leaders however really understand and accept the inevitable casualties of open competition. When a large established firm is near bankrupcy owing to its management mistakes, opinion leaders of all ideologies call for a rescue by the State. As an illustration, the conservative Figaro commented on the government's refusal to bail out Creusot-Loire in the following terms : 'The State has chosen to deprive France of one of its largest industrial groups. Already the Germans are happy about it (...). In the next months, the fall of Creusot-Loire will result in larger trade deficits (...). It is an expensive way to teach a lesson to the private sector (...) the workers are not altogether wrong to stop trains : they symbolize indifference'.

The recent conversion of the French people to the virtues of the market and competition is less the result of influential intellectual leaders than of reverse pedagogy from the bad experience of the 1981-83 economic policy. The danger is therefore that public opinion will turn its back on the new liberalism as soon as the government changes. More fundamental changes have to take place, which can only be done through the role of intellectual leaders and the education system.

The debate on the education system has never been so vivid, and the concern about quality, competition and freedom so acute. The new Minister of Education has given up all Socialist ambitions to unify the schools in a single State controlled system and has announced very pragmatic measures such as the development of technical education, the introduction of micro-computers and a better selection system.

Despite all these changes, France will still have to learn the behaviour of market driven organisations. Of all advanced countries, the French speak the most of socialism and know the least how to live in society harmoniously and productively. They tend to wait for changes in laws, and regulations, or for revolutions, rather than progressively adapt to a changing environment. Will French history for once adopt different paths ?

**A cultural revolution on the way ?**
The conditions might be ripe for the end of the populist anti-capitalist tradition in France, and the emergence of new social values, based on risk, innovation and social mobility. The old patrician families which symbolised a marxist vision of big business (Michelin, Peugeot, de Wendel) are giving way to a new generation of capitalists who appeal to a wider

319

audience and fit in with their time : Trigano, Defforey, Bouygues. Until the second world war profits were still considered as a continuation of the old privileges of the aristocracy, and industry was too protected to be seen as a risky venture. It has taken thirty years of wealth creation, and a decade of brutal decline of many established capitalists, for the French people to realise that open competition and market forces make profits legitimate and necessary . It will take another two or three decades - if time is left - to learn how to stay fit in the ever-changing world of open competition.

There are still three fundamental beliefs which the French Left has transmitted to the collective subconscious of most of the people :

- 'The State can by itself determine economic growth and employment levels'. Many political leaders are still of the age of having been influenced by the economic programme of the Resistance and the successful turnaround managed by General de Gaulle in 1958. Most Socialists and Gaullists of that generation would still advocate a State-led recovery programme, despite all the negative effects on the trade balance, rather than wait for the long and patient route of enhancing the competitive positions and market shares of companies in the traded sector ;
- 'Banks and financial institutions do not take risks and they increase their profits to the detriment of industry'. The French do not treat money as the natural result of commercial activity, but as a shameful way to gain access to power and pleasure. Capital markets, for the majority of the people, do not participate in the mainstream of economic relations, but starve corporations of funds for investments. Industry produces, financial institutions speculate. Most French people think about their economy as a market system without capital ;
- 'Foreign multinationals control the real decisions'. Large and anonymous corporations - particularly of US origin - are still seen as the centre of a mythical power which can dictate its will to local

governments and workers. The international division of labour is not yet accepted. Foreign companies are rarely seen as potential fruitfull partners.

Thus, according to the popular vision, modern capitalism in France should still be greatly influenced by the State, be kept independent the financial markets (and from financial performance measures) and be mainly nationally-based.The coexistence of a strong State and dynamic capitalists is undoubtedly a distinctive feature of France's successful catching up after the Second World War. This will not – and should not – disappear with the changing ambitions of international competition. In all crucial periods of its history, it is the State which gave the French nation its sense of survival. In 1945, the political leaders convinced the people that the country had to, and could, catch up with its more advanced partners. What has to change however is the method which a strong State should use in an economy more complex and more open to international competition than forty years ago. Most leaders in business and government would agree with the inevitable evolution towards a more decentralized market economy open to international partnerships. The traditional gaullist ideology of an ambitious State has given way to the neo-liberal policies advocated by Jacques Chirac. The socialist objectives of a planned economy based on a powerful nationalized sector have given way to a very moderate vision of a "mixed economy". Few leaders however know how to influence the French society in depth, to make it fit to withstand the never ending competitive battle.

Le 'Mal Français'2 is one of bad management. The next French miracle will see the emergence of a new breed of managers in all circles – business, labour and government. France does not need natural resources – oil and gas discoveries have not revitalized Holland or the UK. France does not need more technology or more capital – it has plenty of both or at least untapped reserves of both. France needs the values and the leadership which have always prevailed in successful industrial nations.

---

2
A. Peyrefitte, Le Mal Français, Plon, Paris, 1976.

These values are changing in France today. They call for more responsibility, more freedom, more confidence in the individual, but also for a sustained solidarity between groups in society. France is not America. Like all European societies it will continue to rate quite highly the security of employment or at least of large unemployment benefits and long advance notice of dismissal. It will still be attached to the merits of free education and free health to a better protected environment, to more harmonious social and human relations. But this does not prevent more competition, more quest for performance, more personal rewards.

The French people are more open to change inside the corporation than outside. Progressive companies have already taken the lead in pioneering new forms of work organization, pay systems and labour relations. These are also companies which perform best in international markets against their foreign competitors. The traded sector, exposed to the first waves of change, is also the first place to accept and initiate changes. This is the role of business leaders.

A new leadership is emerging in France which has the crucial responsibility to promote and manage social and economic changes. This book has the ambition to put their role in a long term perspective and give hope to the many talents who claim this responsibility.

 Policy Studies Institute

The **Policy Studies Institute** is Britain's largest independent research organisation undertaking studies of economic, industrial and social policy and the workings of political institutions.

The Institute is an educational charity, not run for profit, and is independent of all political pressure groups and commercial interests. It receives particular support from the Joseph Rowntree Memorial Trust.

The core of PSI's work is its wide-ranging programme of studies, organised and developed under six Research Groups responsible for a series of studies in the areas of the economy and the labour market, industrial development, politics and government, justice and social order, social policy and the quality of life.

The research methods include surveys, case studies, statistical analysis, literature and document search and discussion with practitioners and other researchers in seminars or groups.

A full list of PSI publications, and information about methods of ordering, are available from:

THE PUBLICATIONS DEPARTMENT
PSI, 100 Park Village East,
London NW1 3SR
Telephone: 01-387 2171

Copies of publications are displayed in PSI's reception at the above address, and are available for sale to individual purchasers.